Wait for God to Notice

This gripping, astutely written memoir of adventures and misadventures is also a very moving story of a mother-daughter relationship. One cannot help admiring the heroic stubbornness and resiliency of this naive, idealistic clan of missionaries, as they adjust to near-impossible circumstances presided over by mad tyrant Idi Amin.

—Phillip Lopate, *A Mother's Tale* and *Two Marriages*

The missionary experience occupies a fraught corner of contemporary memoir. Sari Fordham approaches it simply as a girl, growing up in a faraway land. She doesn't celebrate the mission so much as her memories of family and home in a place that, as she notes, was never really theirs. The specter of Idi Amin casts the decency of the Fordhams and their Ugandan hosts in sharp relief—we root for them, and especially for this storyteller.

—Ted Conover, *Newjack: Guarding Sing Sing*

It is so rare to find a book as generous in spirit as Sari Fordham's *Wait for God to Notice*. Fordham's portrait of her childhood in Uganda, growing up in a missionary family during the time of Idi Amin, is sometimes harrowing, sometimes funny, and sometimes beautifully sad. Her love for East Africa and for her stubbornly remarkable parents will make you want to buy one copy of this exquisite memoir for yourself, and a few for your friends.

—Julie Schumacher, *Dear Committee Members* and
The Shakespeare Requirement

Missionaries, even with the best intentions, don't quite know what they're getting themselves into. Especially in Uganda under the reign of Idi Amin. Food is scarce. Driver ants and snakes are omnipresent. Ordinary errands mean dealing with blockades, bribes, and sometimes terror. Sari Fordham has written a memoir of a family both innocent and brave. Written with compassion, humor, and a healthy dollop of skepticism, Fordham creates a world as vibrant and alive as Africa itself. A truly compelling read.

—Fern Kupfer, *Leaving Long Island*

Sari Fordham's *Wait for God to Notice* is both a story of a young girl and her missionary family's life in Uganda in the 1970s among political unrest, and a meditation on landscape; of how our love is made from the stuff of the places in which we grow. Most deeply and poignantly, however, this is a daughter's address to her mother, upon whom the memoir focuses most of all, and speaks to, and loves. I enjoyed this book immensely. It is lucid, careful, expressive, and wryly funny, and searchingly emotive without being sentimental. Sari Fordham takes her time—there is wisdom and authority here. *Wait for God to Notice* is a unique, pleasurable, heartbreaking read.

—Amanda Coplin, *The Orchardist*

In *Wait for God to Notice*, Sari Fordham movingly and intelligently probes the ties that bind us: to our families, our homes, our cultures, our faith. She examines the simultaneously tenuous and unbreakable nature of attachment and identity as only the daughter of missionaries could. I fell in love with the author's family and with the wide-eyed, outsider children she and her sister were. Fordham's writing is funny, affectionate, wise, and socially aware, and I didn't want this beautifully-written book to end.

—Andria Williams, *The Longest Night*

Wait for God to Notice

Sari Fordham

etruscan press

Etruscan Press
Wilkes University
84 West South Street
Wilkes-Barre, PA 18766
(570) 408-4546

 Wilkes
University

www.etruscanpress.org

Published 2021 by Etruscan Press
Printed in the United States of America
Cover design by Carey Schwartzburt
Interior design and typesetting by Julianne Popovec
The text of this book is set in Adobe Garamond.

First Edition

17 18 19 20 5 4 3 2 1

Library of Congress Cataloguing-in-Publication Data

Names: Fordham, Sari, 1974- author.
Title: Wait for God to Notice / Sari Fordham.
Description: First edition. | Wilkes-Barre, PA : Etruscan Press, 2021. |
  Includes bibliographical references. | Summary: "*In Wait for God to Notice*, Sari Fordham writes about a childhood that is by turns dangerous and idyllic, but is always seeped in the peculiar faith of her parents. Her vivid, unsentimental prose observes how it is possible to love someone you disagree with and how a place that doesn't belong to you can turn you into who you are. Reminiscent of *The Poisonwood Bible* and *Don't Let's Go to the Dogs Tonight*, *Wait for God to Notice* explores the complex terrain of being a mzungu in Africa, and ultimately being a stranger anywhere on earth"— Provided by publisher.
Identifiers: LCCN 2019054796 | ISBN 9781733674157 (trade paperback; acid-free paper)
Subjects: LCSH: Fordham, Sari, 1974---Childhood and youth. | Authors, American--21st century--Biography. | Missionaries--Africa--Biography.
Classification: LCC PS3606.O747337 Z46 2021 | DDC 814/.6 [B]--dc23
LC record available at https://lccn.loc.gov/2019054796

Please turn to the back of this book for a list of the sustaining funders of Etruscan Press.

This book is printed on recycled, acid-free paper.

For those who were there: my father, mother, and sister.

*And for my daughter, who is always asking me to tell her
a story about when I was a little girl.*

"We just found out that the price of one roll of toilet paper is $5.00, and its size is not enough to use a dozen times. I've read that the sellers rarely have bananas and beans. Wait for God to notice. We remember you all with love in our prayers."

—*Kaarina Fordham in a letter to her father ~ September 27, 1979*

TABLE OF CONTENTS

Wait for God to Notice

ACKNOWLEDGMENTS

One day, I realized I had been writing this memoir for longer than my family had lived in Uganda and Kenya combined, and I knew then that it was time, beyond time, to finish.

I'm grateful for the magazine editors who published parts of this project as the book was taking shape. Early work appeared in the following literary journals: "Driver Ants" in *Brevity*, "Dividing Up the World Between Us" and "Ugandan Psalm" in *Cerise Press*, "House Arrest in Thirteen Parts" in *Isthmus Review*, and "Shaking Hands with Idi Amin" in *Passages North*. "Ugandan Psalm" was also reprinted in *Best of the Net Anthology 2011* by Sundress Publications, and "House Arrest in Thirteen Parts" was reprinted in *Wrath-Bearing Tree*.

I'm lucky to have studied with so many brilliant professors who encouraged and challenged me in equal parts—particularly Helen Pyke, Fern Kupfer, Sheryl St. Germain, Madelon Sprengnether, Julie Schumacher, and of course, Patricia Hampl, who has acted as my literary fairy godmother. Thank you also to classmates and friends who provided crucial feedback, inspiration, and community—Amanda Fields, Marge Barrett, Laura Flynn, Amanda Coplin, Jon Lurie, Nicole Johns, Jen Johnson, Kevin Fenton, Brian Malloy, Cheri Johnson, Andria Williams, Karen Rigby, Rachel Wooten, Lorissa Gottschalk, Manolita Farolan, Keri Phillips, Synnova Goodge, and Sandy Suh.

Poet and novelist Shana Youngdahl translated my mother's letters into English, and through her translations, I heard my mother's voice singing a song both new and familiar.

I was given time and space to write at Djerassi Resident Artists Program, Soaring Gardens Artist Retreat, The Evered House (for that final push), and the ARIM residency, which came with a community of writing mamas. Though I never attended summer camp, I can't imagine it being more fun than my week at Bread Loaf Writers' Conference.

My colleagues at La Sierra University—Winona Howe, Robert Dunn, Lora Geriguis, Sam McBride, Melissa Brotton, Marilynn Loveless, Erin Banks-Kirkham, Jill Walker Gonzalez, Erica Garcia, and Debbie Higgins (who was also, in that small Adventist world, my composition teacher in college)—believed in this project all these years. Mary and Jim Wilson gave me the gift of friendship and a magical place to write, and Christine Law Fujitani met me for Saturday night work dates.

While teaching writers' workshops at Collegeville Institute, I met fascinating people and learned so much about everything. Thank you especially to Don Ottenhoff, Carla Durand, and Elisa Schneider who provided that famous Collegeville hospitality when I was a terrified young writer/teacher.

This book wouldn't have been written if I hadn't returned to Uganda as an adult. I'm profoundly grateful to ADRA Uganda and particularly to my colleagues and friends Esther Wani, Sabbiti Ruhiriita, and Kephrain Kakende.

Much of this book was written at Jammin' Bread, and I can attest to their excellent lattes and sugar cookies, and while I was there, Jessie Elliot took my daughter for walks around the neighborhood and read to her. There is no one more essential than the person caring for your child.

I am profoundly grateful to Etruscan Press—for their enthusiastic commitment to words and to the writers of those words. Thank you Phil Brady, Bill Schneider, Pamela Turchin, Karen Krumpak, Robert Mooney, Stephen and Jeryl Oristaglio, Julianne Popovec, and Carey Schwartzburt for making this book a reality.

My aunt Riitta Liisa and my uncle Reijo opened up their home in Finland and shared family stories. My sister Sonja is this book's biggest cheerleader and has been so generous with an experience that belongs to us both. My stepmother Karen has been an early reader, providing smart feedback along the way. My father's detailed memory is the stuff of legends, and his habit of saving everything provided the spine of facts I needed. I wrote this memoir in order to find my mother, but while writing, I also discovered how much I have been shaped by my kind and adventurous father.

I was smart to marry a writer. Bryan Bradford—so brilliant, so funny—read through this manuscript many times. His edits have made it infinitely better. Together, we have a kid who makes us laugh and who asks for stories about mambas, lions, and driver ants. What more can you want?

PROLOGUE

Driver Ants

MY MOTHER WAKES to the sound of rain—not a storm, but a steady slapping of drops against pane. She rolls over, her body weary from the plane and the children and the dust. Although our new house is at the top of a hill, windows flung open to catch a breeze, the air is heavy, and my mother realizes with a start that she's in Africa. Fully awake, she sits, pulling one leg against her chest. The room is a watery grey, and the mosquito net hovers over the bed like a wraith. Next to her, my father is stretched out, snoring. Something feels wrong, and so my mother turns and looks out. Their window faces a jungle, dark as a bruise. The branches reach toward the house, nearly scratching the glass. She hears the rain but cannot see it.

"Gary," she says.

"Hmm," my father answers.

"Gary," she says again, nudging him. "Is it raining?"

My father listens to the distinctive patter of water hitting glass. The rhythm is constant, lulling. "I guess so," he says, reaching out to pull her toward him. "It does that sometimes." Perhaps he is tired, or perhaps he has not been in the house during any of the afternoon showers. Neither of them would have made this mistake later. They will learn to know the thickness of rain on a tin roof, the overwhelming timpani of it.

"But it doesn't *look* like it's raining," my mother insists. She might be new to this place, but she knows rain. Laughing, my father sits and looks out the window, and he has to agree: It *doesn't* look like it's raining. They sit together in silence, listening. The noise grows no louder, no softer. It is both constant and close by.

My father untucks the mosquito net and swings his bare feet to the ground. He will later be glad that he got out on the side that he did. Hands outstretched, he feels his way over to the wall and flips on the switch. A single bulb hangs from the ceiling, casting a waxy glow across the room. My parents gaze down, their stare a mingling of horror and curiosity. A column of driver ants, six inches wide, streams across the floor and marches purposefully out of the bedroom and into the rest of the house. The trail begins at the window, where the ants boil out of a slit in the screen and drop from the ledge, landing with small plops.

Driver ants are not interested in picnic fare, in cake crumbs or bits of bread. Mostly, they eat lizards, cockroaches, millipedes, geckoes, scorpions, frogs, chameleons, baby birds—anything that cannot get away. They are partial to chicken coops. They can eat through a trapped hen, leaving behind bones as clean as porcelain. There are even stories of driver ants chomping through a tied-up calf or goat.

With as many as twenty million in a colony, driver ants are more organism than individual insect. Their nest, when they stop, is a living thing, a churning rope of ant linked to ant. They wait only for the queen to lay eggs, then they pick up and leave once again; no plot of jungle can sustain their appetite. When they move, they can cross the road for a week.

My parents follow the trail as it winds down the hallway. My father giggles like a schoolboy. He has heard about these ants: how expatriates have sat in the wrong swath of grass and had to high-step it for home, how the most prudish of missionaries will become a clothing Houdini, leaving behind a shirt here, a pair of trousers there. This is the first time he has seen them. "Look what you brought," he whispers. My mother does not know whether to be amused or dismayed.

The trail of ants turns and travels into my room. My parents walk faster, but I have not cried, and so they don't worry. The worst they expect is that the ants will have surrounded my bed, that they will have to step over the trail and rescue me. When they turn on the light, I stir beneath the blanket.

A river of ants cuts across the floor and straight to my bed. It moves up the thin quilt, journeys over the bump I create under the covers, and continues down the other side.

Only a piece of cloth separates me from a churning mass of mouths. Somehow, the ants have failed to peg me as food. They flow over me unconcerned, as over a rock or log. I am lying on my stomach, both hands tucked at my sides, the blanket pulled to my ears. It is a wonder that I have not kicked off the covers. The air is thick as honey, and I am used to cool, Finnish nights. If even one hand was flung over the edge, I would have been found.

My parents do not try to make connections between what has happened and what could happen. They do not see the ants as a warning, that peril can slip in through the smallest of openings, that Uganda is too dangerous, that we should pack up and leave. Nor do they see my escape as a miracle, a sign that we are supposed to be here, that we will be protected. They are not seeking metaphor or prophecy. They are too practical. The ants have given them a scare, but they do not consider them a threat; there are too many other dangers out there.

My mother eases me from under the covers. As the blanket moves, the ants spread like a blooming flower. She pulls me clear and stands up straight. "There you are," she says.

I blink in the sharp light.

PART I

We Are Still Here

CHAPTER 1

Letters

WATER MOVED ACROSS the land in great sheets. The rain slanted through green-veined leaves and kicked up dirt, which ran down the hill in rivulets. The darkness and the water fell against our house with such intensity that it felt as if we were going to drown in the sound of it. "I can't hear myself think," my mother would shout over the roar. She would take to the couch then, carrying an aerogramme and a large book to write on. If my sister Sonja or I came and asked a question, she'd be visibly annoyed. Sometimes, she would rattle off how to spell *does* or *dog* or tell us where to find the crayons, but more often she'd shoo us away: "Don't be helpless. Use the dictionary," or "Look in your room. Think about where you had it last." My mother would then fall back into her letters, back into a language we couldn't follow.

As she wrote, she turned her predicament over and over. *What would she do?* That first night she had laughed about the driver ants, and she still laughed about them, but as the years passed, she became more and more convinced that one of us would die in Uganda. There were so many soldiers, so many guns, so many fevers and snakes. She did not think she could protect us.

My mother finished one letter and picked up another aereogramme.

Most of her letters traveled to Finland, where the seasons changed. In autumn, the birch leaves rattled, and near my mother's childhood home, the orchard was heavy with fruit. Children gathered apples off the ground. They bit into the fruit, enjoying the crunch as much as the sharp, crisp taste. The air smelled of smoke and the coming of winter. The days were shorter, and the Baltic Sea, cool even in the summer, was a shock. After sauna, men and women ran naked to the water and threw their bodies into the darkness.

There, in a small kitchen close to the Baltic Sea, my grandfather sliced three edges of an aerogramme. After my grandmother died, the receiving and reading of letters fell entirely to him. A meticulous man, my grandfather used a letter opener, which he kept on the table along with some pens, a few apples, a bowl of almonds. He ate seven almonds a day— the perfect number, he said. Perhaps he poured a glass of buttermilk before sitting down. He must have wondered what new dangers my mother had recorded. He had taken to underlining facts he found troubling.

The aerogramme was a delicate thing, and my grandfather peeled it open with care, revealing first the back flap. My mother saved this space for us. He smiled at the childish drawings—a house, two guinea pigs, a beaming sun—before turning the half sheet and revealing my mother's hand.

Dear Father,
It has rained so much it feels as if we're on an island. The tomatoes are in a big sickness. We will see how large a harvest this brings. Gary baked cookies and now comes his message, "eat every meal as if it were your last!"

More than two decades later, I would sit in my cousin's old bedroom, sorting through my grandfather's things. Downstairs, my sister Sonja kept company with her small son. We came to eat Finnish food, go for saunas and swims, and visit relatives. But I was sitting in this room, searching for the vague possibility of something. My aunt had been mysterious.

After my grandfather died a year earlier, she had moved his possessions here, and here they had sat, waiting for a pliant pair of hands. Who could be more pliant? In Finland, I was the youngest, once so eager to play Marco Polo I had forgotten to put on my swimsuit before galloping out of the public restroom.

"Oh, oh, oh," my mother had said, half laughing. "Don't cry. Everyone swims naked here."

"Not in the pool," I said. "And *they* aren't naked"—*they* being my cousins—"and now they're all laughing at me." They *were* laughing, and she knew it.

"So what?" she said. "Let them laugh. You don't have to cry about it." And then, "Good grief. You don't have anything they haven't seen before."

I cried anyway, and often. My cousins remembered me as a weeper. When we were young, they would tease me until I burst into tears and ran to my mother. They reminded me of this now as we played cards, ate candy, and gossiped. I was a keen one for gossip—it was, after all, just another word for *story* and *character*. I'm particularly taken with the past.

At my own home, I sometimes called my father in the middle of the day and asked him about Uganda, comparing his memories to mine. "What happened next?" I would ask. "What were you thinking?" I took to collecting things—photos, letters, books, and diaries. When I visited my father and my stepmother Karen in New Mexico, a box would be waiting for me, always another box. He, too, had been holding on to the past. "Look at this," my father would say. "Isn't it neat?" And whatever it was, he would give it to me, the family historian.

My aunt, though, didn't want to hold on. "Oh boy," she said, surveying the boxes. Some were still packed, but others were opened, their contents laid bare. "What can I do with all these things, things, things?"

I sat cross-legged on the floor, a box of slides beside me. I was drawn to these slips of images, hoping to come upon us while we were still *us*. But most of the slides were bought in museum gift shops. *Oh, Pappa.* I held one after another to the window.

I made piles: ask, keep, throw away. The slides clicked against each other like dominoes—throw away, throw away, throw away—and I wondered what my grandfather would think. My father, I knew, would be appalled.

My aunt rummaged through a box of knickknacks. These, too, must be parsed. She held up an Eiffel Tower paperweight made of glass and high-lighted with gold paint. "Do you want it? You must have a lot of papers."

I shook my head no. I lived in a studio apartment.

"When we were kids," she said, "Pappa would bring us little gifts when he traveled. Even when we had no money and Mamma was screaming at him for spending the last markka, he still would bring us back some cheap little thing. Are you sure you don't want it?"

Before I could say yes, wanting it for her sake, she answered. "No, I don't want it either. Let's try this box."

She had hinted that there might be letters. I was intrigued about running into my younger self. For as long as I could remember, I had corresponded with my grandfather, telling him first about pets and later about my bland high school happenings. He replied with postcards of lovely and scientific things. He favored drawings with ample white space. On the backs, he recorded the day's temperature (in Celsius), how many times he had been cross-country skiing (double digits), a Bible verse (Proverbs).

From deep inside a box, my aunt pulled out a bundle and held it up, triumphant. "I thought these might be here. Pappa was good about saving things." She handed me the grocery bag, the extra plastic spooled around a brick of paper. Even through the layers, I recognized the shape and color of aerogrammes. These were not my letters, not mine. *Please let them be hers.*

My aunt watched, sharply.

On our first night in Finland, a few days earlier, Sonja and I had sat side by side, facing our aunt. It was late, and from the window, we watched the water and sky grow dark. "Do you miss your mom?" our aunt asked. Our mother had died with a swiftness that even after five years still left us feeling raw. We nodded, neither of us willing to talk about our sadness, to expose our soft emotions. My years as a shameless crier had passed. Even when my mother called and told me she was ill, I had waited until I was off the phone before sobbing. "Are you doing your grief work?" our aunt had said. Sonja and I shifted, shifted, looked at each other, looked down, looked up and out the window. *Of course*, we thought but didn't say. Oh, our aunt must have wanted to shake us. "After your mother died," she told us, "I cried nearly every day for over a year. People thought I was crazy. 'This is too much,' even my husband told me. I cried so much my children thought I was loony." Tears leaked out of our aunt's eyes, and she took off her glasses. "See, even now I'm crying." She laughed as she acknowledged it. "I can't look at you girls without crying."

Now, I unrolled the plastic and reached for the aerogrammes. I recognized my mother's hand, could recognize it anywhere. On the outside, she had written my grandfather's name—*Onni Maattanen*—in small, slanted letters. Below it, she had written his address. *She had delicate handwriting,* I thought. I wouldn't have guessed it. In the corner, there were Ugandan stamps, but I was still pondering my mother's handwriting. I knew it as well as my own, and yet I had never really *looked* at it. We know and don't know our parents in equal parts.

Seeing these aerogrammes was like seeing a ghost. They were wispy and blue and had the crunch of old paper. For over twenty years, they had held my mother's words. I felt their heft—more than forty, each carrying a silent message: *We are still here.*

I opened the top aerogramme. My mother's words marched across the page in orderly lines. She didn't cross out a single word. I was willing to bet that she hadn't drawn a line through any words in any of these letters. Erasing and second-guessing and, worst of all, scribbling over a mistake were habits she had tried to pry from me: "Good grief, just leave it. You're going to erase through the paper." Or, "If you *must* cross it out, use a single line. You're not writing state secrets."

The sentences drew closer together as they neared the end of the page. A single aerogramme had to hold all the day's opinions and reports about the seasons—wet and dry—and reports also on who had (and had not) written. In Uganda, our days were marked by letters. Once, in the middle of the week, an extravagance of postage arrived, envelope upon envelope: two letters from my mother's father, one from her sister, one from her brother, one from my father's mother, and hallelujah, the first letter yet from Uncle Johnny in

California. Of this monsoon of words, my mother had written: *It was the happiest I have been in a long time.*

My mother wrote her father in Finnish, a language with rolling Rs and no Bs. It was a difficult language. The words were long; the syntax, a math equation. Though flanked by Swedish words and Russian words, Finnish was as independent as those who spoke it. Its closest linguistic relative was in small Estonia. To listen to a Finn speak was to listen to water and stone. It was a beautiful, lilting song. It was a language I didn't know.

Some Finnish had lapped into our lives, and those words were like the edge of the sea. *Kiitos.* Thank you. *Hyvää huomenta.* Good morning. *Joo. Ei.* Yes and no. My sister and I could pray, count, and sing a Sabbath song in Finnish, but each time we visited our mother's country, we couldn't hold our heads above the words.

How could a daughter not know her mother's tongue?

"I didn't see any sense in it," my mother had once explained. "Finnish just isn't practical. If it was Russian or German . . ." her voice trailed as she considered all the languages that she knew and we didn't. "I probably should have taught you, but we had a lot of other things to worry about when you were small."

"Do you think in Finnish or English?" I had asked another day. "Do you dream in Finnish or English?" *Who do you belong to?*

My mother had laughed at these questions. It was morning, and she was making the bed. From the curtainless window, squares of sun fell on the sheets. I leaned against the frame of the door and gazed at my mother, tucking in the corners, and beyond her at the trees. My parents had bought this suburban house in Atlanta for the forest behind it. We could sit on the patio and watch robins and squirrels—a thin reminder of Uganda and our verandah there. At the time, I was home from college and was in the habit of pulling my parents into short snatches of dialogue. "Why do you want to know?" my mother asked.

"Just curious," I said.

"Well, let's see. When I speak in English, I think in English, and when I speak in Finnish, I think in Finnish."

"And what about when you dream?" I said.

"I don't know. I never think about that—not in English or Finnish."

"Let's go see about lunch," my aunt said.

I took the bag of aerogrammes and followed her down. At the bottom of the stairs, I held out the letters to Sonja. "Look. Can you believe it?" She smiled. My aunt, I realized, had already told her.

My mother used to say, "You'll be glad you have a sister." For years, Sonja and I were ambivalent. We went to separate high schools and rarely saw each other in college, and then I found my way to South Korea where Sonja taught English. Of course, I went because of her.

We were sisters who looked so similar a student once thought we were the same person—this after he had spent a semester in my class, a semester in hers. But then, we also had friends who thought it was a wonder we were related. We shared this: turned-up noses, full lips, thin arms, slouching posture, and a tendency to talk with our hands. Sonja was taller than me and liked pretty dresses and shoes. I preferred jeans and chunky necklaces.

We were both cheerful, though Sonja was an optimist and I was a pessimist. She was romantic; I was cynical. She was a perfectionist and excelled in whatever she did; I took taekwondo and was so awkward my young classmates tutored me during lessons. She was impulsive and flexible about rules. I was the bossy goody two-shoes. When she drove, she would neglect the turn signal, and I would turn into our mother and say, "Blinker!"

A lawyer once looked into our eyes. He had a knack for seeing a person's character. The eyes told all, he said. Our mother had just died, and this must have been his way of distracting us as we signed legal papers. He looked first into Sonja's eyes and said that she was warm and nurturing, a natural mother. Then he looked into mine and told me that I was assertive and efficient, a CEO. He said I could fire an employee without flinching. We were both offended.

In South Korea, where I had once lived and where Sonja still lived and worked, we were known as "You Fordham sisters." Our friends said this as if that was all one needed to say about our competitiveness, our laughter, our compulsion to hike and travel. Sonja's husband added to the mantra. On long trips in the car, he would sigh, "You Fordham sisters and your stories," and we would realize that we had spent the last hours passing familiar narratives back and forth. The stories began like this:

a. Wouldn't Mom have liked this?
b. Remember that time in Africa?
c. We were such outcasts in the States, such nerds.

The last was the most developed narrative. It was the one that started us laughing. It is not difficult to spot a missionary—there is something about the dress, the hair, the earnest eyes. We had all that and more. We were the kind of missionary children that other missionary children found uncool. When we stepped into our respective American classrooms, we never had a chance.

Now, in Finland, we relived our indignities and exchanged more contemporary stories—stories about our lives and about our father's latest obsession with mountain climbing. We could have done all this talking-talking-talking in her country or mine. We met in Finland because the soil here was as much a part of our childhood as Uganda's loamy earth. It was one more home we had lived in and left. We were wedded to the forest, and to the smooth grey stones below the fir trees, and to the moss and lichen that covered the stones. We were children of the lakes and sauna. We were our mother's daughters, and we returned to her home and to where she was buried.

When we were children in Uganda, Sonja and I had believed our mother could do anything. We had followed her from country to country and had never questioned her courage. When she found a snake in her laundry basket, she killed it. When we stopped at a military checkpoint and the soldiers yelled into our car, she smiled and asked questions about their lives. She made a home for us in a country on the verge of civil war.

Once we were teens, we discovered that our mother wasn't just human, she was overly fearful. For many years, she was the only adult I knew without a driver's license, and once she got one, she refused to drive at night, on freeways, on unfamiliar routes. She chewed pills so that she wouldn't choke and took BarleyGreen to prevent cancer.

When our mother was alive, Sonja or I would say, "Oh, you know how Mom is." That was all we needed to say. Now, we weren't so certain. Loss had alerted us to earlier memories, and they sat in contrast to the parent we thought we knew. We had begun to wonder who she really was.

My aunt waved me away when I followed her into the kitchen. "Each potato doesn't need a helper. I'm not that senile yet." Sonja put her son, Aidan, down for a nap and joined me at the table. We sat facing each other, our mother's letters between us. We would have to wait to read them. My aunt was too busy to translate such an abundance of words. A poet friend in the States was fluent in Finnish, and when I returned, I would ask her to translate the letters into English. For now, we pored over our own correspondence.

"Come and draw something for Pappa," our mother would call when we were young. I remembered the seriousness with which I approached the endeavor. I would kneel on a chair, hold the paper flat with one hand, and consider carefully what I should create. Sometimes our mother would make a request—"draw two giraffes"—and the way she would ask made me feel commissioned.

Sonja and I were charmed by our former selves. We held up pictures of houses, flowers, people, and animals. "Look, look," we said, noticing how we gave everything a smile, how we were fond of red and orange. Perhaps these colors represented the last of the crayons. Most of the pictures were mine. Sonja had used her space to compose small letters, which I now read aloud.

Dear Pappa,
I can read and spell too. I teach Sari to read. How are you?
Love from Sonja and Sari.

Dear Pappa,
How are you? I am fine. We have two kittens and two guinea pigs. Sari and I get
them grass. Thank you for the stamps.
Love, Sonja

"Oh, look," Sonja said. "Mom sent him the picture." She held up a photograph she had found tucked in one of the letters. It was a beloved image, much copied, much distributed. I had a larger version framed and sitting on my desk at home. It wasn't just a photograph; it was almost an emblem of our time in Uganda.

Most snapshots from Africa were family fragments: us two girls, the three girls (as my father called us), my mother alone, my father alone. In this one, we were posing together. Furthermore, no one was blinking. Furthermore, the photo was in focus, and we were close enough to the camera. But there was also something else. As clear as prose, this picture said: *missionary family here.* We were wearing our Sabbath best and had the fresh-scrubbed look of Adventists.

It was a beautiful picture for all its innocence. There we stood under the lacy leaves of a mimosa tree. My mother was thirty-six years old, my father was thirty-four, Sonja was five, and I was two. We had lived in Uganda for six months by then, carving out a home in a strange land. I had already lost my hair to a fever, and it was growing back slowly. The photograph was black and white, giving it the appearance of something ancient, a relic from another time. There we were—the four of us, a history of ourselves.

My parents were striking, the way one's parents often are in old photographs. My mother wore a Ugandan dress and a bright smile. She was, in fact, the only one smiling. Her head was nearly level with my father's shoulder. She looked slender and strong and capable. Behind her, my father stood in his preaching suit. His tie was wide and checkered and lay crooked against the formality of his shirt. He was a man who enjoyed a good joke—they both did—but he didn't like to smile for pictures. In this one, his lips and his eyes suggested a smile without actually committing.

My father held Sonja, and my mother held me. We were leggy children who seemed on the verge of bounding out of our parents' arms. We squinted at the camera, held static in a moment that would otherwise be misplaced. The children in the picture belonged to a different time and place—*this* time, *this* place. In the photograph, I was fully part of the land, and I sat forever in my mother's arms.

CHAPTER 2

—⁂—

Soon and Very Soon

"WHAT WOULD YOU do if you knew Jesus was coming in five years?"

Sitting in a hermeneutics class full of men, my father's head jerked up. He was a twenty-year-old theology student, sweet-faced and sincere. In his dorm room, he kept his few clothes and his many books, including his Bible, several Bible commentaries, and Ellen White's *Steps to Christ* and *The Desire of Ages*.

The professor, a preacher by training, paused and repeated his question for dramatic emphasis while my father and his classmates scrambled to answer. Those who were thinking *Get married. Quick!* didn't say it. Instead, they said they would knock on doors, hold evangelistic crusades, make and distribute religious tracts, and go overseas. They would go to India or Norway or Uganda, and they would tell as many people as they could about this urgent good news.

Of course, the professor's question was hypothetical. Of course, it wasn't.

The Seventh-day Adventist church began with the certainty of God's imminent arrival. In 1818, William Miller, a Baptist preacher, read Daniel 8:14—*Unto two thousand and three hundred days; then shall the sanctuary be cleansed*—and believed he was looking at a secret code: the date of Christ's return. If each prophetic day was a year and the countdown began with the rebuilding of Jerusalem in 457 BC, then the second coming would happen in Miller's lifetime. He must warn the world. Humanity, he wrote, was "sleeping over the volcano of God's wrath."

Miller preached at churches near his farm and wrote articles for the Baptist paper, *Vermont Telegraph*. He converted ministers who then converted other ministers who then converted their congregations, all anxious to know exactly *when* God was coming to take them home. For many years, Miller refused to identify a specific day, but after much cajoling, he settled on March 21, 1843—which came and went. Then he predicted March 21, 1844, which came and went again. Samuel Snow—a new convert not only to Millerism, but also to Christianity—had independently searched his Bible and emerged with a different date: October 22, 1844. Initially, this date was rejected by Miller and the other leaders, but eventually—one by one—they embraced it. October 22 became known as the true midnight cry.

The Millerites, as they were called, preached the second coming throughout the northeastern United States. They spent their inheritances spreading the good news. As the date of Christ's return grew nearer, believers left their debts unpaid and their potatoes in the fields. Miller, to a bit of controversy, built an expensive wall around his own farm, but leaders in the movement scoffed at the implication. There were more important matters. Jesus was coming!

On October 22, around one hundred thousand Millerites stood on hills, waiting for Jesus's return. They waited and waited.

The next morning, the sun rose, and New England's farmland spread before the believers, familiar and second-rate. Jesus hadn't come. Hiram Edson, a Millerite leader, wrote, "Such a spirit of weeping came over us as I never experienced before." After the Great Disappointment, as it came to be known to the faithful, Millerites tried to salvage the threads of their ordinary lives while their neighbors laughed and laughed. In town, groups of boys trailed believers, shouting, "I thought you were going up yesterday," and "Have you a ticket to go up?"

Most people left Millerism. You didn't need to be a Biblical scholar to appreciate how wrong Miller was. Even Miller left the movement he had begun. But a small and stubborn number persisted, among them Edson, who reexamined the passages in Daniel and concluded that Miller's calculation was accurate, but his interpretation wasn't. Instead of returning in 1844, God had begun the investigative judgment. He was separating the metaphorical wheat from the tares, and when he was finished, he would return for the faithful. Jesus was still coming soon.

The Seventh-day Adventist church emerged from this new calculation. The early leaders, steeped in millennial fever and the invincibility of youth, began the long and often cantankerous process of creating their own denomination. They would follow scriptures alone, *sola scriptura*, and would be the remnant, God's last church.

Their qualms, and they surely had some, were eased when Ellen Harmon, a frail teen who had stayed with Millerism despite her sorrow and bewilderment, began having visions. In the first, she saw believers traveling to heaven. The road was narrow and the journey arduous, but Jesus shone a light at their feet. When believers doubted, the light dimmed, and they fell to the wicked world below. The vision's lack of subtlety was part of its appeal. The believers had been mired in the Book of Daniel and its complicated symbolism. If they had to explain the investigative judgment one more time, they just might scream. Now, finally, they had the clarity they craved. Ellen's vision exactly reflected their experience. The road really was arduous, and their numbers really were dwindling. How relieved they were that heaven was at the end of their journey. There, God would tell them, *Well done, thou good and faithful servant*.

Ellen's visions—she had nearly two hundred during her long life—were straightforward and easy to interpret. They didn't exactly shed new light. The Bible was the light. Instead, her visions confirmed Biblical interpretations that church leaders, or at least Ellen, were already considering. When Ellen had a vision, discussion was over. No one was bold enough to argue with God.

Whether intentionally or not, Ellen had discovered the only religious authority a woman was allowed in the nineteenth century. William Miller and Hiram Edson weren't prophets, and they didn't need to be. As men, they could be theologians and preachers. Even as they calculated the end of the world, their Biblical scholarship was taken seriously. Women with their weak minds and bodies were relegated to the pews and to the tender ministries of the home. If they were audacious enough to lead a Bible study, it was strictly for other women. The story goes that before Ellen had her first vision, God had tried to give the gift of prophecy to two men. Both refused. As a child, I never thought to be offended at the lesson that God can work through anyone, even the imperfect vessel of womanhood.

Once Ellen's visions were accepted as authentic, she was welcomed into the ranks of male leadership. She married James White, an Adventist preacher and publisher, and they traveled together, instructing the faithful. My favorite Ellen White story was one of the few my mother told: Ellen and James had just presided over a church service, and James was praying for the benediction. His prayer went on and on. A second sermon. Finally, Ellen stood and raised her voice above her husband's and said, according to my mother, "As Brother White finishes his prayer, let's sing the closing hymn."

Ellen White became the informal head of the Seventh-day Adventist church. When she wasn't preaching or raising children, she was writing letters, sermons, and books. She read widely, consolidating an assortment of fringe beliefs into a cohesive point of view. She became interested in health reform and education, and because of her influence, the Adventist church built schools and hospitals around the world. When Ellen White died in 1915, the Seventh-day Adventist church was an established denomination. Much of the church's theology was recognizably evangelical—grounded in Miller's Baptist roots—but there were significant zigs and zags, still evident today.

Adventists worship on the Jewish Sabbath (from sunset to sunset). We believe that when people die, they sleep, metaphorically, until the second coming. We don't believe in a literal hell. Hell is eternal separation from God. Adventists expect Jesus to come soon, and while we wait, we try to live plain and wholesome lives. In his letter to the Corinthians, the apostle Paul asked: *Do you know that your bodies are temples of the Holy Spirit, who is in you, whom you have received from God?* Adventists know. Our rules on temperance and morality have arisen from this awareness. In the past, Adventists didn't season food with black pepper or vinegar, drink coffee, wear jewelry, read fiction, watch films in theaters, dance, play competitive sports, or gamble. Today, most Adventists indulge in at least one of these, if not all.

Nevertheless, we still have a distinct culture. We're mostly teetotalers, often vegetarians, and generally busybodies about other people's health. We joke about the Great Disappointment, even as we watch for the end times. At church, we say "happy Sabbath" when we shake someone's hand, and at potlucks, we fill our plates with Special K loaf and pasta salad. On Sabbath afternoon, somewhere, an Adventist youth group is at the beach. As the day wanes, a teen will bring out a guitar and lead the group in praise songs. If the chaperones find the lyrics repetitive, they will gamely clap along. Someone, maybe one of the adults, will request the Adventist classic, "Side by Side." Adults and teens will arrange themselves into a large circle and reach for their neighbors' hands. The teens might stumble through the verses, but everyone will know the chorus, which they sing together, strong and earnest: "Meet me in heaven, we'll join hands together. Meet me by the Savior's side. I'll meet you in heaven, we'll sing songs together. Brothers and sisters, I'll be there."

My mother was born into Adventism. Her father was a Bible teacher at the only Adventist high school in Finland. Even when he was young, my grandfather was known as the Grand Old Man on campus. Because he was entrusted with the spiritual development of other people's children, his own were expected to be models of Adventist virtue. My mother—studious, obedient, and loyal to her own mother—didn't complain. Instead, when she had free time, she climbed into the attic and read the illicit novels she had somehow procured. If my grandfather knew, he said nothing.

My grandfather, whom we called Pappa, was a shy man, with an elfin face and a generous smile. He was friendly to everyone but unable to form deep connections, even with family members. His most sustained relationship was with Ellen White. When he visited us in the United States, he came with one suitcase filled with her books. My mother reached for that bag, and its weight wrenched at her arm. She loved to tell the story: "I thought his suitcase was full of rocks, but it was only Ellen White."

I never saw my mother reading Ellen White's books, and unless she was pointing out inconsistencies to her daughters, she rarely discussed Adventist theology. She was an Adventist who minded the edges of the Sabbath, read from Psalms and the Gospels, cooked vegetarian meals, and before evening prayers, sang, "Turn your eyes upon Jesus," her attention clicking away from us, her face softening.

My father converted to Adventism when he was a child. His mother, Marjorie, was dynamic, beautiful, and impulsive. She divorced young and had a knack for bad relationships. When men told her they wouldn't date a woman with children, she dropped off her kids at various foster homes, visiting when she could. My father and his siblings were frequently beaten, and at one home, a woman broke my father's arm. My father's uncle intervened, arranging for my father and his older brother, Johnny, to stay at an Adventist home in the Mojave Desert. The couple owned a chicken farm and required the brothers to do chores and mind their manners.

My father attended a one-room Adventist school. He could barely read or write, and during class, he wandered around the room, no doubt annoying his teacher. Yet she responded with kindness, igniting in my father an admiration for the profession and an awareness of how one teacher can change someone's life trajectory. She stayed after school and tutored my father until he caught up with his peers. For the first time, my father felt the pride that comes from academic excellence and the security that comes from a structured home life. He and Johnny lived for two years on that old chicken ranch, attending Sabbath School and church each Saturday. When their mother, who had moved to Hawaii for a job, finally brought them to live with her, she was surprised at how devout they were, particularly her youngest.

The Adventist church became the ballast in my father's childhood. My grandmother moved from man to man, apartment to apartment, job to job. Every few months, she and her children would pack their belongings and scrub down their rental unit. No matter, on Sabbath, my father was at church. Sometimes his siblings came. Sometimes his mother came, too. When he was old enough, my father enrolled himself in an Adventist boarding school, paying his way through work-study programs. In the most secular sense, the Adventist church had saved him.

My father was devoted to his mother, and he was also determined to be nothing like her. As a teenager, he developed his capacity to see things through. By the time my mother met him, he was like a landmass. Once he set his mind to something, he didn't budge. He listened politely to others and remained steadfast, doing precisely what he said he would do. My mother called this his stubbornness.

My father dedicated himself to serving God and dreamed of someday becoming a missionary. The life he envisioned looked so different from his mother's that he didn't recognize their mutual restlessness. By most metrics, they were opposites. She discarded everything. He discarded nothing. She was outgoing and assertive. He was introverted and diplomatic. She was impulsive. He was responsible to a fault. She couldn't sit still. He loved academia and could spend hours poring over his books. While he was studying for a degree in theology, she was having an affair with a married man. Yet beneath their contrasting natures were matching fulcrums tipping them toward adventure— the more reckless, the better. If Marjorie's child was going to be religious, it made absolute sense that he would want to be a missionary.

After asking his class about the second coming, my father's hermeneutics professor listened to their answers, and what he heard were earnest and self-important plans. The theology professor's job was to temper any fanaticism and to teach the value of inquiry. To be of any use to future congregations, these men needed to wrestle with hard questions like, *How could a good God allow bad things to happen?* The professor still studied and prayed over that one, while my father and his classmates had a fast answer, a non-answer: God was coming soon and would make everything right.

"If you knew Jesus was coming in five years," the professor told his students, "the best use of those years would be to finish your education and only then start preaching."

This moment became my father's second conversion. He loved studying and had often felt guilty for his misplaced priorities. Shouldn't he be more anxious to do the important work of evangelism? Now, he was assured of the importance of his interests. Education wasn't just valuable; it was crucial. Jesus said you needed to have the faith of a child, and didn't children question everything, and didn't Jesus say you needed to be as wise as a serpent? If my father really wanted to be a missionary, he should bring something to the table: an education. He filled out paperwork expressing his future interest in mission work, then burrowed down into his studies.

My father finished his degree in theology and enrolled in the Master of Divinity program at Andrews University. He met and married my mother, graduated with honors, accepted a pastoral position in Indiana, had two daughters, and took advantage of his proximity to Ball State University to study part-time for a Master's in Public Health. He hadn't forgotten about the mission field. It just didn't consume his daily consciousness the way parenting did. So when a letter arrived from Adventist Mission, he was taken by surprise. The church was offering my father—and by extension our family—a mission appointment in Uganda.

The job was at Bugema Missionary Training School, a sprawling campus about an hour outside of Kampala. It had a rigorous high school, an on-site farm, and a training school for ministers and teachers. The Adventist church wanted my father to transform the ministerial certificate into an accredited college degree, the first one offered at Bugema. My father had no teaching experience, no Ph.D., no unique connections within Adventism. It was as if someone was flipping through mission applications, read my father's, and thought, *Well, this guy seems earnest.*

My father didn't speculate about why he had been chosen. He assumed someone knew he was up to the task. He also believed in his own work ethic, in his aptitude to learn from others, and, of course, in his ability to see a task to completion. Mostly, he was elated, and even my mother felt the pricklings of excitement. He was being offered the chance to teach in Uganda. Life was finally getting interesting. Of course we would go.

Years later, my father learned that fifteen more qualified candidates had turned down the position before he had been asked. My parents didn't wonder why the others had said no. By then, they already knew.

CHAPTER 3

———— ❧ ————

Jambo

THE LONG RAINS had ended when our plane landed at the Entebbe airport. The ground beside the runway was plush, and cattle egrets stepped through the grass, catching crickets and frogs. Sonja pressed her forehead against the oval window, and beside her, my mother peered past Sonja's nutbrown hair and gazed at the earth with its greens and reds. The intercom crackled, and with the voice of the British Empire in his throat, the captain said, "Welcome to Uganda."

Our plane stopped on the tarmac, stairs were wheeled over, and the door was flung open. It was midmorning, and already the heat seeped in. Passengers stood, gathered their bags, and shuffled for the exit. My mother held a carry-on in each hand and another slung over her shoulder. She set me in the aisle and told me to go on. She was overwhelmed with bags, and babies, and a growing sense of unease. My father had gone to Uganda before us, and without him, she was having trouble just getting off the plane. We were the last to exit.

Our first step into Africa offered light so fierce we shut our eyes before reopening them slowly, a sliver of eye against the sun. Our gaze swept across the tarmac and beyond that to a small, cement airport. Sweat gathered on our faces and bodies as we were embraced by the showy heat of Uganda.

My mother must have reeled at the enormity of our arrival. When she had married my father, she had left Finland behind. For months at a time, she spoke only English. At the bank and at bus stops, she was asked, "Where are you from?"—a frequent reminder that she didn't belong. Now, she was even more conspicuously an outsider. We planned to live in Uganda for six years, and she hoped this place would feel like home to her daughters. For herself, we had become her home.

My father waited behind a velvet rope. He stood, leaning outward, the image of a man who had lived alone the past two months and hadn't liked it. His hair was brown and long on his neck. It was recalcitrant, wavy hair, and he would have looked like a moppet if he hadn't been so tall and thin. He was, in fact, the tallest, thinnest, whitest man in the lobby. His glasses were over-large, and he wore tan slacks and a western shirt with silver snaps. He was the first person everyone noticed as they entered. Still, when we stepped through the door, he waved one hand above his head and shouted, "Jambo! Jambo!"

He had come to Uganda before the academic year, arriving alone because my mother couldn't bear to fly through Europe without stopping in Finland to see her parents. Her mother had cancer, and she carried daughter-guilt with her. *How many years left?* Where our mother went, we her daughters followed. This would become our pattern: my father starting or finishing a school year in Uganda, the three of us in Finland.

Alone, my father moved into the house I would always think of as home, the definitive home: a place of warmth and wonder. It was a red brick house, squat and square, with a corrugated metal roof and a screened-in verandah. Because it was the farthest house from campus, nobody had wanted to live there. "Hurry to Uganda, or you'll be stuck with the house on the hill," my parents had been warned. When it was assigned to him, my father was elated. The jungle surrounding the house was still inhabited by monkeys, civet cats, mongoose, and bush babies. My father could scarcely believe our luck.

I am batching it in a very big house, my father wrote his mother. *I don't know how Kaarina will take to the rudimentary conditions. I don't mind. My needs are taken care of. Except that I have only two pots. It is so hard to transfer everything back and forth since I have no storage containers. So I must boil water for drinking, cook beans, and cook rice, all in the same pot, plus I cook my soup in it. I don't know what to do with one, while I'm doing the other. It would surely help if I had an electric rice cooker. I would appreciate it very much if you could airmail one to me.*

Over the next decade, my parents would ask my American grandmother to send many things, including clothes, which they would ask her to wash first (*and don't iron*) so that the items would look used. *Customs is 100 percent of value, or more*, they wrote. My grandmother wearied of these letters, but that first request, she was quick to respond to: Only two pots, oh my! I'm not sure if the rice cooker arrived before we did; the screens are what my father remembers.

"When is your family coming?" the school secretary would ask. My father's solitary arrival worried the staff at Bugema. It sure didn't seem as if he planned to stay long.

"I'll send for them after the house gets screens," my father replied. He was joking and not joking. Our tickets to Uganda were open-ended, and he had a mzungu's fear of malaria. When we arrived, the screens, such as they were, were in place.

My mother dropped the bags and half ran to my father. They embraced for a time before remembering us. I hadn't seen my father in a long while, and when he bent to hug me, I wiggled away. Sonja placed her arms around his neck and allowed him to kiss her cheek, but she soon pulled away.

"You've gotten so big, pumpkin," he offered. She smiled and took my hand. "You girls have really grown."

"Well," my mother said to my father, hands on her hips. The worry on her face was gone, and behind the smile there was nothing more complicated than brightness.

"Well," my father said. He, too, was giddy. The two months had been long ones, filled with work and wonder and foolish mistakes. Each day, he had been shoring up stories to share with my mother, for she was a fine one for laughing.

"So," she said, "this is Africa." She reached up and touched the hair that looped across his forehead. "You need a haircut."

"How would you like to go shopping?" he said. "I know the best place in town." The truth was that he would have liked to take us straight home. The flight was long, and he knew we must be tired, that my mother must be anxious to see the house, that a woman wants to unpack something. But we didn't yet have a car, and the family who would drive us back to Bugema was now shopping in Kampala, an optimistic pursuit.

The Entebbe airport was outside of Kampala, and so we took a taxi into town. My mother gazed out the window, her first look at Uganda. The taxi rattled past dukas selling bananas and fish, past a dip in the ground where men stood knee-deep in water and washed a Mercedes with old t-shirts, past a marabou stork the same size as me. "Pretty amazing, huh?" my father said, pointing out the window. The stork was standing on a heap of rubbish, fussing over something. "They're all over Kampala, but you won't see many in Bugema." We gazed at the trees and grass, at the ground and sky. Only the words were familiar. The difference between Finland and Uganda was like the difference between watercolors and oil paints. The textures were thicker here, the colors more intense.

My parents hadn't stopped talking. They hadn't been separated this long since they were married. They had met during my mother's last semester of graduate school, her commencement nipping at their heels, her need to get married looming over every exchange. In her dorm room, she would sit with her friends and analyze her dates with my father. Was this significant? Was that? Would he propose before she left?

Though my mother alone knew it, their courtship was being played out under the long shadow of my Finnish grandmother, a shadow that stretched from Turku to Michigan. My grandmother was a formidable woman who had kept a keen eye on all her children's romantic prospects. When my uncle Hannu dated the "Kissing Machine," my grandmother dispatched my mother to the Machine herself to demand the couple break up. My mother complied, as did the Machine. Few, apparently, could say no to my grandmother. My mother's own romantic prospects were scarce. She's too skinny, the family said, too bossy, too shy with the boys. My mother was sent to America to get her master's degree. That she was also to find a husband was not only assumed, but also discussed in exhaustive, embarrassing detail.

If my mother was ever shy, it was certainly news to my father. "You'll have to find another girlfriend soon," my mother announced pointedly near the end of the semester. Her accent was British in its exactness, but Scandinavian in its rolling Rs. As her departure slipped from weeks to days, she intensified her campaign, pointing to girls with their miniskirts and their swinging blond hair. She selected tall, voluptuous girls, girls with twanging accents and large blue eyes, girls who were nothing at all like her. "Is she your type?" my mother would ask. "What about her?"

When my father finally proposed, my mother felt first a rush of relief and then happiness. They told the story of their courtship often, interrupting each other with points of contention, laughing at each other's versions, then listing romantic rivals and complications, including a breakup. My father said he had every intention of proposing. My mother said that he would never have asked if she hadn't compelled him to. If she's right, then it was one of the few times my mother got her way over something significant. Though opinionated, smart, quick tempered, and strong, my mother had a soft spot for my father. That she ever agreed to live in Uganda would surprise everyone for years to come, her daughters most of all.

The suburbs surrounding Kampala were disarmingly rural with banana trees and tied-up goats and tin-roofed homes, and my mother hardly noticed we were nearing the city until the taxi jostled into Kampala. And even still, the capital of Uganda felt more like a town. The tallest building was the fourteen-story International Hotel. The road gave some indication of Kampala's importance. It had become an alarming tangle of cars and bicycles and matatus, each jostling to pass the other. Our driver, sweat running down the back of his neck, poked his head out the window and shouted at pedestrians, then at a kombi driver, and then he turned to my father and shouted, "Nobody can drive here, eh?" and laughed. It was a laugh so full and leisurely that he could have been sitting in a parlor telling stories.

Kampala was built on seven hills. While Rome has Romulus and Remus, Kampala has the Kabaka and the colonizers and long-necked antelope. Imagine a land green enough to overwhelm every other color, though the dirt is red and the sky is blue. Imagine that the land is already separated into distinct kingdoms, each with its own language, culture, traditions, and religion. The monarchies are as distinct as any Europe has to offer. And there, in the heart of Buganda—a kingdom as old as the British Tudors—lies Kampala (before it was Kampala). And imagine Ugandan kob stepping through the brush, moving in herds, their heads tilted, listening and then sensing no danger, eating at the green, green grass. Here, where we hurtle down the tarmac, is where the Kabaka once hunted.

In 1858, British explorers John Hanning Speke and Richard Burton came to Uganda, searching for the source of the Nile. When Burton grew ill, Speke continued without him, traveling north until he came to a virtual ocean of water edged with papyrus. Crocodiles lay upon the muddy banks. Though it was already named Lake Nyanza and owned as much as any body of water could be, Speke called it Lake Victoria.

He returned to England and announced (somewhat correctly) that Lake Victoria was the Nile's source. Burton disagreed. The two men traveled England, giving competing presentations and were about to debate each other in public when Speke died in what was either a suicide or an accidental shooting. For those living in Uganda, it didn't matter. Other explorers were coming, and then missionaries. They would arrive and find Uganda a good land, a lush and temperate place where the sun rose and set at seven, and they would set in motion the destruction that was to come.

Buganda was the largest kingdom and the most powerful. The Kabaka was king, and he lived on a hill surrounded by impala. The British called this place "the hill of the impala," and the words were translated into Luganda as kasozi k'empala, shortened eventually to Kampala.

Kampala became the heart of a new and reluctant nation. Kingdoms were gathered like fish in a net and tossed together under one protectorate: the British Empire. England used one kingdom as an administrator, another as a police force and army. They exploited grievances and pitted region against region. When Uganda's independence came, it brought with it the nationalism of many nations. Each former kingdom carried a reasonable grudge against the others, and with that grudge came fear. Is it any wonder that Uganda was hurled toward tragedy?

We arrived in Kampala ignorant or naïve, idealistic or malevolent, depending on how one would judge us. We carried with us the historical baggage of missionaries: the colonialism, the racism, the imposition of one culture over another, of one religion over another. We also carried the idealism: the sacrifice, the good intentions, the hospitals that had been built, and the schools. For good or for ill, we had come to Uganda. One family can't answer for all the evils that religion has wrought upon the world, nor can it take credit for any mercies. The only certainty about our arrival was its foolishness. Years later, my mother would write in a mission talk: *If we had known enough about Uganda to make an intelligent decision, we probably wouldn't have gone.*

How my parents managed to remain ignorant, I'm not certain. When our plane touched down at the Entebbe airport, the United States had already closed its embassy, moved its ambassadors to Kenya, pulled out the Peace Corps (a volunteer had been shot and killed at an army checkpoint), and advised U.S. citizens against travel to Uganda. Idi Amin had evicted (or "booted out," as he said) sixty thousand ethnic Indians and Pakistanis, stripping them of everything they owned. He had accused fifty-five Catholic missionaries of smuggling weapons. They were lucky to only be expelled. Shopkeepers accused of price gouging were executed. People were disappearing. And Idi Amin had declared himself President for Life. In 1975, the year my parents received their invitation to serve in Uganda, the country's Finance Minister escaped to England, saying, "To live in Uganda today is hell."

The taxi stopped at the market, and together my father and the driver pulled our suitcases out of the trunk and lined them up on the street. "Watch them," my father told my mother. "They'll walk off if you're not watching."

My mother sat on a white hardback and set me on her lap, holding me to her with one hand, the other gripping the strap of her carry-on. "Don't wander off," she called to Sonja. "Come and wait here."

My mother had never lived anywhere hotter than Michigan, though she had visited California, Hawaii, and Florida. She was used to poverty, but not the tropical scent of it. The air of Kampala was heavy with smells: over-ripe fruit, burning rubber, the absence of soap. Flies landed on our arms and faces, their feet tickling our skin. My arms shot up in protest. The flies lifted, circled our heads, and landed again in the same moist places. A few children had gathered. We would have been a peculiar sight anyway, a bulky circle of suitcases and bewilderment, but with the exodus of expatriates, our existence was even more extraordinary. A boy bolted forward and touched Sonja's arm, then ran back, giggling. Other children held out their hands. "Hello, mzungu. Hello. How are you? Give me money."

What was a mzungu if not wealthy?

My mother placed both palms out, revealing their emptiness. "Do you have money?" she asked my father.

"If you start giving money, we'll be mobbed," my father replied.

My mother sat on a suitcase surrounded by children who were as beautiful and as curious as her own. Of their clothes, she would later write *one wouldn't even use them for rags, and many of the trousers have holes where it counts.* She would soon learn that Ugandans placed a point of pride on dressing smart and were appalled that Americans, who could afford better, dressed like hippies. She would learn that most Ugandans earned fifteen cents an hour, and clothing here was more expensive than in the States. She would learn that the stores were mainly empty, that a soldier would kill for a piece of soap, and that soap was, in fact, the perfect bribe. She would learn how to bribe and how to sweet-talk her way out of trouble. She would learn how to move through this city on her own, how to sell items in one place and purchase airline tickets in another. But no matter how much she learned, she would always be aware of the color of her skin, of its otherness. It was her passport as much as anything else.

The children darted forward in ones and twos, laughing. How could anyone be as drained of pigment as we were? They touched our skin and held tentative fingers toward our hair. Their hands were fleeting, like humming-birds. Fingers grazed our bodies and then shot back to the bodies they had come from. The children stared at us, and Sonja and I stared back.

The other missionaries were visible from a distance, and my mother watched them for a long time as they approached. They moved easily down the road and did not seem to notice how they were noticed. Each person turned as the couple passed. They walked up to my parents, smiling. "Jambo," they said, shaking my mother's hand. "You are welcome, as they say in Uganda."

The couple was tall and blond and friendly, and during the drive to Bugema, they took pleasure in trying to shock my mother, their voices over-lapping: "Idi Amin. What a madman! He'll kill us all yet. He's certainly killed enough Ugandans, but don't say that to anyone here, it'll get you killed. He's crazy, all right. He was offering aid to America. He must have sent it, too, be-cause there was nothing in the stores. Nothing! And everyone sitting around selling their nothing. What else are you going to do? I hope you brought lots of food with you. Or ate well on the plane. You've got to smuggle in flour if you want any without bugs, and you can only buy the buggy flour from a VIP store, strictly for expats. Of course, we all eat bugs here. We enjoy a good bug now and then, don't we? Good protein. Good for the vegetarian diet. Some insects actually are for eating. Termites are edible. Did you know that? You just pull off the wings. No, we haven't tried them. We're not that hungry yet. Who knows, maybe next month."

My mother was more amused than anything. They expected her to be horrified, and their expectation was bracing. Besides, she was certain they were exaggerating. If the Adventist church was still sending missionaries, Uganda must be reasonably safe, food must be reasonably available. She smiled as if she couldn't wait to eat a termite, as if she had come for that very reason.

"It can't be all bad," my mother said. She had been to the market and had been dazzled by the fruit. There were pineapples, passion fruit, paw paws, and bananas. So many bananas. She hadn't known so many varieties existed. She had bought a bit of everything and couldn't imagine needing anything else. She gestured to her bag. "There's something to buy."

The wife turned to my mother. "The fruit *is* lovely. But you'll see, there isn't much else, and the political situation, well, it's pretty awful."

The trip to Bugema was at least an hour's journey on the road, which began paved and gave way shortly to dirt. The earth was red, and it rose up from the road and clung redly to the windows, and behind the van, a cloud of maroon hung in the air before returning to the road and to the grass beside the road. The lane was narrow, and when cars approached from the opposite direction, the smaller vehicles had to pull to the side. Bicycles and pedestrians traveled at their own peril. "The road to Jericho," the missionaries called it after the carjackings began.

We passed grove after grove of banana plants. A cluster of trees stood outside every home. Bananas could be boiled, steamed, fried, mashed, made into beer, or eaten raw. The word matoke means both banana and food. Through the shredded leaves, great clusters hung down from stems as solid as a leg. When the fruit was harvested, the stalk was cut with a panga, and the whole bunch, weighing as much as a goat, was dropped in a corner of the kitchen.

The homes were made either with cinderblocks or earth and were roofed with corrugated metal or straw. The kitchens, my mother would later learn, were usually separate, a hut in the back where women squatted beside a fire and where smoke was a second ingredient. Cooked on a stove, matoke could taste bland.

Sonja and I closed our eyes against the adult voices. We weren't jet-lagged. There was only an hour's time difference between Finland and Uganda, between this land of lakes and trees and that land of lakes and trees. But we were tired from rising early, our day beginning with a drive into Helsinki, the checking-in of luggage, the moving from plane to plane, the whine of wheels before liftoff, the jolt of wheels upon landing, and then, finally, Uganda. We were soothed by this rhythm of tires against dirt, and even the bumps couldn't wake us.

Later, we would come to know this road and to love it. We would sit in the backseat of our Ford station wagon, our bodies angled toward opposite windows.

"I recognize that chicken," I would say.

"I recognize that man on the bicycle," Sonja would respond.

It was a joke, this game, as if the same chicken and the same man and the same bicycle waited along this road, waited for us to return. When we came home after a long absence, we would set our happiness to song. We would commemorate what we were returning to in a long and loving litany—our friends, our cats, our dog, our chickens, our house, our hallway, and even our guava tree, the one I had named Bertha. We added verses and changed the tune, laughing at our own cleverness. We played with the words, stretching out the vowels. But the chorus was always the same: *We will soon be home. We will soon be home.*

It was late when we finally arrived at the house on the hill. Sonja and I were sleeping, our heads lolled back on vinyl seats. "Here it is," my father said. "What do you think?" He carried suitcases to the house. My mother carried children. They waded through grass that hadn't been slashed for several weeks. The house sat at the top of a hill in a small clearing, encircled by jungle. In the fading light, it was hard to notice the flowers. My mother was left only with the shadows, the buzzing of insects and frogs, the greens that grew steadily darker, and a vervet monkey that scampered from branch to branch, edging for a closer look.

CHAPTER 4

———— ❧ ————

Every Tree Has Flowers

THE HOUSE MY mother moved into was so infused with snakes that even for Uganda, it was notable. It was as if Medusa lived in our attic. Students later spoke of a science teacher who lived there, a man who kept snakes on the verandah, their aquariums arranged in stacks. They said he bred mambas, pythons, vipers, and cobras, and when no one was looking, he cooed to them as if they were a room full of guinea pigs. Before the missionary returned home, he carried his collection to the yard, removed each lid, and watched as the snakes rustled in the grass, their pulses disappearing into the jungle. The story passed from year to year, class to class, and like the most vivid legends, it wasn't true. What is true is that there were snakes here, a lush and diverse population, and that they would remain long after we had left.

My mother was a woman with many fears: driving, choking on pills, cancer. To that list, she promptly added snakes. Only later would she include Idi Amin and Uganda's "political situation," the delicate phrase missionaries used to refer to the killings. But those early days, our mother's biggest fear was snakes. Each day, when Sonja and I returned from playing, she would peer at the cuts on our legs and arms and ask, "Were you scratched by a stick?" And always we said no—no, no, no—because even though we had assured her we knew the difference between a stick and a snake, she didn't believe us.

My mother had grown up knowing a single venomous snake—the common viper, common only because of the number of countries in which it's found. In Finland, it is as rare as the winter sun, and as mild. Bees are a greater hazard. But the snakes of Uganda were flashy, venomous affairs, the superstars of the ophidian community: a black mamba could chase down a man, a cobra could spit poison. For such glamorous reptiles, they were intrusive neighbors, the kind who would stop by uninvited or linger outside the window. They dropped onto our roof from low branches, hid in the laundry basket, and lunged into the kitchen, their bodies flicking side to side.

In a letter to her father, my mother wrote: *Last Friday, in our yard, very close to Gary's feet was a black mamba over two meters long. When Gary stepped over it, it crept into a tree and from there looked at us. Luckily it didn't attack. Then I really lost my breath.*

The week we arrived, my mother began to clean. She knelt in the living room, a bucket of brown water beside her. "I can't live with them," she told my father. She couldn't fathom creating a life in this house, with its curtainless windows, grey walls, and the cockroaches that scuttled for cover each time she switched on a light. She had learned from her mother that a good scrub could cure most problems and leave the remainder with less heft. Though my father had cleaned for two months, it was as if he had peeled back only a layer or two of earth. "We can't live with them," she repeated when my father didn't reply.

What could he say? At the end of his arm dangled the husk of a snake. It was the size he had thought to impress her with. The filmy membrane was nearly as long as his body. He had found it in the attic beside a nail sticking out from the floorboard. The skin, turned inside out, was as wispy as an onion shell. He had felt a rush of excitement at the discovery, at being so near danger without actually being in danger. A snake, perhaps that very morning, had rubbed its nose against the nail, slicing off its restrictive coating.

"I'm not sure what we can do," he said finally. "We can't kill them all."

"What if that is in the house?" my mother said.

"Well," my father said. He could say something easy—*I'm sure it's not. Don't worry. The skin has probably been there for years*—but he was pragmatic and honest. The snake, he thought, probably was still in the attic; if not, it would probably return, and if it didn't, others would probably come. "Let's just hope it's not poisonous."

They both laughed. It was their favorite kind of joke—subtle and dark. *Of course* the snake was poisonous.

I grew up with Two Truths.

Truth One: When you're outside, make noise. Never creep down a path. Instead, stomp, shout, sing. My mother led the way down the hill, singing songs in English or Finnish. She liked hymns—"How Great Thou Art," "Blessed Assurance," "What a Friend We Have in Jesus." She said the snakes could hear us a mile away.

Truth Two: If you encounter a snake without an adult present, stop dead. Don't run. Don't walk. Don't scratch your nose. And maybe you won't get bitten; maybe you'll live. I grew up believing this, earnest and without question.

When I was six, I saw my first snake, *my* snake, one that existed in that moment (that hour?) exclusively for me. Every other snake had been observed from the safety of my parents' presence. My snake was grey and black and stretched thin against a stone. I almost didn't see it, and when I did, it was only a step away. I halted. It was morning, and the air was cool. I observed the snake, drawing the sun into its body, its tongue flicking in and out, the movement rapid and purposeful like a hand dealing cards. I didn't move. It didn't leave. The morning grew warmer, and I could feel the sun against my back. My neck ached; my arms and legs were heavy with waiting. *What if no one finds me?* The snake lifted and lowered its lacquered head, responding to something I couldn't see. *Not me*, I thought. *I'm invisible with stillness.*

My father found me. He called my name, and when I didn't answer, he called again and walked toward me. "What are you looking at?" I didn't want to risk even the motion of my jaw, and so he had to follow my eyes to the rock and there to the snake.

"The only garter snake in Africa," my father called it. He held his hands six inches apart. "It was so small," he told my mother, "I first thought it was a worm. You should have seen it." My mother assured me that I had done the right thing. She was pleased that I had followed instructions with such diligence. I was a good girl, one she could trust. She told me all this between short smiles and glances at my father and a face that once contorted and then resumed its supportive message. When I went to my room, I could hear them laughing—my father describing the snake again, my mother nearly shrieking.

We had not been long on the hill when Samson joined our lives. He came when the hill was the most beautiful, which was a slippery thing to quantify. The hill was always beautiful, even when the rains were fierce, but in the mornings, it felt as if we were at the top of a steep mountain and the world was all sky and possibility. My mother was inside fretting when she heard Samson's hodi. There was so much pulling at her mind. This time, it was the question of how many insects in the granola were too many. "We enjoy a good bug," the missionaries had said, as if she couldn't hack it. Well, she would show them.

She set down the Tupperware and went to see who was at the door. It wasn't the morning of the passion fruit man, and the women had already gathered water from the tank. Students who wanted to catch my father's ear would look for him on campus, and after the initial flurry of calls by the missionary women, visitors were rare. My mother stepped through the house and onto the verandah. Sonja and I trailed behind.

"Jambo," my mother said through the screen. She smiled, uncertain. Ever since she had arrived in Uganda, she had been overwhelmed by her incompetence. This must have surprised her. She was a woman defined by capability. "Don't be helpless," she told Sonja and me over and over. As a teen, she had spent the summer in the more affluent Sweden, selling Adventist books door to door. The Lutheran housewives took one look at all the Ellen White volumes and then bought the vegetarian cookbook. It was my mother's bestseller. She had laughed at the recipes and fretted about what the women must think. The recipes went like this: Summer Strawberry Salad—wash strawberries, spoon off tops, cut, dust with sugar, place in bowl. She sold enough books to pay for school and, in the process, came to speak Swedish so fluently that the housewives assumed she was a Swede.

But here, here, she was inept. She didn't know how to open a jackfruit or remove the fruit from its thick sap. She didn't know how to cook matoke or make groundnut sauce or even how to fix the taro that grew below the drainpipe. She could have used a cookbook like the one she used to sell. She knew nothing. She didn't know which people were Baganda or Iteso or Basoga or Karamojong or why it mattered. Wasn't everyone a Ugandan? She didn't know the history of this place, the politics, the scars left by missionaries. And when at night she heard drums reverberating in the distance, she sat on the verandah and listened, amazed.

Samson asked for money, and my mother offered him a job. She never imagined she would be someone with personal help. She had grown up on the poverty end of poverty. About her childhood in Finland, she wrote, *I was nineteen when we got a house with a real bathtub and inside plumbing.* Above that sentence, in red ink, she added, *Water had to be carried from uphill. Outhouse was right nippy with the cold and the snow—the visits we made there were very short and sweet.* My parents were self-reliant and proud of working hard, but everyone here had help, or so it seemed, and everyone called the men who worked in their gardens "houseboys," or so it seemed, and my mother—who would later ask Sonja and me, "If everyone jumped off a cliff, would you?"—did the same.

"I hired a houseboy," she told my father when he came home. "I didn't know him from Adam, but I liked his face." As a child, I thought Adam was a university where Adventists got acquainted.

My mother was older than Samson, but she didn't look it. She was childishly thin, dressed like no respectable adult in Uganda, and was a woman. Under ordinary circumstances, Samson wouldn't have taken orders from her. Her authority came from the color of her skin. She was a mzungu, a privilege that missionaries accepted with little reflection. On Samson's first day, she stood in shorts and a t-shirt and asked him to cut trees. The request was absurd. She surely couldn't mean all the trees in the jungle or the fruit trees or the trees that shaded the house.

"Which ones, madam?" Samson asked, leaning against the panga's handle, the point of which he had driven into the ground.

They walked the perimeter of the house, and she pointed at the branches reaching over the eave. "They're too close to the house," she said. "Cut everything touching the roof. Leave the flowered trees, but cut everything else."

"These are good for shade, madam," Samson said. "See?"

They gazed at the shadow a branch cast over the roof. It was dark and cool, like spreading water. "We'll have to do without," she said. She turned to him. She didn't want to be the crazy mzungu. "Our house is crawling with snakes. They just drop out of the trees."

For several afternoons, we listened to the thwack of iron against wood and the crack of branches as they broke against each other and against the earth. My mother read books to Sonja and me, one after another, her voice flowing across words that could be any words, and we fidgeted from her lack of attention.

"No, you can't go outside," she told us again and again. "Why don't you help me wash the dishes?" My mother set me down and pulled over a chair for Sonja to stand on. The two of them washed, rinsed, and dried the plates from lunch, while I helped by watching.

The branches stacked up by the jungle, and yet, when I remember the house on the hill, I remember the trees and the long sweep of leaves. If we were rich with nothing else, it was with vegetation and scrub and star fruits. I can't imagine that when we arrived there were even more.

The last day of the cutting, my mother stepped outside, and she shouted. Beside the road, one of the frangipani trees was lying on the ground. There had been a pair of them, one on each side of the drive. They had reminded her of Hawaii, of leis and beaches and all the pleasures of a vacation. My father had spent much of his childhood in Hawaii, and my mother had thrilled at her proximity. She, little Oili, had married a Hawaiian. She picked up a small branch, and she marched around the house. She found Samson throwing wood into the jungle. He stopped when he saw her. She held out the stick. The wood was so soft it felt like a stem in her hand. The leaves were supple, and the flowers perfumed the air between them. "I told you not to cut down the trees with flowers. What were you thinking?"

"Madam," he said, his voice measured, exasperated. "This is Uganda. Every tree has flowers."

The next morning was Sabbath. My father placed a vinyl record on the stereo, and the house filled with music: "How can I say thanks for the things You have done for me? Things so undeserved, yet You gave to prove Your love for me." We moved to the sounds of Adventism: Del Delker, The King's Heralds, The Heritage Singers.

Our house was as clean as my mother could get it. While Samson had been cutting branches, she had been washing walls, changing sheets, and hanging laundry on the line. As a child, she had hated Fridays. Before Sabbath, piirakka had to be baked, shoes polished, walls and floors scrubbed, and all this had to be accomplished before sunset. During the short days of winter, Fridays were marked by frenzied motion, by small arms moving back and forth like pistons. In her own home, my mother had vowed, she wouldn't fuss over the approaching Sabbath. But when she was a college student in England, living for the first time on her own, she found herself on Friday afternoons washing the floor, ironing her clothes, and missing home.

For a day of rest, Sabbath morning was a frantic time. The teacher and his family couldn't be late for church. We ate breakfast at a clipped pace. My father cleared the table as my mother brushed hair—hers, Sonja's, mine. My father found matching socks for us; my mother put me into my shoes, her fingers working the buckles. And then, inevitably, my father set off looking for something—his sermon, his glasses, his watch. This particular morning, it was his Bible.

With a tie in his hand, my father hustled about the house. "Maybe I left it on the table. Did I have it with me yesterday? Did I leave it at school? Maybe it's on the bed. Did I put it by the door already? Have you seen it anywhere?" We were outside, prepared to leave, regardless, when my father wondered if he had left his Bible in the car. We finally had one. We didn't drive to church, of course; petrol was too precious. But our father did sometimes drive into Kampala for errands, and he would take his Bible and a yellow legal pad with him so that during the inevitable waiting, he could prepare for his Old Testament class or work on a sermon.

My mother, Sonja, and I stood by the verandah as my father walked to the garage and took hold of the door. It was a bulky affair, built like a barn door, and when he pulled it open, a snake dropped.

My father felt the weight of it first, a blow on the back of his neck. For a moment, the viper hung from his shoulders like a lei. It was a bush viper, long and skinny, nearly three feet. Compared to the mamba, it was a benign, mind-your-own-business snake. But a viper on your neck doesn't feel benign. Its venom is a hemotoxin, a blood poison.

My mother watched, her feet tied to the grass, her mind measuring what she would need to do if the viper bit my father. She had been taught about snakebites during the brief training the church had for missionaries. She would need to get a knife first, from the kitchen. How long there? How long back? My father would not wait docilely. He would try to be useful. He would talk and talk and advise her on how best to cut open the bite. He would tell her that there was a sharper knife in the drawer. She would get angry. Her husband bitten by a snake, and there she was yelling at him to shut up. She would try and suck out the poison, spitting blood and saliva on the ground. She would have to go back into the house for something to make a tourniquet with, a dishtowel, maybe. And then she would need to herd us into the car. Who would drive? She didn't have a license but would still insist. My father would hold a towel to his cut and eye the road nervously.

She was a terrible driver. The dispensary would be closed for Sabbath, but she would find someone to open it. She would try to identify the snake, and if she guessed right, there might be enough time to inject the antivenom and save my father's life. But if the snake bit my father's face, where would she tie the tourniquet?

The viper had no wish to linger. It flowed down the length of my father's body like water from a hose and left him shaken and alive. It was a beautiful morning, cloudless and bright. *To God be the Glory.* The trees were still wet from the night, and the leaves were lush and green and vibrant. For the first time that morning, my parents heard the birds singing.

It could have been a generous moment in which two creatures, both dangerous, collided and departed in peace. But my father's mind was lurching with what might have happened. He might have died, leaving his wife a widow, leaving his children to forget him, piece by piece. He bolted into the garage and returned with a jembe. He had learned that a hoe has many uses. One sweep through the air, and the bush viper was dead.

God was watching over us. Surely, my parents thought this. If the viper didn't bite, then wasn't that proof of God's protection? Wasn't that proof of the power of prayer? In letters home, my mother concluded with the simple line: *Thanks for remembering us in your prayers to our Father.*

My mother's quarrel with the jungle hadn't protected my father from the snake. It had probably even been the cause. If there had been a branch stretched over the garage, the snake might have been there and not on the door. But my mother didn't think this. The viper left her more certain that she had been right: She had done something. My mother wrote about felling the trees to the one person who knew exactly what she was up against. Years earlier, a Finn named Sylvia had lived in this house. My mother knew her, of course. The Adventist world was small, and smaller still if you were both Finns. My mother saw the coincidence—that two Finns should live in the same Ugandan house—as a good omen and had begun a correspondence. Sylvia and her family had not only left Uganda alive and healthy, but were nostalgic for this place, this life. Our life.

In her letter to Sylvia, my mother described the destruction of the trees with her characteristic wit. She was hopeful, she wrote, that her actions would keep the snakes away—though so far it didn't look promising. She then told the story of the bush viper, no doubt ending with her now standard joke: *I tell Gary that I missed my chance to tie something around his neck.*

Sylvia's response, like all mail, was slow in coming. When her letter arrived, my mother read it, set it upon the dining room table, and then picked it up and read it again, her mouth pinched. Later, she translated the letter for my father, still fuming.

Sylvia and her family had been the first to live in the house on the hill. The home they had moved into had rested in the clearing like blight on the land, prompting Sylvia's husband to plant trees. The branches, which had rested against our roof and suggested peril, had promised them shade. When they had left, the trees, still young and gangly, had offered something else: a purchase on Uganda. *This I have planted. This I leave behind.*

Sylvia reprimanded my mother for her violence against the trees and implored her to leave the surviving ones alone. The letter was one of grief, but my mother couldn't see it. Instead, she bristled at the scolding and its implication, however unintended: *That is not your home.*

Those first months, my mother would walk into a room and discover children lined up outside the window. They waited, giggling, like one waits before the glass panel at the zoo, hoping the sea otters will emerge, or the penguins. We were strange, exotic creatures, unintentionally hilarious. We didn't belong here. My mother knew this. But with Sylvia's letter in her hand, she was irritated. She would *not* be a guest in her own house. She would create a home here, and if she needed to cut down a tree, she wouldn't apologize.

CHAPTER 5

Fever

OUR CAR WAS out of petrol when one of my vague fevers tipped into something more urgent. My mother kept a washcloth against my forehead. She dipped it into a basin of water, wrung it out, and then turned it over every few minutes.

My fever was one hundred and four degrees and rising, a fact my mother didn't believe until she checked it twice. Her brother was a doctor, her sister a nurse. My mother had gotten her master's degree in English literature. "Study medicine," she told us later. "Don't study English; it's a worthless degree. And whatever you do, don't be an English teacher."

My mother carried a medical book into the bathroom. She read it in the evenings before bed, thumbing through the tropical ailments with their alarming illustrations and their descriptions of all the ways you could die here. With a few practiced flips, she turned to MALARIA. She had read the entry enough times to know the symptoms: chills and fever, nausea, headaches, slight jaundice, tiredness, sweating. My father had already had it. *He was hot and cold at the same time and the whole bed was shaking*, my mother wrote to my American grandmother. *So I ventured out with a flashlight and got some help and luckily the man who ran our clinic came up to our house and gave him a shot of chloroquine.*

For several days, my mother had been spooning liquid chloroquine into my mouth. After swallowing—sometimes for long enough to lull my mother into relief—I would throw up. It was my stomach's impractical joke. If I had malaria, I wasn't getting enough chloroquine to kill it, and if I didn't have malaria, well, that was potentially worse. The only way to know one was to rule out the other. My parents had finally asked the nurse to come up the hill and give me a shot. It was a reluctant request. If injected too fast, chloroquine can cause blindness. The nurse had touched my forehead. "Every child gets malaria," he told my parents before giving me a shot. "In a few days, she'll be better." The nurse advised bed rest, fluids, and cool baths.

But it had been a few days, and I was worse. My mother turned to the back of the medical book and ran a damp finger down the appendix looking for FEVER. It seemed every illness was marked by heat: sleeping sickness, typhoid, meningitis, yellow fever, pneumonia . . . the list continued. We had been immunized for a slew of illnesses, but she couldn't remember which ones. She left the book on the lid of the toilet and fetched a bed sheet. She had run the tub, collecting several inches of water at the bottom. She dropped the sheet in and pressed it into the water until it was sloppy with liquid. My mother's face was set as she drew it up, wrung it out, and walked it through the house.

In my room, I lay on my stomach, hair wet, eyes glassy. My mother gathered me into her arms and peeled off my clothes; she had alternated between bundling me and leaving me bare. She wrapped me now in the sheet. This was one way to bring down a fever.

Heat can swallow a person. It can draw you into a parallel existence, a place where time is slow and your senses are painfully acute. You see more. You see shadows on the walls. Abstract shapes turn into faces, faces turn into a spinning safari of animals. Your body is heavy, but your mind is wild. It chases images and thoughts and terrible fears. You imagine you will be killed violently with a panga. You dream this. You dream your death and the death of everyone close to you. When you wake, you hear the clock and its thick ticking. A fever is monotonous. It is the same sounds, the same nightmares, the same nausea, the same shadows, the same heaviness of limbs, the same taste of peppermint and chloroquine.

Each time I grew ill, my mother would spoon tea into my mouth. In a low voice, she would coax me to swallow. "Okay, one more spoonful. Good. Good. And now, one more." When inevitably I threw up, she would return, her feet staccato on the floor, and she would begin again. I could sense anger below her insistence, and below that, terror. She was sure she would lose me. *Come on, kid. Toughen up.*

My parents liked to say that Sonja was as healthy as a horse. When she got malaria, they were surprised. *She threw up and everything,* my mother wrote in one letter. In another, to my American grandmother, she wrote: *Sonja seems to be as strong as an ox. She goes and shakes all the dirty hands and must get millions of germs and then quickly sticks her fingers in her mouth. Sari also gets her share of exposure. Yesterday in town, she all of a sudden got exhausted and laid her head and chest right on the pavement before I even knew what was up. I was panicky. We just pray she stays healthy and the good Lord watches over her.*

Sonja was the people pleaser, the performer, and I was getting all the attention. As a toddler, Sonja would neigh when asked for the sound of a dog, meow for a chicken, her shoulders jerking up and down as she found joy in her own material. Lately, she had been doing impersonations. She placed my father's overlarge glasses upon her head and galloped through the living room, asking in his voice, "Where are my keys? Where is my briefcase? Where are my glasses? Have you seen them, Kaarina?" Most of the time, my mother would laugh in waves, pausing only to take off her glasses and press her fingers into her eyes.

Left to her own devices, Sonja prowled the edge of the jungle, swinging the Madame Alexander doll she had named Loni. When I was born, my American grandmother had given her the doll as consolation. But I had been a quiet baby, and Sonja was a maternal child, pleased to place a pacifier in my mouth, fetch a nappy, make faces. It was only in Uganda that she was abandoned. "Good grief," my mother had said when Sonja asked for a story. "Can't you see I don't have time for you?"

She wasn't supposed to go into the jungle, little girl with the brown hair and wet eyes, but she left her doll on the ground and stepped into the foliage. First, she stomped on the twigs, then she collected small bunches of flowers, dropping each one as soon as it was gathered. The earth was soft and warm, like bread pulled from the oven. The leaves held moisture from yesterday's rain, and as she moved through the brush, water caught at her shirt. The music of the jungle was a loud vibration, a series of clicks and buzzes. The very grass seemed alive, popping and whirling, announcing the fecundity of insects. Sonja watched monkeys and birds, her chin tipped toward the sky, but she didn't see what did not wish to be seen. There were snakes, surely. There were always snakes: a green mamba in the crook of a branch, a python lounging in the brush.

Sonja came out of the jungle with a guava, a bruised fruit she found lying on the ground. She carried it against her stomach and marched into the house, the screen door slapping behind her. It was a pleasing, smacking sound. If my mother saw the guava she would tell Sonja, "We're having lunch soon. Don't ruin your appetite." Sonja carried the guava up and down the hall, then took it into the kitchen. She leaned against a cupboard and bit into the yellow fruit, which turned into something sweet and pink.

My father came home the day of the fever to a frightened wife. "I can't do this anymore," my mother said. "I just can't." In theory, she was committed to sacrifice. They both were. In Sabbath School class, the teacher would ask, "What are you willing to sacrifice for God?" The daughter of a pastor, the wife of a pastor, what could my mother promise, if not everything?

As a child, my mother had thrilled at the adventure God would provide. Sacrifice meant leaving postwar Finland, a place of chilly poverty. When the missionaries visited her church and asked the children, "Who wants to serve God overseas?" my mother's hand shot up. *Overseas.* Even the word was glamorous. She was an angular, forward-leaning child who, when she remembered, opened her eyes wide, hoping to look like Greta Garbo.

In her school photos, she looks startled. She said she was willing to sacrifice *anything*, a reflex, this thinking.

God asked Abraham to sacrifice his youngest child. Abraham was to take Isaac to a mountain, tie him up, and kill him. It was a test of devotion, total and unquestioning. Before Abraham could strike his child, an angel stopped him, saying, "Now I know that you fear God because you have not withheld from me your son, your only son."

The stories, even the hardest, had lost their heaviness from the retelling.

"She'll get better," my father said. "Kids get sick. They get better."

"She needs to go to a hospital," my mother said.

My father followed my mother into my room. She stood at the door, unsure whether or not to turn on the light. Even this simple decision left her panicked. *Aren't some patients to be kept in the dark?* My father reached his hand behind her and flipped the switch, flooding the room with yellow.

When my mother rolled me over, the direction of my gaze rolled as well. I stared at the ceiling, a hooded stare. A toddler is a mystery anyway, a tiny person who communicates with moods more than language. I had the face of an old man.

My father placed one hand on my forehead, the other on his own. "She sure has a fever. I'll find fuel in the morning," my father said. It was not an easy thing to promise.

Idi Amin had begun a quarrel with Kenya and Tanzania, and now neither nation was allowing oil in. Uganda had run out of petrol. Service stations didn't sell gas, didn't sell anything. Attendants sat on folding chairs, waving away vehicles. The nation waited. Some items were gone for good: cooking oil, sugar, flour, soap. But petrol was likely to return. It was needed for the government's Mercedes and for the lorries that transported soldiers and for the buses and matatus that transported food and people. For now, those in the villages walked as they had always walked, and those in Kampala rode as they had always ridden. Every bus and matatu company had a bit of surplus, a tank behind the garage. Only private owners were out of luck, though to possess a car already suggested more luck than one family deserved.

The next morning, my father asked the principal for a couple liters of fuel. He stood in the office, a jerry can in his hand, embarrassed to make his request. He had come here to be useful, not to take what was already too precious. Bugema had a reservoir of gas, but very little diesel, which he would learn was being saved for the tractors. The school's farm grew maize, which was then crushed into ugali and eaten for breakfast. The students must have food, and only God knew when fuel would be available again.

"These are difficult times," the principal said, and he looked at my father with regret. He was sorry to hear that the mzungu child was ill. "Pole sana. Give her chloroquine," he told my father. "Have the school nurse visit. She has malaria. All the children get malaria." He laughed then, not an unkind laugh, but laughter that came from known worries. "You must pray, Brother Fordham. God is good."

My mother was furious. "What are they thinking?" she raged at my father. "We give and we give and we give, and this is how we are treated? Malaria, my foot. What did he say when you told him she's already had a chloroquine shot?" She buckled a sandal strap and looked up. "You didn't tell him, did you? Oh, Gary, wake up. You have to fight for things. You just have to."

She left us under the care of Faith, the student my mother had hired after Samson. Together, my parents walked down the hill. My father carried the jerry can, and beside him, my mother took short, quick steps. Since I had gotten sick, she had only gone outside to hang clothes or look for eggs in the jungle. Our chickens spent the day running free like good Ugandan chickens, but unlike most chickens, they refused to lay their eggs in their nest.

Her feet hit the dirt with satisfying smacks, and her body leaned into the tilt of the road. The motion jolted her bones and her muscles, loosening the fear she had been holding. As she walked, her body expanded with hope. She would get the fuel. Tonight, we would go to the hospital, and that would be that.

"So," my father asked, "what are you going to say?"

Finns are known for being reticent, for spending the long, dark winters silent by a fire, but when they speak, they speak their minds. My mother was a talkative Finn, giving her more opportunities to be frank. She was quick to laugh, to cry, to shout, and in all these emotions, she was immoderately honest.

"He's my boss, and he's got other worries," my father said.

"I can be diplomatic," she said.

My mother *could* be diplomatic. My father would learn that when soldiers held a gun, my mother could be tactful, even magnanimous. She could smile broadly, engaging anyone in small talk. But my father was right to be concerned. She was smarting under what she considered a betrayal. She didn't appreciate that illness was as common as mosquitoes, and that missionaries panicked at the slightest fever. The principal's job was to consider the school and the students.

My parents strolled onto campus. The grass was trimmed, and the sidewalks were lined with palm trees. Everywhere, students moved purposefully, some pausing to greet them. Each time my mother crossed the main road and stepped onto the campus grounds, she felt as if she was entering a different land. At my father's classroom, my parents parted. If my mother got the principal to agree to lend us diesel, my father would bring it home later.

The principal was surprised to see my mother. She didn't come to the campus often. He saw her only at church or when she invited him to dinner. He must have laughed about that first meal. Like my parents, he had attended Andrews University, and there he had grown fond of spaghetti. He had hoped my mother would serve it. But in her determination to impress him, she had made matoke and peanut sauce. To make matoke, Ugandan women wrapped the green bananas in leaves and cooked them over a fire. My mother steamed them in a pot. They came out bland and overcooked, but throwing away food was a worse sin, and so she served them with embarrassment. The next time the principal came, she baked a tropical pumpkin, and when he ate even the skin, she was pleased with his unspoken compliment.

"Sister Fordham," the principal said. "You are welcome! What can I do for you?" He could not fathom that she was coming for the diesel.

They exchanged pleasantries before she made her request. "Please help me," she said, embarrassing him with her tears. "My girl is so sick. She must go to the hospital."

"Your husband asked already," the principal said. "He should have told you that we can't spare the diesel. I want to help, believe me, Sister Fordham, I do. But these are hard times."

Though the principal promised to send up a nurse, though he promised the egg truck would come in the morning and take me to the hospital, my mother didn't budge. She stayed in his office, smiling, nodding, sometimes crying, but she wouldn't leave. She was like the persistent widow from the Book of Luke. In the parable, the widow wants retribution for a wrong committed, and the judge doesn't want to get involved. He is a hard-bitten character who fears neither God nor man, and so he ignores the widow. But she keeps coming and pleading her case.

If the principal thought of this parable, he must have felt sympathy for the judge. Clearly, the widow was a nuisance, and the judge was misunderstood. No wonder the judge tossed up his hands and relented: *Yet because this widow troubleth me, I will avenge her, lest by her continual coming she weary me.*

The principal didn't think it was necessary (it certainly wasn't prudent), but he finally agreed to sell enough diesel to carry our car to Kampala and back. He could only hope that the fuel shortage wouldn't last long. How would the school run the tractors without petrol? My mother clasped her hands under her chin and looked ready to kiss him. Her joy was as fierce and as available as her anger.

We drove to a Catholic hospital in Kampala. The nurses were nuns, and the one who took my temperature was from Ireland. The first thing she considered was malaria. It would be negligent to do otherwise. Before the doctor would see me, she took my arm in her hand and drew blood. In a lab down the hall, a technician peered at the cells under a microscope, looking for an invasive splash of purple. It was a sight too common on this continent.

Against all conventional wisdom, I didn't have malaria. If I had, it would have been simpler. I would have been given another chloroquine shot, and my parents would have been sent home with easy reassurances. While malaria is vicious, it's also treatable. That it annihilates so many children, still killing fifteeen hundred a day, is a witness to a world sitting on its hands. The doctor was baffled: high fever, no malaria. I had been inoculated against the usual Ugandan suspects—yellow fever, typhoid, hepatitis, polio, measles—and for the less likely ailments as well—mumps, rubella. The doctor did a spinal tap and ruled out meningitis.

The hospital visit, the diesel, the asking for diesel, the chloroquine shot, the liquid chloroquine—each was a resource wasted. The doctor was pragmatic. "I'm afraid there's nothing we can do for her here. Take her home. Keep her fever down." There was a danger keeping me in the ward. If I was contagious, they would have an unknown disease leaping from child to child.

"They were sending you home to be buried," my father later told me.

The nurse had seen the hunger in my mother's eyes and wished to prepare her for the possibility of death. "All you can do now is pray," she said, patting my mother's shoulder.

My parents spoke often of prayer, and in letters, they asked family members to remember them. *Pray for God's blessing on our work*, my father wrote. *Thanks for your prayers which we very much need*, my mother wrote. They believed in the power of prayer, and yet when the nurse told my mother, "All you can do now is pray," a heavy panic entered her heart. Was it really as bad as that?

In church, the congregation sometimes recited the Lord's Prayer: *Our Father, which art in heaven, hallowed be thy name. Thy kingdom come, Thy will be done on earth as it is in heaven.* It was a lovely prayer, and its language invited the speaker to linger on each sound. The words were soft, and the meaning was good and just. *Give us this day our daily bread. And forgive us our debts as we forgive our debtors.*

At home, when we knelt after worship, my parents would pray for the missionaries and colporteurs. I learned this word early—*colporteur*—and found it a tangle on my tongue. A colporteur must be someone who needed a lot of prayer. The word *missionary* went through me like water, like air. It was the most natural of lives. My parents would then offer up more specific petitions—be with Brother So-and-So, be with Sister So-and-So—and if one of us was sick, that would be the center of their petition. Of course, there was also praise. My mother had little patience for people, but she had a heathen's delight for the earth, and she gave much gratitude for the trees, flowers, and birds. Before saying amen and then singing, *Turn your eyes upon Jesus*—a refrain sung with eyes closed—my parents would end their prayers with a fearful and beautiful turn of words: *Thy will be done.* It was an act of surrender. It was an act of trust.

But were Uganda and its inhabitants experiencing God's will? Men were thrown over Kabalega Falls. Others were tied to posts and shot. Their bodies were loaded into lorries and later dumped into the jungle or into Lake Victoria. The whole country was on edge. You couldn't buy soap or oil or rice, and with these new burdens came the familiar ones—the weight of poverty. Below our house, a family lived in mud huts. In the mornings and evenings, the wives and children collected water from our tap. They would fill pails, and my father helped the women lift the pails to their heads so they could carry them. One child complained that her neck ached. She was only ten. If we needed water, we, who were not from this land, could turn on a faucet. Who did God love more? In Uganda, children died easily and often. Babies died of malaria. They died of diarrhea. They died of poverty. This was not God's will.

It was late at night when we returned home. My father carried Sonja into the house while my mother carried me. They hovered over my bed, placing a cold washcloth on my forehead. They prayed that night, as they always did, beginning with gratitude—"Thank you for watching Sari"—and working up to a request, one I would hear often through the years: "Lord, you see us here. Place your hands of healing on Sari. Help her get well."

My parents didn't talk of the nurse's warning; neither was willing to consider it. They took turns wrapping me in wet sheets and coaxing liquid down my throat. They had come to Uganda expecting sacrifice. My father worked long hours, and my mother, alone on the hill, felt increasingly isolated. Compared to most Ugandans, these were mere inconveniences, and luxurious ones at that. We didn't know hardship. We hadn't bargained for it.

What would my parents have done if I had died that first year? My father would probably have been stoic. My mother would have raged against Uganda and against my father. She would have packed a couple suitcases and taken Sonja to Finland. My father would have finished teaching the semester, and then, I imagine, the small family would have returned to the United States, stunned. I don't think they would have remained in Uganda, though perhaps I underestimate their commitment. Of one thing I'm certain—neither of them would have abandoned their faith. They were Adventists in the same the way that my mother was Finnish and my father was American. They couldn't leave the church. Their faith was knitted into their very being.

They were fortunate. Certainly, I was. My fever broke, and little by little, I grew stronger.

As many times as I've heard the story of my illness, how my mother battled to get me to the hospital, how the doctors thought I would die, how my hair fell out after the fever broke, how inert I had been ("Poor Sari," my family liked to tease, "if it weren't for that fever, you might have been really smart"), there is little recorded evidence. In a letter to my grandmother, my father wrote, *It's hard to remember what we have written and what we haven't. I'm sure we told you about the bush viper and Sari's hospitalization (one day). P.S. No relationship between the two.*

CHAPTER 6

———— ❧ ————

Dividing Up the World Between Us

IN THE SAVANNAHS of western Uganda, a family of elephants plodded through the dust and the grass and the thorn trees. They seemed almost to lollygag, the way they ambled, stopping for a bite of this and that. Their trunks curled around branches, pulling down twigs and leaves, which they poked into receptive mouths. Adult elephants eat over three hundred pounds of vegetation a day, and the largest can eat twice that amount.

In the afternoon, the elephants pitched dirt over their shoulders. This second skin protected them from sun and insects. They gathered around the plate of bare earth in a congenial circle. They threw dirt and nuzzled and conversed. They were noisy conversationalists. A mother shouted at her unruly calf, teenagers squabbled, and adults gossiped in low rumbles. The older males preferred to live away from all this racket.

As the elephants flapped their ears, the breeze cooled the blood flowing across the cartilage and then out into the rest of their bodies. Elephant air conditioner. The back-and-forth movement also shooed away insects. In Uganda, a quotient of energy had to be relinquished each day to the tiniest of lives, the tsetse flies and the mosquitoes, the gnats and the termites. Bugs thrived no matter who was in charge.

African elephants are the largest land animals and have no enemies beyond man. If they spotted a crocodile between bodies of water, they might saunter over and trample it. Elephants were the giants of the Ugandan grasslands. They left a trail of leaves and broken branches; they left large prints in the dust. In the morning mist, they moved across the horizon like ghosts.

More and more often, Idi Amin's soldiers entered the savannah. They came with their machine guns and their Land Rovers. These men, these ghost makers—hardly more than boys—searched for elephants. A few years earlier, many of these young men had tended cattle, the tending a serious endeavor. Cows were a family's bank account, and the Ankole cattle of Uganda possessed horns longer than the children who watched them. The boys had walked barefoot in the plains, their feet toughening against pebbles and stickers and heat. They had carried sticks, which they used to move cows. Sometimes they hit a cow, but mostly, they ran beside the herd waving the stick and shouting, or they rested it against a flank: *Go this way*. Sometimes, when the cattle were grazing, the boys pretended to hunt lions. They stalked through the grassland, imagining a pair of tawny eyes in the brush.

The soldiers shouted "tembo, tembo" when they saw the herd of elephants. The noise from so many vehicles had unsettled the group, which was moving away from the rev of engines. The Land Rovers followed, bouncing over rocks and small bushes. The wheels kicked up a river of dirt, which streamed red behind the caravan. The men shouted to each other and used their arms and their hands as a second means of conversing: *Go this way*.

It must have been a relief to ride through the grasslands of Uganda, to be driving under the sky, pure and blue, the world opened up like two halves of a shell. It must have been a relief to be killing only animals. The morality of violence has many hues. It's a job. It's survival. It's to avoid being killed. It's adrenaline. It's revenge. Your people killed my people. It's colonialism. It's oil and water being forced to share the same plot of land. It's for money and power. It's because you have no money, no power, no food. It's because you can no longer remember what it's like not to kill. It's because you don't have a choice. It's because you're here, and now what?

The elephants trampled the vegetation. Calves trotted at their mothers' heels, tails sticking straight out. They lifted their trunks like hands raised in surrender, and they called and called. The grasslands reverberated with elephant terror. The machine-gun fire came in bursts and then a pause and then more fire. The men cheered as one by one the elephants crumpled into piles of ivory. The meat was eaten or left, the tusks were sold to anyone who would buy them. This was one way of propping up the dictatorship after the economic collapse.

Before Idi Amin's coup in 1971, Queen Elizabeth National Park had four thousand elephants. In nine years, only 150 would remain. The buffalo population dropped from eighteen thousand to eight thousand. Lions, leopards, hartebeest, giraffes were decimated. Animals that survived the soldiers fled into Zaire. It would be nearly two decades before they returned, but the park wouldn't be the same. There would never be as many elephants or hippopotamuses or lions.

My parents, oblivious to the carnage, were anxious to go on safari and see Africa's famed wildlife. The relative nearness of lions and wildebeest left them dizzy with desire. When my father went to Kenya to buy oil, flour, margarine, oats, toilet paper, and dish soap, he also purchased a slender paperback titled *Animals of East Africa*. It was written and illustrated by C.T. Astley Maberly. The book had no photographs inside, only drawings, and in the introductory note, the author warned, "In order to be able to devote adequate space to the more popularly interesting animals, it has been necessary to omit mention of the numerous smaller rodents, bats, etc., which swarm in abundance throughout the areas concerned, and which are equally interesting to the keen naturalists."

My mother wasn't a keen naturalist. She had seen enough of the rodents. The *etc.*, she suspected, were snakes. They certainly swarmed in abundance. She didn't mind their omission. She flipped through the book backwards, looking at the drawings: zebras, warthogs, oryxes, mongoose, lions, hyenas, gerenuks, and baboons. They all seemed so improbable. Who would dream up something with that coat or those eyes? God had a sense of humor.

My mother read *Animals of East Africa* as if it were a novel. She sneaked passages while the beans were boiling, and when she smelled something burning, she reluctantly set the book facedown on the couch. She had grown fond of Maberly and his arch prose and couldn't figure out whether he was intentionally being funny. She chose to believe he wasn't, that he was an expatriate even more ridiculous than her. She imagined him sitting on the dry grass, wearing khakis and a pith helmet.

My father always returned home with a story waiting in his throat: "You'll never guess what my students said when I told them about the upcoming test." Or, "Guess who's finally coming to Bugema? You'll never guess." He began his stories at the door, while he was taking off his shoes. My mother was eager to hear something of life beyond the hill, but she was also annoyed at her isolation, at having nothing of her own to contribute beyond the domestic: Sonja said this. Sari did that. My father even carried up the mail. Each day, she gazed hungrily at his hands. My mother had begun to measure her happiness by the number of letters we received each week. The slips of paper were evidence that there was a world beyond beans and rice, beyond Idi Amin's voice on the radio, beyond mosquitoes and malaria, beyond chloroquine.

Now that my mother was reading *Animals of East Africa*, she had something new to report. All day, my mother ached to share what she had been reading. Trivia, like good news, improved when it was spoken aloud. She waited now, first devouring the letters that my father brought: one from his mother, one from her sister. And then she waited further, first for supper, then worship, then until Sonja and I were settled into bed. Only when the last story was read, the last glass of water drunk, the mosquito nets tucked in, the lights turned out, did my mother pick up *Animals of East Africa*.

"Listen to this," she said, flipping through the pages. "Hippos graze like cows."

"Sure. A cow that'll bite you in two," my father said.

"Would you just listen?" my mother said. "So normally they leave the water only at night. But," and here she paused, "in Queen Elizabeth Park—or what is it now? Rwenzori National Park?—anyway, the hippos graze all day. We could see hippos strolling around. Now wouldn't that be something?"

"That would be something," my father said.

"You have to read this. It's hilarious." To my mother, *funny* was a bad smell or a suspicious activity. When something made her laugh, she called it heelarious. It was one of the few words where I could hear her accent. "Listen to this guy. I love him," she said. *"Generally speaking, the hippo is an inoffensive beast, provided he is left alone.* But here's the best part." She looked up and down the page, trying to find what she had laughed at earlier. "Oh, here it is. *To get between a hippo on land and the water is a most dangerous proceeding."* She looked up. "But he doesn't tell you what to do."

"Run," my father said, "fast."

It didn't seem that we would get off the hill anytime soon. Petrol was too precious, and my father was too busy. He taught five classes, one before breakfast and the rest after. He spent his early mornings biking up and down the hill. In the afternoons, he attended committee meetings; at night, he attended the school's worship service; and when he finally came home, he worked on curriculum for accreditation.

My mother was adjusting to what life meant in Uganda. Each evening, she boiled water and left it to cool. The next day, she tipped the pot against a Tupperware container and poured. Her mornings began with water. She would make breakfast while my father, in the background, dashed through the house, looking for his pens, his students' papers, his book from yesterday. If my mother had traded soap for passion fruit, she would rinse them in the sink, two by two. They were the size and shape of eggs and looked the way rotten eggs ought to: wrinkled, purplish-brown, soft. She would slice each one in half and set them on our plates. Cracked open, they became cups of orange pulp, which we ate with magnificent slurps.

After breakfast, my mother washed the dishes, had worship with us girls, washed laundry, hung it to dry, thought about lunch. She could leave the hill if she wished, but it usually seemed too much of a hassle. In the afternoon, when Sonja and I were napping (a ritual so fiercely enforced that it was nearly religious), she would reread *Animals of East Africa*, perusing it for instruction. She underlined snatches that struck her as important: *Impalas both browse and graze.* She underlined and starred facts that seemed of particular significance. *The steenbok has no lateral, or "false" hooves.* When she needed to, she would know the difference between a steenbok and a duiker, two miniature antelope so delicate they looked as if they belonged in a dollhouse.

We had been in Uganda for nearly six months when a medical technician needed a ride to Ishaka Adventist Hospital. My father was fast to volunteer. The town of Ishaka rested in the western dip of Uganda, a hundred kilometers away from Rwanda, the Congo, and Burundi. It was a dusty strip of a town: a few restaurants, a few empty stores, a few bars, a few inns. The main attraction was the eighty-bed hospital. To my parents, Ishaka meant safari. The road through town also led to Rwenzori National Park.

The game reserve was part of Idi Amin's Africanization campaign. Colonialism had left Uganda with artificial borders and crisp British names. On December 17, 1972, Idi Amin announced that the Ugandan government would take over British tea plantations, media companies, and country clubs, and that meaningless, imperialistic names would be changed to good Ugandan ones. Murchison Falls became Kabalega Falls; Lake Edward became Lake Idi Amin Dada; and Queen Elizabeth National Park became Rwenzori National Park. These names wouldn't last. It wasn't so easy to shake off colonialism, or even the names of colonialism. In 1991, Rwenzori National Park—the longest holdout—once again became Queen Elizabeth National Park.

To drive through Uganda was to be charmed. The road west was a patchy stretch of tarmac, with frayed edges and a center lavished with potholes. The ground, it seemed, was trying to reclaim its own. "These roads are horrendous," my father announced every few hours. It was a congenial complaint.

The roads might be worn down, but the terrain was starkly beautiful. There is no land as lovely as Uganda. If you drive long enough, you will begin to hear its music, the song of earth and leaves, of jacarandas and river bean trees, of crested cranes and cassias. The song is also of banana plants, the leaves an emerald green. They color the hills and small yards. Their leaves, like bolts of silk, rustle in the breeze.

Women walked beside the road. They wore dresses—bright and voluminous. The patterns were a geometry of colors: turquoise flowers, tangerine paisley, magenta circles. On their heads, women balanced jugs and pots and jerry cans. This was the way things moved across the land. The journey might be miles of aching necks and cracked feet. The anomaly of a private vehicle was as ostentatious as a yacht, and we, its privileged inhabitants, traveled west.

My mother sat between us, her daughters. We were sticky, eager creatures. We hadn't left campus in months, and she had worried about how we would manage the long car ride. How much whining would she have to endure? But we were entranced, mainly staring out the windows, turning to her for snacks. She doled out fresh bananas and dried bananas—she liked to joke that bananas now came out of our ears. Never mind, at least we had something to eat. At least there were still bananas in the countryside.

Sometimes, she wondered at the wisdom of bringing two young daughters to Uganda. She had anticipated snakes—maybe not their sheer numbers, but she knew they lived here—and she had even prepared herself for malaria. You took the medicine, everyone said, and you got better. No one had warned her how terrifying it was to watch your daughter or husband trembling under a hundred blankets. Ugandans could have warned her. In the far villages, women watched their children die because they couldn't get chloroquine. It was criminal. And yet, she still complained about how difficult life was here, and at least once a week, her husband reminded her that everything was harder for Ugandans, and she would snap back that she could see that, couldn't she? She had eyes, didn't she? And then she would feel contrite. She was not an easy wife. When she cooled down, she wrote letters to relatives, asking them to send some shoes or clothes for the family who lived down the hill. Such a small thing.

We left the medical technician at Ishaka Adventist Hospital. My father shook his hand, and my mother invited him to visit. He was welcome anytime. The hospital was a cement building with a cement floor. The cots were thin, and the wards smelled of illness and urine. In less than two years, the hospital would be commandeered by Idi Amin's soldiers. For a time, the clinic would be a barracks. My parents didn't hear again from the technician. They didn't hear him spoken of, either—and by this, they knew he had found a safe way out of Uganda. When an expatriate was killed or injured, everyone heard of it.

Rwenzori National Park, as it was called then, was exactly how my parents had once imagined Africa. "Look, look," they told Sonja and me, pointing out the window. The grassland stretched out yellow and disheveled and brimming with possibility. You just knew there were elephants here, and all manner of antelope. "This is it," my mother said.

The park was bordered by two large lakes—Edward and George—and the Kazinga Channel ran between them and was famous for the hippos slumped along its shores. The crater lakes attracted an abundance of birds. On a lucky day, you might see the whale-headed stork, a bird that looked both ridiculous and terribly authoritative.

We drove through the reserve, searching for wildlife. A guide sat in the front seat beside my father and laughed at our enthusiasm, at my mother's frequent referencing of *Animals of East Africa*. The guide was as knowledgeable as he was kind, and he taught my parents tricks not found in books. We would become champion spotters, all of us. We looked for shapes and motion—two triangles, dipping and rising above the grass, might be a silver-backed jackal; a grey tassel dashing through the brush was perhaps a warthog. And always, always, we watched the sky for vultures. A carcass was the surest way to find lions. Another was to know where they napped. The guide directed my father south. We bumped through the savannah, our eyes searching. If there were fewer animals to be seen, and there surely were, we didn't notice. In the distance, Sonja spotted zebras. "Look, look, look," she shouted, her bottom bouncing up and down, her finger outstretched. I climbed over my mother's lap to join Sonja at her window. The zebras looked as if they had stepped out of our Noah's Ark picture book and had multiplied. I looked. We all looked. We couldn't look enough.

The guide was determined to show us tree lions. No more dillydallying over zebras or Thompson's gazelles; we would stop only for important game. Elephants? Of course. Giraffes? Maybe. When he indicated my father could stop for antelope, my parents were surprised. "Ugandan kob," he told them. "You can see these ones on the Ugandan coat of arms." The kob looked at our vehicle, their tails twitching. They were a beautiful antelope, reddish-brown with dark ears and a sturdy build. The males had swooping horns like Grant's gazelles, of whom my mother could read plenty. Maberly, however, had written nothing of the kob. He had titled his book *Animals of East Africa*, but he focused exclusively on Kenya. "And why is that?" my mother asked. None of us could answer.

We were driving to Ishasha Plains, and the guide seemed confident that if we only stopped stopping, we would see tree lions, emphasis on *tree*. The lions of this park were famous for climbing into the acacias, which dotted the grassland, and tourists came here, back when the tourists were still coming, specifically to see them. Our family had never seen any lion outside of a zoo, and while the trees were an interesting accouterment, our interest was most firmly on *lion*.

My mother flipped to the lion entry in her *Animals of East Africa*. "*Descriptive Notes: General appearance well-known.*" She read the line to my father, and he laughed. She repeated, "General appearance well-known."

She reached out and touched my father on the shoulder. "Listen to this," she said, "*Although seemingly phlegmatic, lions are very nervous and highly-strung, and their mood can change with astonishing rapidity.*" She set her book facedown on her knee. "So don't even think about getting out of the car for a better picture." She said it teasingly, but they both felt the tension. It touched on what was starting to become a point of conflict, but was still largely ignored. His risk-taking. Her nagging.

My father said nothing.

The guide told him to turn off the main road, and he did. There were tire tracks in the long grass where other vehicles had turned off. My father drove slowly. Branches slapped the windshield and squeaked as they slid down the length of the car. "Sure hate to get a flat," my father said. "Or bust the oil pan."

We pitched back and forth. Occasionally, my mother's hand landed on my back and held my shirt in her fist. "This is *it*, girls," she said happily. "Keep your eyes open." We were in the wilds. At any moment, a secretary bird or even a hyena might step out from between the acacia trees.

"Okay, stop here," our guide said. "There. Right there. Can you see the lion?" We looked and saw nothing. He pointed through the grass. We saw an ear at first, the same tawny color as the grass, and then the head turned, and a lioness looked at us. We gasped. Her liquid eyes twitched and blinked against the flies.

Our guide suggested that my father pull the car a little closer. He released the brake and we rolled forward. The pride of lions gazed at our vehicle with wary resignation. *You, again!* My father cut the engine. A few lions lounged in the branches of the acacia, but most were in the grass. As we watched, they sank into acceptance. My father took out his camera and rolled down the window. We were all quiet. We could hear the click-click of my father's camera, and the whir of insects, and the crunch of grass as lions shifted positions.

It was a revelation that first day, everything new and hopeful. My parents' worries about the political situation dropped away. Surely, God had brought them to this country. Idi Amin might rumble and shout, but it was God who set up rulers and debased them. *Besides, Paul exhorts us to pray for those in authority*, my father wrote in a letter to his mother.

My parents were still innocent about how bad things had gotten, and like the ignorant often are, we were rewarded with dumb luck. We were the only tourists at the game lodge, and for once in our time in Africa, we could afford to stay in one. In pictures, the three girls, as my father called us, sat on an elephant's skull, the lodge's mascot. How long it had been there, we didn't know, but twenty years later, it would still be there. We took turns on the seat, a macabre prop, and we were not aghast. In one photo, I'm sitting alone, bottom resting on a skull, a smile nearly swallowing my face.

The last day, we drove to the Kazinga Channel to see a wealth of hippos. My mother learned from Maberly that hippopotamus is Greek for "river horse." My father was quick to point out that he taught Greek and could have told her as much. He then expanded on Maberly to break down the word: *potamus*, river; *hippos*, horse. It later seemed to me a strange word, river horse— a misnomer. Hippos looked more like pigs or warthogs, or even Cape buffaloes. They were not elegant like horses, not svelte. Yet they stood as tall as horses, and they were said to gallop thirty miles an hour. If a horse lived in a river, why not in this voluptuous body?

Hippos became my favorite safari animal, a decision into which I poured considerable thought. Sonja and I divided up the world between us: She liked red, I liked orange; she liked spaghetti, I liked baked potatoes; she liked cheetahs, I liked hippos. She selected first, and there could be no sharing. Those were the rules of ownership.

At the channel, hippopotamuses slid through the water, and from the side, we could see a half hippo—an eye, an ear, a nostril, a pinkish-grey jowl. On the shore, more lounged companionably, one upon another. While hippos are cranky animals, given to flashes of anger, and while they carry with them the scars of their quarrels, they looked in repose as if they were smiling. It was a closed-mouth smile, and it gave them a beauteous glow.

It is a rare thing to see a hippo standing. While they have no natural predators, it is just too hot to graze under the sun, carrying all that bulk. They leave the water at dusk and make up for a day of lounging. A hippo can eat nearly ninety pounds of grass in a night.

We were on the river during the watery moments between day and night, the magic hour. We stood, together, and watched. My father hoisted Sonja onto his shoulders so she could see better and he could take better photos. She balanced herself by holding onto his hair and tucking her feet behind his back.

"Ouch, ouch," my father shouted, even hopping in his jest, and on his shoulders, Sonja giggled and clung tighter, causing my father to hop more and shout more, one hand now gripping her feet.

"You two," my mother said. She held me against her hip, an arm free for pointing.

"Look, look," our parents told us, and we looked, amazed.

The water stirred with hippos. They moved from the middle of the river to the edge, and while it appeared as if they were swimming, they weren't. Adult hippos can't swim. They walked along the river's floor, occasionally propelling themselves to the surface. In the water, the hippos rose and dropped like ballerinas. Those already on the bank seemed to hitch their trousers and haul themselves up. In the distance, there was snorting and flashing of teeth. The river boiled around two or three angry hippos— it was hard to know—and then the water and the vegetation settled as they resolved their differences. The hippos moved up the bank, a hippopotamus migration, and they stood, majestic, on the shore.

This was how you would remember: You took a picture. You would later have something concrete to hold onto. That hippo would be yours. You could make as many copies as you liked, and you could show people. See, this really happened. You would have tangible proof. And you would own something magnificent.

In a black and white photograph, my father captured three hippos as they surged out of the water. On the bank, a fourth was already grazing. This is one story about hippos.

Here is another.

A few weeks or months after our visit, the soldiers came to the Kazinga Channel with machine guns and stood on the banks and on boats, and they killed hippos. They cruised the length of the channel and slaughtered hundreds. The animals were easy targets. They floundered in water slick with blood. Hippopotamus meat is high in fat and valued for its ability to fill a stomach. Yet even an army couldn't eat so many hippopotamuses. Most of the bodies were stripped of teeth and left to rot. The water turned putrid.

In Kampala, my father walked from the market to the post office. It was a warm day and growing hot, the kind of afternoon made for sitting under a tree, and indeed, in the shade of a courtyard, some men were sitting. When they saw my father, they called out a greeting. He walked over. Even after the devastation of colonialism, even after the harrowing echoes, even as Idi Amin was putting nails into the heads of his enemies and a single roll of toilet paper cost $1.50, Ugandans treated my family with more generosity than we merited. In a letter home, my father wrote, *I've been enjoying Africa immensely. It's a joy to work with Ugandans.*

The men in the courtyard pumped my father's hand up and down.

"Hello," they said.

"Jambo," my father said.

They were strangers and had no reason to stand in a courtyard on a Friday afternoon and talk, but one didn't need an agenda. Talk was the reason. Good humor and fellowship were the reasons. My father enjoyed this about Uganda, this talking without an immediate purpose. The men spoke of the coming rains, the United States, Uganda, my father's job, the men's jobs, and as they spoke, my father learned he was in the courtyard of a government building. The talk though was mild, and my father wouldn't have thought much of it, except his eyes kept catching on several cardboard boxes filled with ivory.

"Hippo," the youngest man said, following my father's glance. "You've seen him?" He reached into a box, pulled out a tooth, and handed it to my father who marveled at the plaque. The tooth was so yellow it was nearly brown. In a hippo's mouth, that same tooth would have appeared white. Everything was relative.

My father ran his hands over the curve. When he had heard of the slaughter at Kazinga Channel, he had let out his breath and shaken his head. *Terrible. Terrible. Terrible.*

"Do you want it? You can buy it."

"It is legal," another man offered, seeing my father's expression. "The government can sell ivory."

Confronted with a tooth, my father discovered that he wanted it. He wanted to own something so unique and magnificent. He ran his hand over the curve and was already imagining how he would use it as a prop at church. Certainly, he would someday tell a hippo story, and to have this tooth to show would be a wonderful thing. And so, for a pittance, my father bought two teeth (if you buy one, why not two?) and was given a certificate that stated that the ivory was legal. One was scrubbed clean, the other was dark with plaque.

Later, I would ask my father—a man who voted for the Green Party, who donated money to conservation efforts and who got up at night to feed a puppy with a cleft palate—"How could you? How could you buy them?"

"Don't be such an idealist, Sari," my father said. "The hippos were already dead. All of them. There were no more hippos to kill in Uganda."

CHAPTER 7

A Trip to Town

MANY WERE DISAPPEARING. At night, they vanished. Under the sun's unblinking eye, they also vanished. Bodies reappeared in the most unlikely places. At Owen Falls Dam, someone worked to keep the turbines cleared. In the Nile, amongst papyrus green as spring, the crocodiles grew fat and indifferent.

Fear is a scent, an actual pheromone that animals can smell. Fear is also a weight across the throat, a pressing against thin bones. It moves in a flutter of voices, the sound of Bat Valley at dusk, the pulse of wings. Uganda had become a land of whispered stories told in the half-light. The worst were not the ones about nails pounded into skulls or the severed heads said to be resting in Idi Amin's freezer, or even the prisoners made to kill each other with sledgehammers. The worst were of benevolence, even the word hinting at violence under goodwill.

A man gives a woman a ride from Kampala to her home in Jinja. "These are hard times," the stranger says after they have been in the car for an hour. "Yes," the lady replies. There is the thump of tires over speed bumps, more than twenty through this town. They discuss Idi Amin cautiously and then with less care. Bad things are happening, they agree. Terrible things. "Asante sana," the lady says when she is dropped off at her door. The stranger smiles, accepting her gratitude. That night, the soldiers come and take her away. That is one story.

Or there is this one, so common it is almost a nonstory. A man on the street is accused of treason—maybe he offended the wrong person, sold oil on the black market, asked an unfortunate question, or worse, came from the wrong town. He is accused and knows that he is a dead man. And then, suddenly, he isn't. He is clasped on the shoulder, everyone is a friend, and he's obligated to join in the laughter. His lips stretch until his cheeks ache from the benevolence. Maybe, he thinks, maybe he will return home after all, eat a meal of matoke and peanut sauce. Then the mood shifts. Laughter becomes a blow to the torso, a bruising of scalloped bones. A machine gun caresses the back of his head, and he is swallowed into the State Research Bureau. These are the stories. And there were more. Stories nobody was telling.

Idi Amin, anxious to be loved even as he was killing, couldn't ignore the stories. My father would later remember the addresses on the radio, how one night, Idi Amin spoke directly to the ladies of Uganda: Don't blame the government when your husband does not come home. Don't blame the soldiers. Your husband has run away with another woman. It is not the task of the government to keep your husband from chasing after ladies.

Each night, over the crackle of Radio Kampala, Idi Amin addressed the nation. He used English, a tongue both cumbersome and foreign. When Queen Elizabeth asked a journalist about one of his speeches, the pressman supposedly replied, "Your Majesty. That was President Amin of Uganda speaking a language similar to English."

It is peculiar that Amin fashioned his messages from the words of colonization. He was a man to spurn European custom, an African first, a nationalist who wished to change the official language of Uganda from English to Swahili. Why not begin with the radio? Yet his choice was also not peculiar. It was cunning, even vain. Idi Amin knew he was speaking partly to his people, but also to an outside world, now riveted. How many knew Kenyetta? How many knew Nyerere? They, too, were presidents, but it was His Excellency, Field Marshall, Al-Haji, Dr. Idi Amin Dada, Life President of Uganda, Conqueror of the British Empire, Distinguished Service Order of the Military Cross, Victoria Cross, and Professor of Geography who was fretted and fawned over in the West. During an American drought, he volunteered to send baskets of matoke and cassava to the States. He addressed Queen Elizabeth as "Liz." About Henry Kissinger, he said, "He is apparently not a very intelligent man. He never comes to Kampala to consult me about international affairs." Idi Amin was audacious, and yet he was also right. Why shouldn't an African nation be a world power?

Listening to Idi Amin became my parents' nightly entertainment. They tucked us into bed and turned on Radio Kampala. "You can either laugh or cry," my father later said. "Laughing is always easier."

They sat across from each other at the dining room table, my father with a stack of papers, my mother a half-written letter. It was almost a game, these evenings. There were the phrases and half stories passed back and forth. There were the pens, the ones that still worked, which they each claimed and guarded with fierce banter. There were the finger bananas; the pile of peelings grew beside my mother only, for my father had already brushed his teeth.

The lampshade was bright yellow, a crown above our table. It was from Finland, a complexity of plastic loops casting a spell of buttercups upon the wall. It had been a wedding gift. The objects my mother cherished most were from Finland, and most of these were from her wedding. A gecko ran up the buttercup wall. It could cup the ceiling with its toes, and if a ruse was needed, it could drop off its tail like so much excess baggage. In this house, as in all Ugandan homes, geckos were welcomed guests. They ate mosquitoes, our most immediate adversary. We had all gotten malaria.

On the radio, Idi Amin urged Ugandans to kill American soldiers. The Ugandan army would shoot the fighter jets out of the sky. As the U.S. soldiers parachuted to the ground, Ugandan civilians were to introduce them to the business end of a jembe or a panga. There were, of course, no American soldiers, no F-5s waiting near Mombasa. My parents laughed at the radio. "Who is he kidding?" my father said.

"Oh boy, oh boy," my mother said, both hands resting on her stomach. "He says the craziest things." She removed her glasses and wiped at her eyes. She put her glasses back on and took a long breath. "You don't think anyone will take him seriously, do you? I mean, people won't see us and run for their jembes?"

We were known as the Americans on the hill, never mind that my mother was not American, and that Sonja and I didn't know how to be. In 1984, we would arrive in Texas, and we might as well have been aliens. But here, by virtue of absence, we were as American as the apple pie I had never eaten. More people knew of us than we could possibly suspect.

The local chief visited Bugema's principal. They spoke first of the weather and the students who must study hard for Uganda's future, about children and grandchildren, about the peanut and maize fields. Finally, the chief looked past the principal's shoulder. "Tell your American to be very careful. The tall one, he is being watched."

My parents thought they knew who was watching. A family lived down the hill from us, and we had gotten to know the wives and the daughters as they came for water. My parents saved clothes for the family. The husband, an army man, would sometimes beat his wives. At night, my parents could sometimes hear wailing. Once, the sound didn't stop, and my father got out of bed. "Oh, Gary," my mother said. "Please, please, don't go. You'll get yourself killed. It's not our business." My father was pulled between the tears of his wife and the tears of a woman he knew vaguely. He had no firm plan, and when the sound stopped, he climbed back into bed, relieved. The next morning, my father took the man's third wife to the hospital. She held both hands over an eye that had been knocked out of its socket. She had been hit, she told my father, because she hadn't ululated when her husband returned home.

When my mother saw the man, she refused to lower her eyes. She smiled, hands on her hip. These days, he was overly interested in conversation. "Ah, madam," he would say, clucking his tongue. "You are having a difficult time."

"Oh no," my mother said. "We really love Uganda. It's such a beautiful country." It was one truth.

During these months, my parents wrote their usual letters, but few arrived. Only one flight left Uganda each week, and mail was opened and read. Idi Amin didn't want negative stories pouring across the border. My parents were careful about what they wrote, but still, from the stack of aerogrammes I later transcribed and organized, none existed between November 5, 1976, and February 24, 1977.

My mother spent most of her days on the hill, boiling water, reading stories to her daughters, sitting on the couch and gazing at the gap in the jungle, wondering, *Will anyone come up the road today?* My father made a few trips to Nairobi, and while my mother longed to join him, our vehicle didn't have the proper papers to cross the border. The stories my father told about the bus made her reluctant to take two children on it.

In November, our car permit finally arrived, and we drove to Kenya. My mother, sister, and I marveled at Nairobi, a city of milk and honey. We shopped in the morning, my mother walking in and out of stores, Sonja and I trying to keep up. People turned their eyes toward us, cataloging us as missionaries. My mother wanted no part of this narrative. She wore a Ugandan shirt, bell-bottoms, flip-flops, and had a baobab bag slung over her shoulder. She hoped to be mistaken for a humanitarian or, best of all, an ambassador's wife and we the ambassador's children. But there was something too plain and simple about her bearing. With different children, maybe. We were skinny and dirty, always dirty, despite our baths and our mother's swipes at our faces, and we marveled too extravagantly at the goods. "It was like they had never seen food before," my mother later told our father.

We returned to the guesthouse for lunch. Restaurants were for real diplomats and for children who weren't vegetarians. My mother set the groceries on the table. She had bought mostly British staples—marmalade, Weetabix, noodles, tomato paste, and Marmite. She put the perishables in the fridge, the rest in the cupboards, and made three sandwiches. *This is it.*

Now, what about supper? Maybe she would make spaghetti, and for dessert a pudding—and yes, she would buy greens from the truck, which came in the afternoons. The vegetable truck was magic. When I was older and we visited Nairobi, I would wait for it in the afternoons, and when I saw the battered vehicle, I would run into the guest apartment shrieking, "The vegetable man is here! The vegetable man is here!" My mother would follow me out and buy artichokes.

That first evening meal, we ate greedily. Nairobi, to our family, came to mean food. Spaghetti was Sonja's favorite dish, but we were all enthusiastic about a meal without beans or rice, without tropical pumpkin, without avocados, without bananas. We couldn't speak enough about how good it all was. We were lucky, and my parents knew it, and even Sonja and I knew it. My mother cleared the table; my father gave us a bath and read us a story. Sonja and I drank hot milk with Milo, had our prayers, and went to bed, trying out a phrase we had recently heard, "Shadrach, Meshach, and To-Bed-We-Go."

We repeated it many times, until our mother finally said, "Okay, okay, we get your point."

The apartment finally quiet, our mother addressed an aerogramme to my American grandmother and her husband, Gordon. The relationship between the two women was fraught. They were both independent, outspoken women, and my grandmother had a way of giving advice that made my mother want to howl. Family, though, was family. The adversaries were drawn together in their common concern for our safety. My mother, her body slanted toward the blue page, wrote:

Dearest Mother and Gordon,

Thanks for your letters. We finally got permission to drive our car out of Uganda and are now in Nairobi shopping frantically for foodstuffs and other supplies. Nairobi is quite a modern city, and it is almost too much for Sonja to see so many things in stores. She keeps constantly wanting this and that. In Kampala the stores are virtually empty. The Ugandans are beautiful people—smiling, not complaining, walking in rags. In fact, we wouldn't even use for rags what people are wearing. There is a desperate need for shoes of all sizes and kinds, shirts, pants, dresses, sweaters, sheets, anything and everything.

My mother asked my grandmother to collect clothes and shoes at church and to send them to us. When the items arrived, the beneficiaries thanked my mother and then turned and sold everything. A shirt could pay for chickens and the subsequent eggs could pay for school fees. Shoes could purchase a visit home. Taken on the women's terms, the church charity gained a bit of dignity. The only people who kept the clothes were those whom my mother made trades with or those who had done her a favor.

My mother ended her letter by writing again of the glories of Kenya. Her optimism almost gleamed off the page. *We got Time and Newsweek. It's nice to get some news. These magazines are banned in Uganda. We're also enjoying some cheese, candy, and soft drinks.*

My father took up where my mother left off: *Tomorrow we expect to see a game park within the city. Recently, over 20,000 wildebeest entered, so we will see a large herd. Also we will go to the animal orphanage. The children will like that.*

He folded the aerogramme into a rectangle and tucked it into his briefcase. This blue slip of paper would be the last letter my grandmother would receive for many months. It was a benign, hopeful letter. Politics were a backdrop to our quiet hilltop lives.

Before returning to Uganda, we drove through Nairobi National Park. I would carry with me this memory: my hand on the back window, the click of the camera, an antelope as large as an elephant, its skin striped and velvety, its horns splendid spirals. It seemed to step out of a fairy story. It glided past our car, and then back into the pages of pushmi-pullyus and Aladdin's treasures. I don't remember the migrating wildebeest or the lions. I remember only the eland, handsome and otherworldly.

We returned to Uganda as everyone else was leaving. "If everyone else jumped off a cliff, would you?" my mother often asked Sonja and me when we were older. After the hustle of Nairobi, my mother welcomed the quiet of Uganda. She was filled with a surprising joy and a sense of home. She was glad to return to the rhythms of the jungle, particularly after our experience at the border. It was her first time smuggling and bribing and waiting, waiting, waiting, bored except for the fear in her throat. She would never get used to it. "The borders," she told a missionary, "were *hell*." The raised eyebrows encouraged her, and she went from house to house saying, "The borders were *hell*."

That the borders were horrendous was not news to anyone. Kaarina's profanity? Now *that* was news.

CHAPTER 8

———◆———

Ugandan Psalm

MORNINGS WE SAT on the verandah, the three of us; my father had long vanished into the reaching branches and tangle that surrounded our house, despite violent spats of slashing at the underbrush. He would reappear in the evening, a stack of papers under a looping arm. This was our world, this hill. It was early, and the air was still cool. A breeze shifted the top branches of the bougainvillea. My mother sat looking outward, toward her tomato garden. There was a sole survivor, a pinkish fruit she had been thinking about plucking. Today or tomorrow, she wasn't sure, but she had been watching it ripen all week.

My mother hummed as she opened her slim Bible. She opened directly to Psalms. It was always Psalms, and the words dropped out of her mouth like music:

I will lift up mine eyes unto the hills, from whence cometh my help. My help cometh from the Lord, which made heaven and earth. He will not suffer thy foot to be moved: he that keepeth thee will not slumber. Behold, he that keepeth Israel shall neither slumber nor sleep.

My mother read chapter 121 at a leisurely pace, relishing the milk and honey of David's language. She was drawn to his metaphors and found company in his ambivalence. In a green felt pen, she underlined a single verse, a passage I never heard her read aloud. It is the rumination of the exiled, and the question must have resonated: *How shall we sing the Lord's song in a strange land?*

After my mother read the scripture, Sonja and I bowed our heads and folded our hands. We turned one ear to our mother as she prayed for our protection, for our deliverance from snakes. It was a prayer we have heard often, but the words were spoken with fresh urgency. A story had been passing like ashes from mouth to mouth, from mother to mother.

The story was this: A young girl climbed the mango tree, the one that sat between the dispensary and the college gate. The girl must have been the daughter of a new student, for we had not played with her, would not, in fact, ever play with her. Still, I see her, slight and smart, ankles freckled with scars. She stops at the base of the tree, searching the dark foliage until her eyes rest upon the top branch, upon fruit hanging down like small, green hearts. Unripe mangoes, white fleshed and sour, are best dipped in salt and chili powder. The girl stands, hands hanging at her side, eyes sweeping the trunk as she considers the best way up. I want to tell her now—*Keep walking. Today is not a good day for green mangoes*—but she cannot hear me, and so she must hitch her skirt and dig her toes into rough bark.

A few men squatted in the shifting shadow of the tree, paying little mind to the girl clambering up the trunk. Fruit was communal, and we children climbed with ease. The men squinted against the sun and discussed everything except politics. It did not do to share too much of what you were thinking. Instead, they wondered when the rains would come. It was the dry season, and the leaves gathered overhead were coated with earth. They were still talking when the girl screamed and, a breath later, fell to the ground, landing in the dirt with a thud. The men hovered over the frail, birdlike form, uncertain what to do. Finally, one man turned her over, placed burning fingers against the curve of her jaw, against the stillness of her artery.

A nurse saw the huddle and ran out of the dispensary. He was prepared to handle a broken arm, a concussion, even a snakebite, for my parents smuggled antivenom for the clinic. Each time they visited Kenya, they carried back vials marked *viper, mamba, cobra*. The men were grateful to turn responsibility over to someone who knew what to do. The nurse directed one of the men to gather up the girl and carry her into the clinic. He laid her on a cot stained with urine. And that was all anyone could do. "She died before she hit the ground," they would later say in soft voices, a refrain that would be repeated from house to house. Somehow, this fact gave the story its urgency. Other children died and would die, but hers was the death we remembered.

The girl was bitten by a green mamba, a lovely snake—sleek skinned and graceful. She was bitten several times, machine-gun bites that left a row of punctures on her angled arm. It seemed impossible that marks so small could amputate slender bones from breath and sinew, impossible that the green ballerina, gliding from branch to branch, bore death as well as beauty. Yet there lay the child, a girl whose mother would later kneel on dry earth, arms outstretched, lashing the air with the songs of her grief.

You are never safe. You are never too young to die. Those were the lessons, clean and simple, but my sister and I would not learn them. We were children, fearless in the tradition of all children, and there were many interesting matters. There was the star fruit tree to climb and the dirt pathways we pressed into the jungle floor with our matchbox cars. There were the friends on campus to play with, dolls to dress and parade, and there was a missionary's cat who had just had kittens we were aching to see.

"We shall see," my mother said about the last item. She held a rubber band between her teeth and slid a brush through Sonja's hair. Sonja sat on a stool between our mother's knees and scowled. She had a tender scalp and long, slippery hair that my mother pulled back into merciless ponytails and braids, a ritual I was spared, for my hair was short. In the mornings, my sister would often dissolve into tears, sobs my mother had little patience for.

"Hold still," she said. "Good grief, I'm not trying to kill you."

And then, unexpectedly, my mother shrieked. The nearly completed braid slipped from her grasp, unraveling like a living thing. My mother paid no heed to the plait as she stood and lunged for the screen door, leaving us to sit in astonishment, mouths agape, eyes alert, our whole beings wonderfully interested in whatever phenomenon had interrupted our morning. We watched as our mother hurled out the door and down the steps. She shouted again, but it was too late. A monkey had run off with her tomato.

The monkey loped through the brush and up a small tree, cradling the tomato against his chest. He sat on a branch, his tail hanging down like an anchor, and faced my mother. He turned the pink tomato over, sniffed it and took a bite, almost daring my mother to get out the slingshot. She stood three paces from the verandah, hands resting on hips as she weighed her options. She was a terrible shot, and the monkeys all knew the radius of her anger. They gathered on branches just beyond the range of her slingshot to observe and to mock, she was certain.

There was a fondness that the monkeys commanded with their cuteness and their ease. They were deft and clever, and when they carried off our jackfruits, arms straining to encircle fruit larger than themselves, bodies swaying under the weight, my parents called out to each other—"Come quickly"—as one or the other stood at the window and laughed. A brief truce in the war. The monkeys began it, my parents maintained.

Uganda's food, like everything else, had been vanishing. It was a disappearing act set to the pulse of soldiers. We were lucky for the beans and rice, lucky for the tropical pumpkin, lucky for the accompanying wedge of avocado. No matter what pestilence might befall us, Sonja and I could rely on avocados. Six trees lined the yard, and like diligent aunts they foisted buckets of sustenance upon us. My father delivered most to his students, but four a day found their way to our table. Sonja and I abhorred avocadoes, and Sonja pointed out to our parents that even the monkeys would not touch them. My parents, who moved into the house delighted at the bounty of avocadoes, were in truth growing weary of them.

"Beggars can't be choosers," my mother would say, and then make a point of praising its vitamin value, its healthy fat.

"All right, avocado," my father would say, scooting his chair closer to the table.

Sonja and I looked at our plates. "Yuck." We held our noses and stifled dramatic gags.

"Listen," my mother would say. "Skip the show. That's all we have, so you're just going to have to eat it."

To supplement our diet, my father decided to plant a garden. He hired two students to clear the plot of semi-level jungle and plant rows of peanuts, pineapples, and corn. The seeds grew like Jack's beanstalk. The hearty leaves meant peanut butter to my father, corn on the cob to my mother. We would have peanut sauce on our matoke, cornbread with our beans, pineapple juice and fruit salads. Greedily, my parents carried water down to the shoots and yanked at the weeds, which seemed to creep up each night through the jungle floor. The garden held the promise of a bumper crop.

A family of monkeys observed the flutter of activity with keen interest. Humans had been living in the house on the hill for years, passing through the jungle on cautious paths, keeping mainly to themselves. It was only the little ones who scattered through the underbrush, climbing trees and going where they pleased. The monkeys perched on branches high above earthly cares, combing fingers through each other's fur and biting the exposed fleas.

It was dusk when they came down from their trees to investigate. They spread across the garden, sniffing leaves so rich in color they appeared to refract the fading light. The monkeys began with curiosity, examining the roots and finding peanuts. They moved on to a row of pineapples, a prickly plant whose serrated edges did not say welcome. The monkeys, small magicians each one, reached soft hands into the hearts and pulled out ripening fruit. They approached the corn, still too young. The stalks offered up nothing. The harvest was over, but the monkeys gave themselves over to the tactile delights of annihilating a garden. They scrambled over the rows, leaving the plants scattered above the earth that once embraced them.

"Well, so much for that," my father said as he stepped into the kitchen through the back door. He rested one hand against the wall and leaned down to untie his shoes. "The garden's gone."

"What?" my mother said. She was baking tropical pumpkin, and she could be certain that no one would rejoice when she brought it to the table. Avocadoes teetered on the chopping board, ready to be sliced in two.

"You're going to love this," my father said, the pleasure of getting to tell the story already taking some of the edge off his disappointment. "The monkeys came in and harvested everything. And when I say everything, I mean *everything*. They pulled up the plants, just to see what was on the other side."

"Oh, Gary," she said. "Please tell me you're kidding."

Later, my father rummaged through the garage until he found a slingshot. He took it outside and walked about the yard, head tipped toward the earth. He did not take many steps before he stopped, reached down, and picked a smooth stone. He tossed it in one hand, testing the weight. He hadn't used a slingshot since he was a teenager shooting coots, a practice he and his friends abandoned as soon as the girls noticed and disapproved. My father faced the jungle, hand full of stone, and he searched the trees for a victim. He hoped only to scare off the monkeys, to be able to grow corn and peanuts, to harvest a few jackfruit. He skimmed the surface of the trees until his eyes rested on a monkey who had been preening on a low branch. She looked up, and they considered each other. The monkey was sleek, with a tan body, a white chest. She was the size of a housecat, and more curious. She scratched her back and watched as my father placed the stone in the sling, held it up, and closed one eye. The aim was nearly good, and the monkey screamed as the rock slashed a nearby leaf. She rushed into the jungle, moving with a one-two swagger. My father smiled in the hollow of our yard and listened as the sound of breaking twigs traveled into the jungle, grew distant, and disappeared.

The monkeys went nowhere. They learned only to know when my father carried his slingshot and when he didn't, no matter how stealthy his attempts. When he carried it, they slipped away in deference to his aim and range, returning as soon as the screen door slapped shut behind him. When he didn't carry the slingshot, they stayed in the trees and chattered. The sounds drifting down were not alarmed, like the calls that warned of a mamba; they were just neighborly noises, with perhaps a hint of ridicule: *We are smarter than you think*. Which was not exactly true; my parents had begun to think that the monkeys were small Einsteins.

Try Ex-Lax, my father remembers someone suggesting in a letter, *The monkeys might get sick and leave*. They helpfully included several bars of the recommended product. My parents called Sonja and me into the room. As soon as we walked in, we spied the slim package resting between our parents on the couch and eyed it with guarded interest. Boxes from overseas were a hit-and-miss affair. Sometimes we got candy, but more often it was underwear—or worse, hand-me-down underwear.

My parents held up the Ex-Lax. "This is not for you. It's to chase off the monkeys, to make them ill. This is *not* chocolate. You are *not* to eat this." Eating had become one of our great obsessions. We climbed trees for fruit, picked bunches of sour grass, and roamed the fields with other children in search of dodo, a spinach-like vegetation that my mother would add to our meals. At supper, Sonja would admonish the rest of us, "Don't eat my food while I'm gone," before she slipped off her chair and trotted to the bathroom. When she returned, she would examine her beans and rice (the fate of the avocado was of little concern), and only then would she be satisfied. At night, my parents would have to remind me that we had eaten three meals that day.

"Remember," my father would say gently, "we had uji for breakfast, rice and beans for lunch, pumpkin for supper. You didn't miss a meal." But the next night, I would again feel there was a void in my day, a morsel that had been overlooked.

Our books were filled with fairytales designed to make the mouths of small children water. There were houses built of gumdrops and licorice, cookies that dashed down country lanes, chocolate eggs won by diligent schoolchildren, and trucks that cruised neighborhoods, offering up music and ice cream.

The Ex-Lax, with its crisp wrapper, balanced on my mother's palm. "Trust us, you don't want to eat this," my parents said once more, before plotting the downfall of the monkeys. The Ex-Lax would go out in the evening, they decided.

In a pinnacle of self-control and filial obedience, Sonja and I gave the Ex-Lax a wide berth. So did the neighboring children, who had also been warned. So did the monkeys. Only the ants were drawn to the slabs of exposed chocolate resting on a rock. After a week, my father retrieved the Ex-Lax, ants running up his hand. The monkeys watched from the branches as if to say, *We are here to stay.*

My mother's response to the garden tragedy was to plant another, this one closer to the house. There was no room for a crop, only a few tomato vines. "I need something new on the table," she told my father. Together, they tilled the earth, planted seeds, weeded the patch of ground, and tied the vines to stakes, but it was my mother who found particular pleasure in the pale stems that rose toward the sun. When the first fruit appeared, she hovered over the plant like an anxious nursemaid, inducing Sonja and me to take our Fisher-Price toys outside and play near the garden. Constant vigilance, however, could not be maintained. Sonja and I grew tired of staying in the yard; my mother grew tired of posting herself in front of a window.

As soon as the first tomatoes were big enough, they were picked green and placed on the windowsill, where they would inexplicably rot. The rest were allowed to ripen, both my mother and the monkeys biding their time, wondering how long they could wait before the other would pluck the fruit right out from under their noses. Sometimes my mother won, and a slice of tomato appeared beside our avocado. More often the monkeys won, the novel fruit carried up a tree and devoured.

There was only one tomato left when my mother called Sonja and me to come for worship. As she read from Psalms, she was not listening to the rhythm of the words or to the language that was usually violins and oboes; she was instead deliberating over when to pick the tomato. *Today,* she had finally decided, *just as soon as I put Sonja's hair into braids.*

"Of course the monkey got it," my father would later say. "Murphy's law."

"I don't know," my mother would respond. "I had a hunch, and I should have followed it." Sonja and I would add nothing to the conversation, listening only as the bitter tomato was tasted again and again.

The loss of the tomato put my mother in a bad mood, worse because she was aware of how pathetic it was for a tomato to throw her off-kilter. All morning, she refused to take us down to see the kittens. "I have to make lunch," she said. Then she had to wash dishes. Then she sent us to our nap. Then she threw clothes in the washing machine. "I have to be here to hang them when they're done." My sister and I lurked behind every corner, pleading, *Can we go now? What about now? How will the kittens learn to love us? You promised, remember?*

"Why can't we go alone?" Sonja asked. Our mother didn't believe in close supervision of her daughters, and despite her fear of snakes, we roamed the hill without much observation; a trip to the bottom wouldn't be so different. Of course, there was the mamba. Few of us children knew the little girl, but our mothers all now knew the mother, and they saw the event as both a tragedy and a warning: *Watch your children.*

"All right. You can go," my mother said.

"We're going to see the kittens, kittens, kittens," we sang to the tune "Ring Around the Rosie," our arms outstretched, our bodies spinning in widening circles. When we collapsed on the rug, she stated the rules: Stay together. If you see a snake, don't move. Take the road, not the path. Stay an hour, then come straight home.

"Go and change into something clean," she said, swatting our bottoms as we raced past her and down the hall.

My mother was not watching as we set across the yard toward our usual shortcut, a mouth slashed into the jungle's flank. It was not an act of disobedience but of habit.

"Mommy said take the road," I said. Trust me to remember.

"Oh," Sonja said, and we paused at the edge of the yard, straddled between two fates. "We're already here." The unspoken knowledge passing between us was that the path was much faster. Yet there was something else compelling us forward, something we felt but could not articulate: our mother's hypocrisy. We had been scrambling about this jungle for months; the danger of mambas was no less then, no more now.

If I was a goody-goody, Sonja was pragmatic. "Come on," she said and plunged down the trail. I followed, as I always did.

It was a bright day, and then it wasn't. A canopy of leaves muted the sun, and though it was the dry season, the air was cool and damp. The ground held its own moisture and gave off a loamy scent of *here* and *home* that I would carry with me like a puzzle piece. It was the smell of crushed leaves, lemongrass, pods, earth, and something else. Years later, I would breathe in this smell and then, only then, would I know I was back.

Somewhere on the trail, I elbowed past Sonja, anxious to prove I wasn't slow. I held my arms out, parted branches that swung shut behind me. The bush vibrated with insects, and a rattle in the elephant grass could be heard for several paces. Our feet were clad in flip-flops, the worn rubber slapping our heels as we walked. Grass scratched at our calves and our steps perturbed locusts, which leapt from blade to blade. They were large, and their sudden movements startled us. It was a delicious fear. A chance mamba gave drama to what would be just a random walk on a random day. We were edgy enough to sing—noise an inoculation against the snakes drawn to our disobedience. Children's books had taught us what happened to those foolish enough to disobey their parents. They burned a hole in their mother's favorite dress, ate all their Halloween candy and got sick.

At the top of the hill, my mother reached into the washing machine and pulled out wet clothing. She was pleased to snatch moments away from us. She carried the basket to the line. She was humming, always humming, as she clipped a pair of jeans to the line and leaned down for another. She looked before she grabbed.

A snake once appeared in this plastic basket—jeans, then sheets, then coiled viper. It must have slid across the yard and crawled through a tulip-shaped hole in the basket, and my mother only noticed when she saw motion under a sundress. If she was scared, she kept it to herself as she marched to the garage, grabbed the jembe, and returned with Sonja and me at her heels. A snake in the laundry was something new. "Step back," my mother had said. She held the blade of the jembe and dipped the wooden handle into the basket. Her biggest concern was that the clothes might get dirty. She pushed aside her flowered dress, and there it was, twisted like a lady's fancy hairdo.

My mother used a stick to pluck each item from the basket. She picked around the snake like it was a bit of avocado she didn't want to eat. She pulled out jeans, dresses, underwear, t-shirts, pants; the viper curled tighter, muscles rippling under glossy skin. Our water came from the rain barrel, the supply dependent on afternoon showers. It had not rained in days, and there was not enough water to rewash the clothes. She pulled out everything except a dishtowel; then she killed the snake with the jembe, teeth gritted as the blade swept the air in its downward arc.

My mother would never quite feel comfortable hanging clothes again. She moved down the clothesline, first pinning the sheets, then the pants and dresses. The motion between basket and line was no longer a smooth one. She was tentative each time she reached down, even as her mind was caught on the puzzle of the day—how to cook beans and rice and make it taste like something else. If only she had a tomato.

"I was hanging clothes when I heard you scream." This was how she would always begin the story of that day. The cry she heard was continual, one long siren, and she was not sure whether this was good or bad, only that it was coming from the path and she must hurry. She dropped what she was holding back into the basket, and then she began to run.

We were not so far down the path, maybe halfway down the hill. The noise was coming from my mouth, gaping like a baby weaver's, tears and mucus smeared across my face. Sonja too was crying, though she had not thought to pull me off the path. We both were rigid. *Don't move, don't move* a litany through our heads.

I was standing in a river of driver ants. My feet had vanished in the tide, my ankles nearly gone, my calves streaked, my arms and chest spotted. Ants were even crawling on my scalp. My legs were ablaze, the soldiers' pincers as sound as sutures. They say if one is lacerated in the jungle, driver ants can close the wound.

A thousand needles against my skin, and my mother nearly smiled from the relief of it. She yanked me off the trail, my two flip-flops lost in the boiling path—my father would get them later—and scooped me against her side. I was a heavy burden, and a loud one. My mother clucked her tongue in sympathy and brushed at my feet. She jogged for home.

I was still crying when my mother carried me into the bathroom and heaved me into the tub like a sack of cassava. She turned on the tap—we had no shower—and held each foot under the precious flow. She cupped the liquid in her palms and poured it over my body, stripping off my clothes as she went. The tub filled with black, a film of ant clinging to ant. They tried to crawl up the porcelain, back up my legs. Some held to my wet skin. It would be a long time before my mother could remove all the ants, wash them down the drain, and wrap a towel around my body. It would be a long time before I pulled off the last ant that had wedged itself behind my ear. Finally, I curled on the couch, looking down at my welts. My mother sat on the couch and held me to her side.

Later, Sonja and I went to our room to play, my mother returned to the couch. She picked up her Bible and turned to Psalms. *I will lift up mine eyes unto the hills, from whence cometh my help.* She still felt the fear constricting in her throat, remembered the bargains struck with God as she hustled down the path. Now held, she saw the gift of protection as a frail thing. She saw her own two daughters as foolish and impetuous, and no more worthy than another. What role does luck play? What role does God? She turned her head toward the wall and wept. She cried for the child who died in the mango tree, for the mother who was still mourning.

CHAPTER 9

————— ❧ —————

Archbishop's Murder

IDI AMIN'S ADDRESSES on the radio grew more bombastic, the whispered stories more frequent and horrifying. Idi Amin had come to power through a coup, and despite what many in the West believed, he was not a buffoon. When Amin had overthrown Milton Obote six years earlier, there had been long celebrations, and the streets of Kampala echoed with ululation. Now, Idi Amin could feel the will of the people shifting from jubilation to silent anger. He was one man with many enemies, and the land was ready for a change. In Tanzania, Milton Obote was waiting like a spider.

At the beginning of 1977, a small army rebellion was thwarted. Amin's response was swift and terrible. He killed everyone in Milton Obote's home village and purged the army again of Acholi and Langi soldiers. They were bundled into lorries and taken to Mugire prison. A refugee who fled to Kenya told *Time* that he'd seen soldiers herded into prison cells. The refugee was a prisoner, too, and how he escaped, he didn't say. He described instead the sounds of Idi Amin's own soldiers being murdered. "You would hear a short cry, and then sudden silence. I think they were being strangled and then had their heads smashed. Next day, the floors of rooms C and D—the elimination chambers—were littered with loose eyes and teeth . . . I was forced to load battered bodies of my cellmates into lorries."

A public execution was announced in Kampala, and my parents learned of it on campus. "Are you going?" they were asked. My mother wanted nothing to do with it ("What a question!"), and even my father's curiosity had a limit. Later, they heard how the prisoners were tied to posts in the traffic roundabout. The men wept, their eyes wild. When someone gave an order, the soldiers opened fire, their machine guns pointed low. They began shooting at the men's feet, then moved slowly up. The prisoners screamed and thrashed against the ropes, before falling limp and silent.

The most influential religious leader at this time was Janani Luwum, the Anglican Archbishop of Uganda. Like Idi Amin, Archbishop Luwum was a product of Africanization; nearly one hundred years of missionaries in Uganda and Janani Luwum was only the second Ugandan archbishop. He was a rare man, both a warm individual and an innovative, effective leader. He encouraged theology students to take classes in Developmental Studies, and promoted a Christian practice that looked African, not European, and when parishioners came to him with names written on slips of paper, he would go to the State Research Bureau and secure the release of someone's brother, someone's husband.

On January 30, after the waves of violence, one of Luwum's bishops preached a sermon he had titled "The Preciousness of Life." Six days later, Archbishop Luwum's home was searched for weapons. He responded by writing an open letter to Amin and sending copies to government officials and to the church in Kenya. Seventeen bishops signed the letter, and Archbishop Luwum personally delivered it to Idi Amin. Their voices were like those crying in the desert: *We have buried many who have died as a result of being shot and there are many more whose bodies have not been found . . . The gun which was meant to protect Uganda as a nation, the Ugandan citizen and his property, is increasingly being used against the Ugandan to take away his life and property.*

On February 16, Archbishop Luwum and six bishops were arrested at a rally. They were accused of smuggling weapons into Uganda. Idi Amin asked, "What shall we do with these traitors?" The crowd answered, "Kill them now." No, no, Amin responded, Uganda is a civilized country. Luwum would be tried in court.

The next morning, Radio Uganda announced that Archbishop Luwum and two government ministers had died in a car accident. According to the official report, while the three men were being driven to the interrogation center, they attempted to overpower the driver, causing the car they were in to crash into another vehicle. A sealed casket was sent to Luwum's hometown to be buried. People said that before the funeral the family pried open the coffin, and that the archbishop's body was riddled with bullets. There were whispers that Amin himself had shot Luwum in the mouth and then shot his body again and again. There were other rumors, darker rumors. My parents heard that Luwum had been decapitated, that Idi Amin kept the head in a fridge and, from time to time, would take it out and scold it.

After the archbishop's murder, even expatriates were anxious. The thing to do, the missionaries all said, was to be unobtrusive. Don't make waves. It went without saying that you shouldn't travel unless you had to. Any time you drove, you risked getting stopped by soldiers or carjackers, soldiers being preferable of the two, but with the country on edge, who knew? It felt melodramatic to speak about getting killed. It felt presumptuous to clutch your passport and assume you were above it all.

For months, my father had planned to drive into Kenya for some administrative meetings. My mother had always intended to stay with us on the hill because it was safer and because crossing the border was, as she noted, "hell." She had created a shopping list for my father that might as well have said *buy all the things*. Now this.

"No one expects you to still go," my mother said. "No one."

"I'm not that kind of missionary," my father said. It was his favorite line.

My mother could feel the tug of their old argument. She sometimes veered away, setting her mouth and saying nothing further. More often, she railed. "Why can't you just once put your family before the church?"

On the morning my father left, she was cheerful. My mother might shout during a fight, but she didn't stew. As my father dashed through the house—"Where's my Bible? Where's my passport? Have you seen my glasses?"—she pointed him toward the items he needed, and when he was ready to leave she handed him a stack of aerogrammes that had accumulated on our table. For the past week, missionaries had been dropping off letters for my father to post in Kenya. Mail sent from Uganda was opened and read by someone, we all knew.

My father said goodbye to us in the yard. I sat in my mother's arms and watched him go. It was a familiar sight. He left, and then he returned, often with presents. The best were matchbox cars. Sonja and I loved them because we loved him. At night, he would get on the floor with us and push cars around the legs of the dining room table.

"You better get going," my mother said. "Don't do anything stupid."

She didn't have to say that we'd be fine. Of course we'd be fine. If you didn't count snakes and malaria, life on the hill was uneventful.

My father was in Kenya when Jimmy Carter held the second press conference of his presidency. Reporters wanted to know how Carter's campaign promises were holding up to the realities of office. No one anticipated that Uganda would be mentioned or that the press conference would have international consequences.

Halfway through, a reporter asked Carter, "What, if anything, do you plan to try to do to help victims of political repression in these countries?" The countries in question were Iran and the Philippines, and the reporter noted that despite human rights abuses by both regimes, the United States was aiding their governments. Carter spoke vaguely about changes his administration was making, then pivoted to Uganda. Uganda was a small, politically inconsequential country, one the United States was not supporting either covertly or overtly, and the archbishop's murder *was* shocking.

"Obviously, there are deprivations of human rights, even more brutal than the ones on which we've commented up till now," Carter said. "In Uganda, the actions there have disgusted the entire civilized world, and, as you know, we have no diplomatic relationships with Uganda. But here is an instance where both Ambassador Andrew Young and I have expressed great concern about what is there. The British are now considering asking the United Nations to go into Uganda to assess the horrible murders that apparently are taking place in that country, the persecution of those who have aroused the ire of Mr. Amin."

It was a throwaway line. The press conference, broadcast live on television and radio, continued for fourteen more questions, none of them about Idi Amin. Jimmy Carter didn't mention Uganda again.

The next day, Idi Amin announced that Americans couldn't leave Uganda and were to report themselves to Kampala on February 28 for a personal meeting. No one was quite sure what this meant. It could mean nothing. It could mean we would be deported. It could mean we would be imprisoned or held in Kampala. There were only 240 Americans in Uganda. Most were missionaries like us who had ignored the State Department's travel warnings. There were also a handful of airline employees, oil workers, and technicians. Sonja and I were some of the youngest Americans. With our father in Kenya, we were likely the only American children without an American guardian in the country.

"Goddammit. Why couldn't our first crisis have been a more dignified one?" a White House adviser reportedly said.

———— ❧ ————

CHAPTER 10

House Arrest

NEWS OF THE house arrest, as the missionaries called it, moved swiftly through campus. There was news, and then there was *news*. What were the Fordhams going to do now? Would they be deported, or worse? What was Carter thinking? The other missionaries were relieved that the leaders of their respective nations—Philippines, Australia, and Canada—had sense enough not to irritate Amin, and it was fortunate, they all said, providential even, that Gary was in Kenya. They knew my mother was Finnish, and they speculated on whether or not Sonja and I were dual citizens. (We weren't.) That my mother was the last to hear the news said more about living on the hill than anything.

After the midday rain, a missionary hustled up to tell us. She called out, "Hodi," and my mother's heart lurched. "Gary's fine," the missionary said as she sat on the couch.

In the dining room, Sonja and I were building a puzzle. We began singing because we liked to sing and because we finally had an audience, even if it was only a missionary. The women spoke as if we weren't there, and so we responded in the only way we could: We raised the volume. "God is so good. God is so GOOD. God is SO GOOD. HE'S SO GOOD TO ME."

"Please, can we have some peace and quiet?" my mother said. "We're trying to talk here." Her voice was sharp, and I began weeping. "Oh, for goodness sakes," our mother said.

To the missionary, she asked, "What does this mean? What's he thinking?"

After we went to bed, our mother turned on the radio. She confirmed the date and time we were to present ourselves in Kampala and wondered whether or not she should take us. Who would even drive us? Surely the Ugandan government wouldn't seek out two children. Did anyone even know we were here? Who kept track of these things?

Termites flew against the glass with steady pings. A few had gotten into the house, where they fluttered on the floor, lattice wings propelling thick bodies. They were a delicacy. When they came flying out of the ground, children would leave whatever they were doing and run out into the fields to gather them. The termites were roasted and eaten. My mother carried the mugs into the kitchen and set them in the sink. She stood in the green darkness, water running through her hands, and cried.

In Kenya, my father sat down to write his mother and stepfather. Despite attending meetings all day, he must have felt as if he was on vacation. No teaching, grading, or lesson planning. And the food! In Uganda, we spoke often of such meals: toast with Marmite, potatoes and green beans, spaghetti and peas, cake.

My father dated his letter February 24, the day after Jimmy Carter's press conference. Either he hadn't heard the news or the detention hadn't yet been announced.

Dear Mother and Gordon,

Wanted to let you know all is well with us. There is trouble in the land, but we have not been bothered.

He filled the front page of the aerogramme with the minutia of our daily lives: Mail in Uganda was censored, the dairy farm was down to six cows, wages for Ugandans were only fifteen cents an hour, fellow missionaries were requesting transfers.

Four days later, my father, fully aware of the events in Uganda, returned to the letter. He had left the back flap empty, and so he turned to it and wrote in the date: February 28. So much could happen in four days.

I am still in Kenya (Union Session finished yesterday) and Americans are detained in Uganda. We are not sure what to do because Kaarina, on a Finnish passport, can leave more easily if I'm not there. We expected to get an indication today, but now the meeting [with Idi Amin] is postponed until Wednesday. I may go in tomorrow to be there for the appointment with the president and I may wait.

I wish I could contact Kaarina, but the phones are cut at the border. We know the Lord will watch over us, but feel it may be wiser to see what's going to happen before complicating matters. The Lord Bless you. Love, Gary

My father was a phlegmatic man who liked to say, "Don't make a mountain out of a molehill." After hearing we were under house arrest, he had continued attending meetings. He was a delegate, after all. Let the world burn around him, Gary Fordham would fulfill his duty. The letter to my grandmother, however, suggested that my father had identified a mountain as a mountain. Over and over, he used the pronoun *we*, as if he and my mother were in consultation: *We are not sure. We expect. We know. We feel.* Unable to contact my mother, he was conversing with her in his head.

Two decades later, after my mother died, he returned to this unconscious habit. *We think. We hope. We feel.*

"Who is this 'we'?" I finally asked. "You and mom?"

"Yeah," he said, and smiled. He never used *we* in the same way again.

The soldier came in the morning. We were on the verandah when we heard the crunch of tires on a road that led to us and nowhere else. The rumble was a back and forth sound, a jostling of vehicle against washed-out road, against mud, against potholes. My mother set down her Bible, and the three of us watched the Land Rover jut out of the jungle, roll across the yard, and stop beside the frangipani tree. A soldier dressed in green, sleeves rolled past elbows, climbed out, and there, from the passenger's side, emerged Joseph, my father's student.

"Good morning, madam," the soldier said.

"Good morning, bwana," my mother said. "Morning, Joseph." The soldier was tall and dashing. His eyes followed our chickens, Rebecca and Sarah, as they snatched termites in the yard. "Can I help you?" my mother said. "If you came to see my husband, he's not here."

"Can we come in?" the soldier said.

My mother led them up the cement steps and through the verandah. She removed her shoes at the door and asked them to do the same. "All the mud," she said. She motioned toward the couch, and as the men sat, she asked Joseph how he was enjoying his classes. He answered that he was liking them very much.

Sonja and I scooted behind her. A soldier was sitting next to Joseph on our couch. Any other day, Joseph would have been the occasion. I would have climbed into his lap and demanded a story, but Joseph was not the point. There was a soldier in our house. He was wearing a beret, and there were holes in his socks.

In the kitchen, our mother made cherry Kool-Aid out of water she had boiled the night before. We hadn't had Kool-Aid in months—or as my mother liked to say, not in the memory of man. Sonja and I hoped the visitors wouldn't drink it all. My mother hummed as she moved, reaching for our tall cups, then opening a Tupperware of dried finger bananas. She carried the Kool-Aid out first, giving a cup to both Joseph and the soldier. Then she brought out the dried finger bananas and held them out, and they each took one or two. Bananas were, well, bananas, but the Kool-Aid had made an impression.

"These are my girls," my mother said. "Sonja and Sari." We ducked and smiled. "What do you say?" she said.

Sonja stepped up to the soldier and said, "Hello." The soldier took her hand and shook it. "You are welcome," he said. I pressed my face into my mother's waist, and they laughed.

"Okay," my mother said. "You can go outside and play. Take the cat. Stay near the house, and for goodness sakes, don't get too muddy." And so we went, the reluctant Kissa looped through Sonja's arms.

Our mother frowned as we left, feeling what, exactly, I shouldn't know, but I've heard this story so often I can't separate my memories from hers, my feelings from hers, and so I see her standing in our house, irritated. She was irritated at the excitement of her daughters, irritated at her husband for being gone, irritated at Jimmy Carter for opening his big mouth, irritated at Joseph for accompanying the soldier, irritated at herself for not smiling more pleasantly, irritated that she had to smile. Underneath all her peevishness was fear. Quite absent was the triumph she later had while telling this story.

She sat in the La-Z-Boy we had brought from the States. It had come in a great shipment of things that had taken a year to be released from customs, and only then after my father had overcome his scruples and bribed the custom official. Opening those crates had been like a bad Christmas. So much bounty, so little practicality. Better to have brought more soap, more children's cereal, more watches for bribes. Instead, there sat our La-Z-Boy.

My mother now looked at the soldier with as much pleasantness as she could muster. Even if she could remember where my father kept the watches, she didn't dare bribe an official. It might be exactly the wrong thing. She wasn't going to give Idi Amin any reason to throw her in jail.

"If there's even a speck of mud outside, my girls will find it," my mother said. "So today, forget it. Mark my words, they'll be filthy when they come back in. Do you have children?" When the soldier nodded, she rattled off her Questions For Soldiers With Kids: *How many do you have? How old are they? What are their names? Are they attending school? Do you like being a father?* If we had been at a roadblock, she would have concluded the conversation with a small present for the children (a pencil or a nob of soap), but today she was too anxious.

"Where is your husband?" the soldier asked. "Where is Gary Fordham?"

"Joseph didn't tell you? He's in Kenya." It was not lost on her that the soldier knew my father's first name. She was certain she hadn't told him.

"He's attending the East African Union meetings."

My mother hadn't expected this visit, but now that the soldier sat across from her, his visit seemed inevitable. Of course he was here. But what about Joseph? Why had he come?

The soldier explained that he had been sent with orders from Idi Amin Dada himself. All Americans were to appear before Idi Amin on Monday and couldn't leave the country before then. He was here because the Ugandan government wanted a list of our family's valuables. There was nothing menacing in the soldier's voice. It was the message itself that was menacing. Soon we would be separated from all that we owned. If we were lucky, we would only be kicked out of the country like the South Asians. If we were unlucky, well, no one wanted to consider it.

"This is a misunderstanding," my mother said. "I'm European, not American." She excused herself and returned with her Finnish passport, which she handed to the soldier.

He flipped through it, giving the pages a cursory glance. "Gary Fordham, he is American? Your babies, they are American? Madam, why is your husband gone now? Why are you all alone?"

My mother smiled blandly.

"Thank you," the soldier said, handing her the empty cup and the passport. He was polite. She was polite. "I must inventory your belongings now," he said. He had brought a clipboard with him into the house.

"The furniture doesn't belong to us," my mother said. "It belongs to the school. A fine Ugandan school, as you saw driving in. That couch isn't ours. The table and chairs aren't ours. The refrigerator isn't ours. If you take them, you'll only be hurting the school." She shot a look at Joseph.

"This is Ugandan?" the soldier asked, nudging the La-Z-Boy.

"Oh, goodness," my mother said. "Of course, you're right. That's ours. Actually, it's mine, and I'm not an American citizen. It's not an American belonging."

The soldier looked at her pointedly, though he didn't write anything down. He walked into the kitchen.

"The stove is the school's," my mother said, "But the pots and pans and dishes are mine. The Tupperware is mine."

The soldier began to pull open drawers. "Does the silverware belong to the school?" he asked.

"No, it belongs to me," my mother said. She claimed everything in the kitchen. She claimed the rice cooker my grandmother had sent from the States and the transformer that allowed it to work here. She claimed the cheese slicer, cutting board, and ceramic bowls (which actually were from Finland), and the can opener, dishtowels, and colander (which weren't). In the back room, she claimed the washing machine. She smiled and nodded. Mine. Mine. Mine. They went through the bedrooms, attempting to separate the property of the school from the property of the Fordhams. The beds belonged to the school, as did the mosquito nets, the dressers, and the bookcases. The sheets and blankets and books were ours. The typewriter was ours, as Joseph pointed out. So were the matchbox cars, the Fisher-Price toys, our Sabbath dresses, my father's ties, a Swiss Army knife, an old perfume bottle, the radio, our hens, the dog. My mother claimed them all.

The car, our most valuable possession, was in Kenya, but Joseph suggested that the bicycle should be here. "Pastor Fordham bikes to campus every day," Joseph said.

"Yes, Joseph," my mother said. "He needs the bike to get to campus." She wanted to hiss in his ear—*Whose side are you on anyway, Brother Joseph?* Bicycles were impossible to buy in Uganda. Everything was hard to come by. Even our pots and pans would be snatched up on the black market. But the bicycle? Well, people had been killed for less. "I can show it to you if you think it's necessary." The soldier nodded. "But I think you should know, it belongs to me."

"Your husband's bicycle?" the soldier said. His incredulity sat between them.

"Yes," my mother said. "I bought it, and I'm European." Let them prove she didn't own that bicycle.

"Madam, what is your husband's? What belongs to him, eh?"

My mother said nothing.

Jimmy Carter set up a command center to monitor the crisis in Uganda and redirected a nuclear aircraft carrier to the coast of Kenya, along with five naval vessels. The ships, which had been cruising the Indian Ocean on routine missions, were not prepared to rescue us. *Time* later reported that between all of them, there were fewer than two hundred Marines. Still, the message was delivered. "The President will take whatever steps he thinks are necessary and proper to protect American lives," the White House Press Secretary announced. So much promised effort, so few endangered lives. Of course, every life is precious to its owner.

Idi Amin must have felt conflicted. When a British professor had insulted Idi Amin in 1975, Queen Elizabeth had apologized, and England's Foreign Secretary had come to Uganda to secure the professor's release from prison. After a much more public criticism, President Carter was offering nothing but a show of force. Moreover, if Amin had seen the inventories taken by his soldiers, he must have been happily considering the political support he could secure with all those washing machines and cars.

But Idi Amin had learned what even a small country might do for its citizens. A year earlier, Palestinians had landed a hijacked plane at the Old Entebbe airport and held Jewish passengers hostage. Idi Amin had played host to both terrorists and hostages. He was a Big Man, courted daily by Israeli negotiators. And then the raid happened. Israel commandos freed most of the hostages, killed the terrorists and the Ugandan soldiers on duty, destroyed the Ugandan air force, and left Idi Amin looking weak and inept. He might not survive another such fiasco.

Idi Amin sent Carter a telegram stating that "the Americans in Uganda are happy and scattered all over the country" and that "Uganda has the strength to crush invaders." He postponed the meeting with Americans, and then a few days later, he canceled it. The fun was over. Idi Amin assured us we could leave the country if we wished. But why would we? Uganda was a beautiful country, and he had just wanted to thank us for our service.

My father was in the Finnish embassy when the final announcement was made. The clerks were creating counterfeit Finnish passports for Sonja and me, which they planned to smuggle into Uganda through a diplomatic pouch. It was as James Bond as anything we would be associated with. On hearing the news, my father thanked the clerks. Now for his errands.

Of course, the Fordham family would stay in Uganda. The crisis was over. Why make a mountain out of a molehill?

My father walked to the nearest duka and bought two matchbox cars.

For years, the only accounts I had of the house arrest were my own memories and my parents' stories. I looked for confirmation in Ugandan histories, but amidst the atrocities of the Amin years, the event was too small to matter. Then one day, I stumbled upon *Time*'s online archive and discovered articles written in the midst of the crisis. Once I found one piece of coverage, I found more and more. I listened to Carter's press conference and watched an ABC News report that was broadcast during the crisis. Experts called Idi Amin a "butcher" and said that while Amin didn't usually kill foreigners, nobody knew what to expect. My American grandmother likely saw the news story weeks before my father's letter arrived.

For most of my life, I considered this my mother's story. My mother stood in the living room and made a rash decision. She hadn't known, until she claimed that first item, what she would do. She was angry, and that was part of it. A soldier was informing her we might lose everything we owned. She had grown up poor, and possessions mattered to her, never mind that she was a missionary. She was also anxious about us, her American daughters.

When we were born, she hadn't wanted us to be dual citizens or even to learn the Finnish language. She wanted us to be fully American, unable to return to the land she had left and still missed terribly. Our U.S. passports were to be talismans, offering protections and opportunities that we—as Americans—would never fully appreciate. As she stood across from Joseph and the soldier and claimed everything we owned, she felt utterly alone, and so she did what she did. She was courageous. I think this still.

My mother stood across from a soldier who carried his own stories and fears. He held all the power in their interaction, and yet, he must have known that he was far more likely to be killed by Idi Amin than she was. Surely, there had been whispers about what had happened to the soldiers at the Mugire prison. They weren't just killed; they were killed with sledgehammers because bullets were too costly. If Idi Amin stayed in power, this soldier might join the disappeared, and if Amin was overthrown, he might be killed as retribution.

Standing beside the soldier, inexplicably, was Joseph. Joseph had no obvious reason to be at our house or so helpful. My father was a popular teacher who often ate breakfast in the cafeteria with his students. He was a hard grader, to be sure, but he was also funny and kind. I don't think Joseph came because he was angry at my father. His anger—if it was that—was probably broader. Why should expatriates have so much and Ugandans so little? Upon graduation, Joseph would likely be hired by the Adventist church and assigned a district that covered hundreds of miles and included multiple churches. He would work more than forty hours a week, but he wouldn't be able to afford a car, and if he owned even a bicycle, it would be through charity. A rural church in Ohio or North Carolina might send money for one as their mission project. They would expect a thank-you note and photographs. Where was the dignity for Ugandans? Where were their opportunities?

My Finnish grandmother knew that some people were more valued than others. The church might teach that God loved everyone equally, but in this world, citizenship determined worth. My grandmother had tended cows as a child, and as she stood in the dung, warming her bare feet, she decided that if she had children, she would urge them to move away and to matter. In Uganda, an entire town was murdered and my parents didn't hear about it. How many residents lived in that town? There were surely more than 240 people, but they had no advocates. Even today, the only record of their existence is their annihilation.

After the detention, *Time* put Idi Amin on the cover, titling their piece "The Wild Man of Africa." One of their sources, a Ugandan who had fled to Tanzania, described Idi Amin's foreign policy: "He always acts the same way. He threatens a group of foreigners, and then he says everything is okay. Then he threatens them again, and then he says everything is okay. The foreign government dances back and forth—and everyone forgets about the thousands of Ugandans who are dying."

We were the foreigners, or some of them. We weren't thinking about political dances or how Idi Amin might be using our presence in Uganda. Officially, my parents were thinking about God. In addition, my father was thinking about teaching, and my mother was wondering whether there would be any letters in the mail. She was also wondering about the church's wisdom and good intentions. She now knew that the church would send missionaries to a country that was too dangerous. She wondered how much, if anything, the church would do for missionaries caught up in political difficulty. Would the church have protested if the soldier had confiscated our belongings? She suspected not. What would church administrators do if we were arrested or imprisoned? What could they do?

She began to suspect we were here on our own.

Believing my father would be home soon, my mother used the last of the whole-wheat flour to make piirakka. "We'll see," she told us. She stood over the stove, stirring the rice, stirring the rice. If she let it burn, she would feel even more foolish than she already did. Who makes piirakka in Uganda? It was a Finnish staple, on every table, and for months, Sonja and I had been begging her to make it. She had waved us off, saying it was too hot here or that we didn't have enough powdered milk or that piirakka wouldn't taste right without rye flour. Well, she was making it now, and we would see.

My father had originally planned to return today, and my mother expected that he still would. "He has class tomorrow. He'll be back," she said. Sonja and I spent the morning arguing about who would tell him about the soldier. We sat for a while on the patio steps, giving each other shoves.

"I'm telling."

"No, me."

Our mother poked her head out the door. "Daddy's probably sitting at the border right now, just wishing he could hear you two fight. Oh boy. He doesn't know what he's missing." And then, "As long as you're out here, keep the monkeys away from the tomatoes."

By the afternoon, Sonja was building a puzzle and I was pushing my matchbox cars around the kitchen floor. "Daddy's bringing me a car," I told my mother.

"Don't count on it. We'll be lucky if he brings flour. And, good grief, if I step on one more car, I'm taking them away."

By supper, my father still hadn't come. My mother set the table. "Never mind, he still might come. Or he might stay the night in Kampala and come in the morning. We can wait another day. Right, girls?"

She put the piirakka and some finger bananas on the table and told us that it was probably the first time they had been served together in the history of mankind, making us feel very important indeed. The piirakka had a salty, creamy bite, and though my mother had been complaining about their looks, she smiled after trying one. "This is a nice change of pace."

We were almost done eating when we heard a car. We ran for the door. My mother was out of the house first, feet bare, but once she got outside, she slowed to a walk. She kissed my father and asked how the border went.

Sonja and I were jumping and shouting, *soldier, soldier, soldier,* and also, *Kool-Aid.*

"What's this about a soldier?" my father asked. "Did you have any problems? Did you get to meet Idi Amin?"

"Nothing like that," my mother said, "Someone came to the house to find out how rich we are. The girls are dying to tell you. But," and she lowered her voice, "you'll never guess who came with the soldier. It wasn't Idi Amin, I'll tell you that." She turned to us. "Okay, girls, let's go inside, and you can take turns telling. Let's not talk out here."

My father picked me up, and I whispered in his ear, "Did you bring me something?"

"Do you mean oil?" he said.

"No," I said. "A present."

"A present? Like a matchbox car?"

I nodded.

"Oh, man! I just knew there was something I was forgetting. I've been driving all day today, trying to remember what I had forgotten. At least, I think I forgot it."

Each time he returned from Nairobi, he did this. He said he forgot to buy matchbox cars or that he forgot to pack them. When he finally found them in some obscure corner of his luggage, I would be near tears or full out crying. "Gary," my mother would say.

"This is just terrible," my father said and smiled at me. I looked into his eyes and believed him. I was sure that it was the most terrible thing in the world.

That night, we sat at the dining room table, the four of us. Sonja and I were still damp from our bath, and my mother was still cheery from our father's arrival, despite his confession that he hadn't brought back flour or oil or any of the staples on her list. Never mind, that was tomorrow's problem. Sonja described the Kool-Aid and how the soldier had asked for glass after glass. I nodded, as if it all meant something grown-up and important. In my lap, I held an orange matchbox car and ran my thumb over the silver chrome.

My father asked what flavor the Kool-Aid was and if there was any still in the fridge. He got up to pour himself a glass and our mother told us that it was past our bedtime. "You'll see Daddy at breakfast." Our father carried us to our rooms and had prayers with us, asking God to watch over us and all of Uganda.

With my father back, I felt content and full. From where I lay, I could see the orange glow from the dining room light and hear the hushed turn of my parents' voices. I couldn't make out what they were saying, but the sounds were soft and companionable. Sonja was in the next room, and our cat—that villain—was probably curled at her feet.

I imagined we were on a dhow, just the four of us. The jungle was the ocean, my mosquito net was a mast, and the thrumming frogs were the waves. The moon shimmered on the water, and far below us, whales sang songs to one another. We were together, a family of four. I closed my eyes and listened to the wave, and I felt completely secure.

CHAPTER 11

Branch Sabbath School

AFTER MY FATHER came home, it was as if we had never been under house
arrest. He continued to teach, pedaling his bicycle to and from campus.
Joseph continued to attend class, and neither of them spoke to each other
about that day on the hill. Sonja and I continued to play with our matchbox
cars and to whine about eating avocados or squash. Our mother continued
to hang laundry on the line and to write letters, amusing herself, if no one
else: *For supper we may have fresh bananas, dried bananas, and banana bread
with a banana shake (made with soyagen and frozen bananas). Doesn't that
make you hungry?*

She also began teaching Sonja how to read. If we had lived in the States,
Sonja would be in first grade. My mother was a relaxed Finnish teacher; you
might learn your letters today or tomorrow, but eventually you would catch
the hang of it. Why worry? They read books together, and a few afternoons
each week, my mother quizzed Sonja with alphabet cards. I hovered in the
periphery, trying to be the smarty-pants. "No, D is for Daisy," I shouted
from the couch.

Yes, life on the hill was quiet.

My parents began to imagine their families seeing Uganda, being
charmed, as they were, with our hilltop life. They imagined them eating
jackfruit and watching monkeys from the verandah. They invited everyone,
in general, but my American grandmother in particular. *We wish you would
come before 1979,* my father wrote. That was the year we were scheduled for
furlough, three months to see family and to shop. My grandmother and
her husband Gordon were currently driving across the United States in a
Winnebago, but she was thinking about her next adventure. What could be
more adventurous than Uganda?

The end of May brought mangoes. When my father carried up a basket of them, a gift from a student, my mother rummaged through the kitchen cupboard, emerging with several bars of soap. "Give him these after class, and tell him he made Mrs. Fordham very, very happy." She began cultivating mango partnerships: soap for mangoes, magazines for mangoes, clothes for mangoes.

My mother would cut mangoes into slabs and slice the flesh into tic-tac-toe grids. We spooned up these cubes or pressed them directly to our mouths. My parents stood at the sink and ate the seeds. They declared mangoes "good" or "bad," depending on their stringiness. To me, they were all wonderful.

On Sabbaths, my mother tried to make a special lunch. If she was out of ideas and the cupboards were sparse, she would at least find a Kool-Aid packet in her desk and serve the outlandishly red juice alongside our beans and rice. Other Sabbaths, she might grate and fry the taro that grew by the spigot. If Sonja and I had collected dodo—wild amaranth—she would boil it and serve it beside rice. And when she had made bread, she would cut us each a generous slice. But the best Sabbath meal was spaghetti, "the food of heaven," as the missionaries called it.

My mother had been saving a box of noodles. When she noticed there were small holes in the pasta, she decided we had better eat it before the bugs did. She dropped the noodles in the boiling water and skimmed insects off the surface. To make sauce, she used a can of tomato paste, some boiled water, and the last packet of Lawry's Spaghetti Sauce. If we were going to finish the noodles, we might as well finish everything.

Fish-lipped and sauce-smeared, Sonja and I spent the meal slurping down one strand of pasta at a time. Sonja had lost a front tooth and used the gap to her advantage. "Don't play with your food," our mother said, absently. "Your Nana would be shocked."

"Horrified," my father said.

My mother smiled. She was glad to have him at the table. He worked such long hours. In Indiana, he had been gone throughout the day and well into the evening. My mother, unable to drive, sat at home stewing. Once, when she heard his car turn into the drive, she hid in the hall closet. Let him think she had left him. It was winter, and after stepping into the house, my father went to hang his coat and found my mother. How she shouted. At least he should have spent some time worrying.

In Uganda, her days opened up into a marching progression of mornings and afternoons, and still, my father was gone. He taught too many classes, sat on too many committees, and on occasion, had to preach. My mother sympathized with his duties. It was when he volunteered for something that she would set her mouth into a line. In the mornings, when my mother felt she could expect to see her husband at the breakfast table, he had taken to biking to campus and eating with students. Once he learned the truth about weevils in the campus-provided porridge, he mostly ate with us. Still, he told my mother, teachers ought to eat some meals in the cafeteria.

As a child, I didn't notice that my father was mostly gone. He seemed so present. Each evening, between supper and bedtime, he would sit on the floor with Sonja and me and play matchbox cars, something my mother had little enthusiasm for, and then he would read stories, adding made-up lines to the familiar words. "Tell it like it really is," I would howl, a stickler for the truth.

After lunch, my parents cleared the plates and washed the dishes while Sonja and I marched through the house. We were the Israelites crossing the Red Sea. Sonja carried our cat close to her stomach, determined to bring Kissa into the Promised Land. The cat twisted and meowed and clawed, and when she finally found her freedom, she darted into our parents' room and under their bed, and there she hissed at our attempts to retrieve her. We resumed our journey with our matchbox cars and our dolls, leaving Kissa to enjoy the cucumbers of Egypt.

We were still marching when my father announced he was going to campus to see about Branch Sabbath School. I asked if we could go, but our mother spoke ominously about nap time. She wasn't happy.

Sometimes, we did all go. Branch Sabbath Schools were interesting, if overly long. They were held at what seemed to be nowhere. A stretch of grass. A tree. My father's students would tell Bible stories, illustrated with a looping scroll that they would hold up or hang on a tree branch. For a long time, I thought this was the reason it was called Branch Sabbath School. The scrolls were from the missionary barrel. In the pictures, blindingly white men and women wore robes and pointed, or they bent over babies in bulrushes, or held beautiful jars of water. They had pink cheeks and perfectly coiffed hair.

As if by magic, children gathered. They came without adults. No parents hovered on the periphery. No mothers called daughters over and wiped their faces with a finger and some spit. Sonja and I envied the children, and our parents admired them. Daily, our parents compared us to our Ugandan peers and found us wanting. Ugandan children didn't whine about eating avocadoes. Ugandan children picked up their toys (if they had them) and worked in the garden and took care of the family's cows and tended their younger siblings (and didn't bicker).

At Branch Sabbath School, Ugandan children didn't exactly listen attentively, but Sonja and I never said this. We admired non-campus children, even as we felt awkward around them. At Bugema, we were just the girls on the hill, and if our friends called me a mzungu, I didn't mind. At Branch Sabbath School, Sonja and I were a spectacle. Children would creep closer and closer until a brave boy or girl touched our hair and ran off shrieking. And no wonder. We looked as if we had stepped out of the Sabbath School scrolls.

"Ugandan children don't take naps," Sonja said. "Why do we have to take one?"

"If everyone jumped off a cliff, would you?" our mother said.

"Yes," Sonja said. Our mother ignored her.

"I should go and see what the students are up to," my father said. He walked through the house and gathered up his things. "I'll be back soon."

"Don't be gone forever," my mother said. "Your daughters would like to see you. And me, too." She turned to Sonja and me and told us that the sooner we started our nap, the sooner we would be done. And no fussing.

My mother walked into the kitchen, and she did what mothers do when their children are not around: She opened the cupboards looking for something to eat. The spaghetti was gone, of course, and we hadn't had real chocolate since she could remember. There was a tin of Milo, the last bag of sugar, and enough flour for one loaf of bread. And there was the fruit she would long for when she later remembered Uganda: mangoes, passion fruit, papayas, and bananas.

She carried several finger bananas into the dining room and picked up the aerogramme my father had been writing on. She scanned what he had written. *We have started a new semester and the Division Education Secretary is arriving tomorrow to inspect our school and our degree program. Our fate is weighed in the balance—I'll probably be found wanting.*

The Education Secretary would be staying at our house, and my mother knew she would have to bake bread tomorrow. If he was smart, he would smuggle in some flour and oil. Then she wouldn't have to force a smile as he ate seconds and thirds.

My mother used the same blue pen my father had written with and began writing:

We are thrilled at the prospect of your visit. Sari is already saying: "When Nana comes she will read me a story." And if we refuse to do something for her, she says, "When Nana comes, Nana will do it!" I'm sure your visit will be a memorable event—also for you. We'll be mentioning a few things from time to time we would like. Of course, I've been dreaming of Almond Roca ever since we got here. A few Lawry's spaghetti sauce mixes would be nice. Actually, it's Sabbath now and I shouldn't be writing about needs. The girls are both napping and Gary

*just bicycled down to school to see about attending a branch Sabbath School. It's
so beautiful and peaceful here. I'm sure you'll love it just as we do. We can hardly
wait for Christmas to roll around. Sonja's grown so much. She's lost one front tooth
and is in the process of losing another.*

If my mother thought about the word *need* and the irony of missionaries using it, she didn't elaborate. How could one family need more than an
entire village? In Uganda, most needs went unresolved. Instead, there was
resourcefulness. In the market, you would find an old man sewing together
pieces of cloth. He could turn a nightgown into a man's shirt, a man's shirt
into a child's shirt. Trousers, blouses, and underwear were patched up under
his trestle.

My mother heard the laughter of children coming up the hill. "Sonja,
Sari," she called. "Your friends are here. You can get up."

We charged out of our rooms, slipped our feet into our flip-flops, and
ran across the verandah, the screen door slapping at our heels. Our friends
lived on campus, and most were the children of my father's students. We were
jubilant that they, too, had skipped Branch Sabbath School today.

We knew our mother was not watching us out the window. She was
somewhere in the house, writing letters or reading or napping, and as long
as we kept our noise outside, she would leave us alone. Still, we minded the
Sabbath. God was watching. Not the legalistic God of our mother's childhood
who demanded perfect obedience, but a loving God who would, nevertheless,
be disappointed if we broke a commandment. Our friends were as devout as
we were. Someone had created a version of Bible freeze tag, and it was one of
our favorite Sabbath games. We ran through the yard, dodging the unfortunate child who was It. Each time we unfroze our friends, we recited a Bible
verse. "Jesus wept," we shouted. "Rejoice in the Lord always," we shouted.

The chickens ran into the jungle.

When it was no longer Sabbath, my parents spoke about what my grandmother might bring from America. "Just you watch, she's going to fill her suitcases with velvet dresses and artificial flowers," my father said, and my mother laughed because it was true and because she wanted my father to know that she had forgiven him, and she hoped that he would forgive her, too. She was trying to be more charitable about his time.

They smiled at each other and decided they needed a plan. They would send my grandmother a comprehensive list of things they wanted her to bring, and if she also brought velvet dresses, well, so be it. They created the list together.

If you are a missionary family in Uganda, this is what you ask for:

1 Canon electronic fully automatic camera

1 men's digital electronic watch

1 pair of child's nylon panties (size 3)

1 slip (size 7)

1 pair socks (size 11, girls)

Ponytail holders with marbles and 1 pair of barrettes

Vitamin pills (500 children's with iron and 1 bottle of adult's with iron),

Calcium tablets (300)

1 bag kosher gelatin

1 can dehydrated cottage cheese

4 toothbrushes

About the last item, my father wrote: *Two Oral-B for us and two Walt Disney ones for the girls with pictures on them of Donald Duck, Mickey Mouse, or Goofy—this is not essential, but we have seen the Disney ones in the grocery stores while we were there—actually any children's will do.*

CHAPTER 12

———— ❧ ————

Adventist Church Banned

O N SEPTEMBER 20, 1977, Idi Amin banned the Seventh-day Adventist church, along with most other protestant denominations. The long rains had just begun, and in the afternoons, water rushed across the horizon in sheets of silver. It was a machine-gun rain. It pelted against the classroom roofs and caused all instruction to halt. The sound of rain was louder than any single voice.

My parents heard about the ban over the radio. They sat in silence and kept sitting long after Idi Amin finished speaking. My father leaned back in his chair, his hand against his cheek. The power was out, and the candles, with their yellow-tinted wax, were growing short. My mother watched the flames, the yellow orbs against the night. She used to paint with oils, filling canvases with land and water. She was interested in the light, in the way it played against the walls, the back of one chair, my father's face. It was the chiaroscuro of Caravaggio, the glow as warm as honey. My mother nibbled at a fingernail. She was uneasy, certainly, but there was also something new—a guilty gladness. My mother was sure we were leaving.

My father didn't know what to do. It was the middle of the semester. If the seminary closed, the graduating class—the students who had stayed despite how irrelevant school must now seem, those students who had clung to this school like barnacles to a sinking boat, those students whom my father loved—they would not likely have another chance to graduate. If the school closed, they would return to farms and fishing and family obligations, and if the school reopened in one year or ten, they would no longer know how to make their way back. Much could happen in a year. Already, they had told him this.

My father took the train to Nairobi, and after a day of meetings, he wrote his mother: *I came over to Kenya to try to discover what the future holds for us in Uganda. Haven't been able to find out much yet. At least not enough to give directions concerning your trip here.*

Even with the ban, my father was expecting my grandmother to visit. Presented the opportunity, who wouldn't want to see Uganda? He just needed to ensure that the ministerial program, and by extension our family, would still be in the country.

I waited for my father on the verandah steps, pulling kernels off a cob. Our three chickens took jerky steps toward me, then away. I had learned not to chase them. "Rebecca," I called. "Isaac, Sarah." I dropped grains on the ground beyond my toe. The rooster turned his head and stepped forward with resolve. He gobbled the maize and pecked at my hand. I stroked his coarse feathers.

"Hodi," my father said, walking up the hill. He picked me up and swung me onto his shoulders. "You've gotten heavier," he said. "What's your mother been feeding you? Beans and avocadoes?" He staggered under my supposed weight.

He was full of humor, or the façade of humor. When my mother told him that she had saved him some beans, he said, "Yum-my," exaggerating each syllable, and then chanted, "Beans, beans, the musical fruit, the more you eat, the more you toot."

My mother reheated the beans on the stove while my father served himself rice. When we asked and asked about matchbox cars, our mother told us to please wait, *for goodness sakes*. She had her own questions. She sat across from my father and watched as he prayed over his meal. When he said amen, she leaned forward. "So? What did they say?"

"Nothing," my father said.

"What do you mean, nothing?" she said. "They had to have said something."

"No, nothing," he said. "They said, 'Keep the school open. Nothing changes.'"

"What? Are they crazy? Well, I suppose they aren't the ones living here. I'd like to see them move here and then see what they say. This is asinine. You know that? This is really asinine," she said.

"Don't shoot the messenger," he said. There was silence as he chewed. He got up, refilled his cup with water, and returned to the table.

"You're not going along with it, are you?" she said.

"Well," he said. There was another long pause. "Well, it would behoove us to wait and see. If things don't change in Uganda, I think they'll eventually move the program to Kenya. It shouldn't take long. A couple months. Half a year. Whatever happens, I'll need to stay and arrange things. If you're worried, you should take the girls and visit Finland. Mamma will be glad to have you. Come back after everything's settled."

"That's what you'd like, isn't it?" my mother said. She started to cry and didn't try to stop. "You just want to get yourself killed in peace, don't you? Well, forget it. We're not leaving until you leave." My mother walked into the kitchen and began washing the empty pot of beans. We could hear the clang of metal as the pot knocked against the wall of the sink.

My father finished his meal, then sat on the carpet. He reached into the pocket of his jacket. "I've been trying to remember if I'd packed those cars, and you know what? I didn't. I put them in my pocket." He pulled out two small boxes and handed one to each of us.

I pushed the jeep across the carpet and off the tangled edge. The world felt both manageable and wide open. We were staying put. My mother would come around because she always did. Uganda was still our home.

My mother woke each morning with a gnawing at her throat. We were still here.

The Adventist church was banned, and the government knew we were Seventh-day Adventist missionaries. They knew our names, what we owned, where we lived. My mother was certain that the army would come to campus and that if my father was home, he would be arrested. All the men would be, including the students. The women and children, she believed, would either be ignored or deported.

She imagined herself walking alongside a soldier and asking him, "Do you have any children? How many do you have?" as her husband was loaded into the back of a lorry. With a daughter at the end of each hand, she would watch as the truck drove off. And then what? We would somehow catch a ride to Kampala and sit in the West German embassy. When a consulate asked, "You're Adventist missionaries? Why are you still in Uganda?" she would be too exhausted to answer. She would press this government and that. She would get my father's name in the news. My father's students would become the disappeared, but at least my father's murder, if it happened, would be reported. Even in death, there would be inequalities.

Missionaries weren't supposed to fear death. My father preached that if your heart was right with God, then dying would be like taking a nap, and when you woke, Jesus would be returning and you would go to heaven. We sang joyfully about shedding our earthly bodies and moving to heaven. "This world is not my home; I'm just a passing through." No dirge, this. Sonja and I clapped our hands and swayed. "My treasures are laid up, somewhere beyond the blue. The angels beckon me from heaven's open door, and I can't feel at home in this world anymore." Heaven would feel more like home than even Uganda. Heaven was better than anything I could imagine.

In theory, death was a pretty good deal. In truth, we were all fond of *this* world, filled as it was with sin. Life could be violent and hard and unfair. It could also be interesting and fun. Even for Adventists. My Finnish grandfather, who traveled with his suitcase of Ellen White books, wanted to live to a hundred. It wasn't just the world we were attached to; we were attached to each other. Would families even exist in heaven? The scant Biblical evidence wasn't reassuring. Of course we wanted to go to heaven eventually. We just weren't in a rush. And nobody wanted to be violently killed. Even John the Baptist had sent Jesus a message asking why he was stuck in Herod's prison while out in the countryside, Jesus was healing strangers.

If none of us wanted to die, why were missionaries staying in Uganda?

I now think we stayed for the most prosaic of reasons: We didn't expect to die. As we prayed for protection each night, we didn't probe the audacity of our faith. Ugandans also prayed nightly for protection, and nobody knew how many had been killed. The number was too vast, the violence too terrible. We didn't believe God loved missionaries more. Still, we stayed. Nobody said it aloud, the truth was too terrible—we had put our trust in our foreign passports.

"What is the church thinking?" my mother asked another missionary. When he started to lecture her on faith, she said, "Spare me," and walked off.

During this time, my father made several trips to Kenya. We stayed on the hill, a trio of girls. My mother washed clothes, read the religious magazines her father had sent from Finland, walked down the hill to teach health at the clinic ("Put an iron nail in the beans while they're boiling," she advised), and when she returned home, she watched the swallows build a nest or she read to Sonja and me, and in the evenings, while we were asleep and when she must have keenly missed my father's steady presence, she sat at the table and wrote letters to Finland. Long sentences flooded the aerogrammes.

The church was locked, and the seminary was now presumably a secular program. My father continued teaching his classes: Greek, health, church history, and world religions. They were all relevant, my father rationalized, even if you weren't preparing to be an Adventist pastor. The homiletics teacher turned his course into public speaking. The Adventist theology class was canceled mid-semester. The Adventist high school, middle school, and elementary school stopped teaching Bible classes and no longer held worship, but otherwise continued on as before. Most parents, even the non-Adventist ones, left their children in the schools. To live in Uganda was dangerous, and education was one door out of poverty.

It felt as if the end of days were nigh. Adventists who had left the church, for one reason or another, returned. Weddings were turned into one-day evangelistic crusades. Funerals were turned into one-day evangelistic crusades. Converts were baptized in bathtubs. On Sabbath, the Adventists on the Bugema campus left their houses, as we always had, a little before 9 a.m. The church was locked, as were the school buildings. We carried our Bibles and wore dresses and suits, and when we crossed paths with other Adventists, who carried their Bibles and wore dresses and suits, we smiled and waved. It was almost amusing. They didn't say "Happy Sabbath," and neither did we. Nobody said where they were going.

My mother held my hand, drawing me along. I knew boredom awaited. We knocked on someone's door and walked into a crowd. All the chairs in the house were pushed into one room, and still men stood in the back. It was dark. Sabbath School scrolls decorated the walls, and doilies adorned armrests. Because the windows were closed and the curtains pulled, the room smelled of our bodies. I wiggled and whispered a complaint in my mother's ear. She whispered back, "Hang in there."

During Sabbath School, men sat on the edges of the couch, resting their elbows on their knees, holding their Bibles out before them. The talk was fervent, a pantomime of gestures. Only the men spoke, and when one made a point about obeying the laws of God, there was a chorus of agreement. My mother's body grew tense. As a child, she had been told that all believers must strive to live sinless lives. The remnant, those still alive at the second coming, would be able to keep the commandments of God perfectly. "It's legalistic rubbish," my mother would say. She interrupted now, but at least her words were more diplomatic: "Works are important, but I'm not saved by what I do. I'm saved by faith. We're all sinners: you, me, my husband." The men pretended not to have heard her, and my mother didn't speak further.

Church closed with "What a Friend We Have in Jesus" and "Amazing Grace." It was a companionable time. The songs were sung fast and happy, and the women weaved new echoes into familiar choruses. My mother swayed back and forth, tapping her hand on my leg. I could feel the vibration of her body, the warmth of her breath as she sang, "Oh, what peace we often forfeit. Oh, what needless pain we bear." I knew these songs well, and though the words were often mournful, everyone was smiling. I leaned my head against my mother's thin shoulder and bobbed my toes to a beat that could get us all arrested.

CHAPTER 13

———— ⌒◇⌒ ————

Not the Time for Prayer

DESPITE THE BAN, church administrators considered Uganda safe, or at least safe enough, and then one day, they didn't. Nothing particular had happened, as my mother liked to say, just the usual killings and violence. And the passage of time. The administrators had been hoping Idi Amin would rescind the ban, and now that he hadn't, they made their fast decision: Bugema's ministerial program would move to Kenya.

For our family, leaving carried its own, almost satirical, complications. My father needed a Kenyan work visa. Until he received one, we had to maintain Ugandan residency. As residents of Uganda, we needed authorization to emigrate. But we couldn't emigrate until my father had a Kenyan work visa. "All these months, and nobody thought of this," my mother said.

My father shrugged. He was usually a straight arrow. When classmates cheated off of him in middle school, he wrote in the wrong answers—then quickly changed them before turning in his exam. In retaliation, a group of boys cornered him in the bathroom and dropped him on his head.

"What can you do?" he told my mother.

"What can you do?" she said. She was already singing the song of Leaving.

She fixed our breakfast to Leaving, combed our hair to it, and as she settled our squabbles, her ears tuned in to the gentle melody of Leaving. To that music, my mother wrote my grandmother and asked her to redirect her ticket to Kenya; we would no longer be in Uganda.

We planned to come back, though, and this was my father's song. Idi Amin's dictatorship would collapse, everyone could feel it, and when it did, the ministerial program would return to Bugema, and we would return, also.

My father packed my mother's wedding gifts and stored them in our Ugandan house, in a high closet. He boxed photo albums, family mementos, the wall hanging my Finnish grandmother had weaved. He made sure all our knickknacks were out of the way and the house was ready for someone else to use while we were away.

My mother packed for Kenya, putting boxes by the door. The birds of the air and the lilies of the field might not carry much with them by way of personal belongings, but she was raising daughters, not flowers, and she didn't want to leave Uganda unprepared. She boxed up dishes, utensils, blankets, pillows, towels, several changes of clothes for each family member, shoes, books, and even a few toys.

"It has to look like we're just going on vacation," my father said.

"And if we need sheets, how are we going to pay for them?" my mother said. She didn't say what she was thinking—*what if we never return?*

My parents bought tickets for two first class train compartments. What kind of missionaries were we? The kind with too many things. Each time my parents carried boxes past the train attendant, they gave him a bag of flour. They made five trips while Sonja and I sat in one of the compartments, swinging our legs and enjoying the theatrics of it all. At one point, Sonja dropped to her knees and loudly beseeched God to watch over us as we escaped. "Now is not the time for prayer," my mother hissed.

My father stacked boxes and suitcases into one compartment, building a platform. My mother tossed blankets on top, and Sonja and I climbed up. "How's that?" our mother asked. "Comfy?" As the train began rolling, we lay on our stomachs and gazed out the window. We were blooming with train-wonder and with the clickity-clack of the wheels.

We ate supper in our parents' compartment. Our room and theirs. We thrilled at the distinction. Supper was a Tupperware of dried bananas, a tin of biscuits, and milk made from powder and from water boiled earlier at home.

My parents said the biscuits tasted like sawdust, but I liked them. They were tawny and dry, and while the first left my mouth parched, they had a nice crunch to them. When I let the biscuits dissolve in my mouth, they were sweet and mushy. Tins of biscuits and the rocking train and the rushing-by land.

In the evening, my father read us a story, his voice booming or snorting or whispering, depending on the character. We asked for another and another, until my father tossed up his hands and said, "No more." And then we said our prayers, and when we each prayed to arrive safely in Nairobi, our mother said amen. Sonja and I placed our pillows by the window. The moon washed over the ground, casting shadows that suggested trees and rocks. We listened to the clickity-clack of the train.

It was hard to know what woke us. The absence of motion. The voices outside. The still and heavy air. Sonja and I pulled our stray legs and arms under the sheet and stayed as motionless as we could. Our father had left our window ajar, and mosquitoes, drawn to the warm train and the warm bodies inside, found this opening. We listened to their ominous whine and then a sharp silence. We slapped at our faces and our necks, careful to return our hands beneath the sheet, to pull the fabric closer to our faces. The moon hung just outside the parameters of our window. If we turned on our bellies, we could make out the shape of a building and the motion of soldiers and passengers.

There weren't many compartments in the car, maybe four or five. We could hear the soldiers knocking and shouting. Why so much shouting? We were already frightened. The whole country was frightened. We were expecting knocks, waiting for them, but when they came against the door of our room, our bodies still jumped. My parents had been expecting the soldiers to come to their door first, and they leapt out into the hall. We heard our mother's voice, "There's only children sleeping in there. Please, don't wake them."

On the other side of the wall, a soldier flipped through the passports my father had given him. We had a work visa for Uganda and a multiple entry visa for Kenya. The policewoman shined a dim flashlight into my parents' compartment. There wasn't much to see: my mother's purse, my father's briefcase, his papers and his Bible, a small suitcase, a Tupperware of dried bananas. It was a modest amount, certainly less than the average mzungu would travel with.

The soldiers had banana beer on their breath. My parents, teetotalers like most Adventists, were uncomfortable with alcohol under even the most benign of circumstances, and this was not benign. One of the soldiers pointed his machine gun at my father and demanded that my mother open the door.

She opened it slowly as if the soldiers might leave before all our things were exposed. As the thin light streamed into our cabin, Sonja and I sat up. The flashlight battery did not seem as if it would last much longer. Everything in Uganda was exhausted. The light moved over the rug, toward our night-gowned forms.

"What is this?" the soldier asked. He was furious. He threw a few boxes into the corridor, then shouted at my parents for attempting to leave Uganda without the proper authorization. My father held out his vehicle logbook, proof that we had left our car in Uganda and therefore that we were planning to return. The soldiers wouldn't look at it.

My mother turned to the policewoman. "We don't have emigration papers because we aren't leaving permanently. My husband teaches at Bugema. Our car is still there." The policewoman said nothing. It was too dark to make out the expression on her face.

"You think we're foolish?" the jumpier soldier asked. His gun was making an impression, and he clutched it occasionally as he shouted, then released it, letting it clack against the metal in his hip pocket.

"Oh no," my parents said, their words tripping over each other. "No, no. Not at all."

"Tell me then, where is your emigration visa? If you don't have an emigration visa, you will get off this train with us. You cannot leave Uganda without an emigration visa."

The quieter soldier reached for the flashlight and flicked its light over our worldly goods. Some people could carry all their possessions wrapped in a bundle and placed firmly on their heads. "You are trying to run away and take all these goods out of Uganda," he said, as if explaining something difficult to children. "It is very illegal. Very wrong to do this."

"You see," my father said, his voice suggesting that a long explanation was forthcoming, "It's all very complicated—"

The soldiers looked at my parents in disgust. They were like fish pulled from Lake Victoria, their mouths opening and closing. The soldiers would be justified in dragging them off the train. "There is no complication. You need emigration papers," the soldier said.

Showing off their guns, my mother wrote, *they shouted that we were taking too many things and they were going to throw us off the train. We were treated as traitors and criminals. We didn't even dare to imagine what would happen to us if they threw us off the train into the darkness.*

"Do you have children?" my mother asked.

The quieter soldier held up his hand. "You will wait here," he said. "We will be back to settle this matter."

The world was a hazy grey, and we were still on the train. "Maybe they won't come back," my mother whispered.

"We should all just try and get some sleep," my father said.

To wait: to rest, to stop, to halt, to mark time and to stand by, to be delayed or placed on the back burner, to be in limbo. We sat on the train and waited for soldiers who did not wish us well. The train waited also, as did all those passengers who had the misfortune of journeying with us. My parents prayed that the conductor's patience would wear thin. How much waiting could he endure? Perhaps he was not waiting. Perhaps he was sleeping. Or perhaps he was sitting in a duka with a glass of banana beer in his hand and a story on his tongue. *These wazungu boarded my train with more belongings than Queen Elizabeth.*

All night, vendors walked the length of the platform selling fish and roasted bananas. Now it seemed there were more of them. Voices rose and fell like kites on the hill. It was as dark as ever, but there was a bustle. My mother purchased some finger bananas from her open window and felt hopeful.

It would have been easy to miss the man walking the length of the train. He clapped his hands and punctuated his Swahili with an "okay," and then the train whistle blew, and by this we understood we were leaving, suddenly, serenely, and after so much waiting: leaving.

The selling sounds shifted to hurry-hurry voices, and passengers clambered back onto the train. Sonja and I brightened at the resurrection of our journey. We peered out the window and watched the conductor walk beside the track. His strides were clipped, and he paused here and there to tap the train with a stick. We saw no soldiers.

We were hoping to leave, expecting it even, yet we were still surprised when the wheels first turned with a jerk. The train pulled out of the station and gathered speed, settling into a clickity-clack cadence. We crossed the border, leaving Uganda farther and farther behind.

In the east, the sun rose red against earth that was also red, and against a herd of red elephants, stained from the earth, and against red-tinged grass, and against a train moving slowly through the savannah. To watch that sunrise was to watch something holy. We were too full for words, the four of us: my sister pressing her palms against the glass, my father resting a hand on the hollow of his cheek, my mother with me in her lap, her chin on my hair.

The savannahs of Kenya were yellowed like the leaves of an ancient book. All morning and afternoon, we cut through waving grass and acacia trees and termite mounds, tall and red beside the track. The savannah was such that one expected to see ostrich or bushbucks or giraffes with their lurching stride. We did pass impala, who stood on spring-trap legs, ready, even as they ate, to bound away.

The train sang out safenow-safenow-safenow, and the song filled my mother's ear as she tipped her head against the glass, against the rushing-by land.

PART II

Civil War

CHAPTER 14

Civil War

IDI AMIN ONCE told a documentary filmmaker that he knew the date and time of his own death. He laughed when he said it, as if it were a joke. It was also a warning. Everyone who wanted him gone should weigh the value of their own life and the lives of their family members and the lives of everyone in their hometown. He wasn't a mere man; he was magic. He was Big Daddy, the nation's authoritarian father, and he would be president for life. His enemies must have wondered. Idi Amin had an uncanny ability to escape assassinations.

By 1978, Idi Amin felt the political winds, already blowing against him, whipping into a fury. To rally the nation around a common enemy, he started a military skirmish on Tanzania's border. It was the wrong country.

Julius Nyerere, Tanzania's intellectual and soft-spoken president, had grown more and more irritated at the mouthy dictator at his border. Once when Nyerere criticized him, Idi Amin had replied with a telegram meant to put Nyerere in his place: "I want to assure you that I love you very much and if you had been a woman I would have considered marrying you although your head is full of grey hairs. But as you are a man that possibility does not arise." Idi Amin was a living caricature who confirmed every prejudice of the West. For years, Nyerere had been welcoming Ugandan refugees and dissidents into Tanzania.

When Ugandan soldiers entered Tanzania's territory, Nyerere ordered the Tanzanian army to invade its neighbor. Ugandan resistance fighters joined the Tanzanian soldiers, and together they moved through the country. Kampala was captured, and Idi Amin fled into Libya. The impossible had happened: Uganda was free of Idi Amin. In Kampala, families ran outside and danced.

During Idi Amin's dictatorship, Uganda had been like a slow-burning room. Once he was gone, it was as if someone had opened the door. The country exploded. Ugandans wanted vengeance: Your brother killed my brother. Your kinsman killed my kinsman. *Time* reported that there were so many bodies on the streets of Kampala that cars just drove over them.

In Jinja, a city east of Kampala, the violence was particularly acute. In April, *Time* reported that ordinary Ugandans were killing Libyan soldiers. Sent by Muammar Gaddafi to assist Idi Amin, these soldiers were now conspicuous targets. Their bodies were hung on trees, and their heads were put on stakes that now lined the roads. A month later, *Time* reported more carnage in Jinja. This time, pro-Amin soldiers had captured 130 Catholic parishioners, driven them into a military stockade, and shot at them with machine guns. There were no survivors.

Tanzanian soldiers stayed in Uganda as peacekeepers. Many were conscripted schoolboys, faced now with shocking violence. What were they supposed to do? They took on the role of occupier. They took over apartments, commandeered cars, and set up military checkpoints.

Yet, there was now hope in Uganda. Idi Amin was gone. Exiles were returning. Shops were opening. Yusufu Lule, a former university chancellor, was acting as Uganda's provisional president. Free elections were to be set. In a speech, Lule said: "Ugandans from every tribe and every family have suffered from [Idi Amin's] murders, torture, terror, robbery, and plunder. From this day, Ugandans must resolve never to allow a dictator to rule them again."

Below the optimism was anxiety. Everyone had their own ideas about what direction the nation should take and about who should be in power.

A civil war loomed. Almost everyone was certain.

CHAPTER 15

Too Dangerous for a Dog

"COME, LORD JESUS, come," my mother said when she read the news about Uganda.

We had temporarily moved to Florida. Once my father's students had graduated in Kenya, he had asked for and received permission to return to the United States and complete his Master's in Public Health. He hoped that while we were gone, Uganda's political situation would stabilize. If not, we would return to Kenya, and he would resume teaching at Bugema's provisional campus.

My mother was hoping that inertia and proximity to my grandmother would keep us in Florida. When my grandmother drove over, my mother hustled us out with towels and water wings. "Let's not keep Nana waiting." She gathered her own things, locked the apartment door, kissed my grandmother's powdery cheek, and said cheerfully, "Hi, Nana." My grandmother had visited us while we were in Kenya, and now, my mother was trying to pack away any irritation in deference to their mutual goal: our family's resettlement in Florida.

We drove to the pool at the retirement center, where my grandmother taught water aerobics and organized fashion shows. "Look at me," I shouted as I jumped into the water. "Look at me!" My grandmother and mother, lying side by side in pool chaises, glanced up and waved. We all wore bikinis.

For a week in the summer, Sonja and I attended Vacation Bible School. The theme was *Heaven*, and it made me lonesome for Uganda. In the painted illustrations, heaven was as green as the jungle surrounding our house on the hill, and the trees all had flowers. The animals were ones I knew, mostly lions and lambs. Heaven looked a little like Kenya and a lot like Uganda, and there on a bench sat Jesus, surrounded by children.

When the VBS teachers asked what my family had been doing in Uganda, I said, "Teaching people about Jesus." In truth, my friends were also Adventists, as were my father's students. My answer was reflexive, like the pleasantries grown-ups exchanged.

The adults had their own scripts. They beamed. "Oh, how wonderful," they said. "You're bringing souls to Jesus." I began to wonder what happened to people whose souls hadn't been brought to Jesus. Voice creaking, I asked my mother. It was my first theological crisis. "Oh, kiddo," she said, petting my head. "God is far better and kinder than we are. We'll all be surprised at who is in heaven."

On the last night of VBS, a man from the wildlife center brought animals into the sanctuary as we children sat and swung our legs. He showed us an opossum and a baby alligator and told us about their habitats. Afterward, the teacher talked about the animals that would be in heaven, how we would be able to sink our hands into a lion's mane and trade in our teddy bear for a grizzly. On the drive home, Sonja and I discussed the pets we wanted in heaven. She settled on two cheetahs, while I wanted a hippo and a rock hyrax. My father, heroically, stayed silent.

At home, we listened to the Heritage Singers, an Adventist gospel group. My mother would pop their cassette for kids into the stereo, and Sonja and I would swoop through the house, providing interpretive dances so beautiful that if my mother had stopped to watch, she would have wept from the loveliness of it all. "If I Were a Butterfly" had the best lyrics for dancing, but my favorite song was "Heaven Is for Kids." You could hear the Heritage Singers smiling as they sang:

> "Lion cubs and wooly lambs and big fat fuzzy bears
> Roly poly elephants leaping with the hares
> Monkeys climbing tall giraffes and tickling their ribs
> Heaven is a happy place and heaven is for kids."

At the end of my father's internship, Florida Hospital offered him a job, and he turned it down. "No conferring with your wife?" my mother said. The upbeat vocals of the Heritage Singers streamed from our stereo—"Lion cubs and wooly lambs and big fat fuzzy bears."

All these months, and my father had assumed my mother was as anxious to return as he was. Who on earth would choose to stay in boring old Florida when they could live in East Africa? "But Florida was always temporary," my father said.

My mother dumped laundry on the bed and began to fold it. "I know. I know. This was *always* the plan. I am well aware of your plans, Gary Fordham."

For several days, my mother narrated the tranquil life we could have had in Florida, and then she began to shop for Kenya. The more she prepared, the more accepting and even enthusiastic she became. The program's temporary campus was beside the Indian Ocean, and the months we had spent there had been restorative. Though my father and his students were building the school and studying, their days had felt almost leisurely. My father had no committee meetings, no sermons to preach, no unexpected obligations. After classes, he went swimming with his students, often inviting Sonja and me to join them. On weekends, my parents had walked hand in hand to a fishing village and bought coconuts and limes.

At the Nairobi airport, a friend was waiting to pick us up. He shook hands with my father, hugged my mother, and told Sonja and me that his daughters were happy we were back. As we drove to the guesthouse, the adults talked Ugandan politics, a hushed wah-wah-wah sound. The brake lights gleamed red on the Nairobi highway, and I leaned against my mother's warmth. Being back felt like Christmas Eve.

Our friend told my parents that with Idi Amin gone, the Adventist church was no longer banned in Uganda. He hemmed a bit and then continued; the ministerial program had just moved back to Bugema. Classes were starting in a week. I felt the jolt of my mother's body.

"Any bigwigs moving to Uganda, or are they just sending us?" my mother said. "Would you take your daughters?" No one spoke. "Of course not," she said. "You're not crazy."

Once we were alone, my mother started crying. "Are they asinine?" she said. "Do they think we're that stupid?"

"Give it a chance," my father said. "Things are always better than what's reported in the news."

"Forget it," she said. "The girls and I aren't going."

As my parents spoke, they worked together to put sheets and blankets on the beds. They told us to brush our teeth and put our pajamas on, and still they disagreed. "No stories tonight," my mother said, and we didn't object. Our bodies were too heavy. We climbed into bed, and as our parents' voices vibrated in the next room, we fell asleep.

My mother had made threats in their marriage before, but she had always come around. She gave in because my father was patient and good. When people took advantage of his conscientiousness, she stood beside him, often seething, but always there. My father counted on her loyalty, and so he stayed quiet and waited. And waited. As the days passed and the presumed date of our departure neared, he became concerned. When missionaries asked my mother about Uganda, she would say breezily, "Nothing's been decided yet."

My father wrote his mother:

The college has moved to Bugema and I'm to go there next week. Kaarina doesn't want to go and keeps talking about returning to the States. I can't see it. We just got here and have not even seen how things are in Uganda. We are told that things are bad in Kampala but peaceful at Bugema. Kaarina says she's not going so I will probably go alone and what next, I don't know.

My mother didn't know, either. She wished my father would tell his bosses that we wouldn't go to Uganda. They would grumble at first and then find another assignment for us in East Africa. But she might as well wish to be married to someone else. Gary Fordham would never shirk what he considered his duty. He would do what the church wanted him to do because he believed it was also what God wanted. Above all else, let it be observed, Gary Fordham was not fickle like his mother. He would return to Uganda. Now, what was my mother going to do?

She had drawn herself into a maze and neglected to draw the exit. She wanted to take us to Finland, but she was afraid that was the same thing as divorcing my father. Instead, she told him she was returning to the United States. It was magical thinking. America was not her home. She had no money there, no place to live, no driver's license, no citizenship, no job. She had said America because she wanted to make her point while still aligning herself with him. She wanted him to understand how serious she was about not returning to Uganda. But where could we go?

She prayed and felt angry with God. She prayed and felt angry with my father. She prayed and felt angry with the missionaries who lived safely in Kenya. Why couldn't we stay, too? She prayed and finally she felt some clarity. She would try to keep her daughters in Nairobi. My father had a new boss who was—*praise God*—half Finnish. She made an appointment to see him.

In a letter to her father in Finland, she described their exchange.

I confided in him, asking if I can get clemency with the children to wait in Nairobi while Gary goes first to Uganda to look at the house and the grounds. Then this old man secretary shouted at me for a long time. I could not believe that the faithful can conduct themselves in such a way. Now I, of course, no longer want to ask anything of him. He said that I am not suitable for mission work and it is better that I go home and so on and so forth. He said not to depress six million Ugandans with a missionary worker who wants to leave. He said it was very important to him that God sees hearts.

When my father came home, my mother was so angry she was nearly crying. My father was a sympathetic listener and when she was done talking, he told her that her fears were completely reasonable, and for someone living in Kenya to treat her with such contempt was really rich indeed. My mother's fury shifted. For the moment, it felt as if it was the two of them against the world.

My father offered my mother the olive branch he had been preparing: If she would give Uganda a chance, he would find her a guard dog. As he spoke, she sighed, her face slack with resignation. My father had won, and he knew it.

He jumped up and began extolling the merits of the hypothetical dog. It would be company on the hill, would scare off any thieves, and would make soldiers more inclined to wave us through military checkpoints. My father brought out a newspaper and showed her the advertisement he had circled. An employee at the British embassy was returning to London with his family and they wanted to find a home here for their Rottweiler. They had specifically advertised for a family with children.

My mother brightened as we drove to the fancy part of town. She would finally glimpse the lifestyle she had tried to emulate each time we crossed the border. The roads had fewer potholes and the homes were farther apart and shielded by flowering hedges. At some of the entries, there were armed guards. The house we were going to was as lavish as we had hoped: The driveway was paved, the lawn manicured, and bougainvillea vines climbed a wrought iron fence. The embassy employee and his wife welcomed us into a large foyer. Their children were too upset to meet us, they explained. They gave us Fanta to drink and asked polite questions about our countries of origin. Sonja and I sat on their plush carpet and petted the dog, Bear, a sweet and friendly male. While the wife asked if we would be willing to send photos of their dog from time to time—"of course," my mother said—my father was making arrangements to collect Bear the next day. And then he mentioned our upcoming departure.

"You live in Uganda?" the husband said.

My parents looked at each other; we weren't getting the dog. The husband kept apologizing, but he and his wife were also annoyed. "Have you read the news? It's a bloody bloodbath in Uganda. Bear would get shot or worse, and then what would we tell our kids?" he said.

"And there's no food in Uganda," the wife said to my mother. "Even if Bear wasn't killed, you couldn't feed him properly. And you know," she said, lowering her voice, "they're eating dogs in Uganda."

"No, they aren't," my mother said.

"Too dangerous even for a dog," my mother said later. It was a refrain she repeated often. When my father suggested finding another guard dog, she shook her head. "Never mind. Anyone who could shoot us could shoot a dog."

When we left Nairobi, my mother held her purse in her lap and said nothing. She wore a skirt voluminous enough to hide the cooking oil and flour she had placed at her feet. She would bake bread in Uganda if it killed her. *Ha ha.* She patted her hair.

A friend had cut it short and given her a home perm. My father had blanched when he first saw the hairdo. He had then tried to compliment it, but she had laughed and waved him off. "The ladies all say I'm *very* stylish." The only other time she laughed was when she told people that Uganda was too dangerous for a dog. But not for the Fordhams.

As we drove, she gazed ahead. Every couple of miles, she patted her hair, which still smelled faintly of chemicals. At the border, she handed back a bag of candy and told Sonja and me not to eat them all.

They were hard candies, the colors of Aladdin's jewels, each one wrapped in cellophane. I took a long time choosing which candies to eat, settling finally on green and red: emerald and ruby. I wanted the candies to linger in my mouth, but I couldn't stop my teeth from crunching down into the sugar. Sonja—superior as always—was still enjoying her first piece after I had eaten mine.

As we waited, our mother kept her skirt over the oil and the flour. She didn't turn and inspect our faces or tell us to look like diplomats. She didn't say anything. Sonja and I organized our remaining candies, first counting them all, then counting them by color, and then dividing them between us, our mouths anticipating a sweet future.

"We can go," my father said, climbing into the driver's seat. "It was that easy." Sonja and I returned the candies to their bag and coaxed our parents into a game of I'm Thinking of Something. Even our mother agreed to play. She was thinking of something in the animal kingdom when we came upon our first military checkpoint. There was a strip of metal across the road and a group of men wearing khaki. They gestured for us to stop. "Here goes nothing," my father said. My mother pushed the flour and oil back under her skirt, and without looking down, she adjusted the fabric.

The men—teens, I realized later—had machine guns hanging off their shoulders. My parents rolled down their windows. My father answered the first few questions, and then my mother began chatting. She asked the Tanzanian soldiers about wives or girlfriends. She asked about what they had studied in school. She told them they looked like good students. She handed out Adventist magazines. She smiled. She did not look at her feet.

One of the soldiers saw our bag of candy and pointed. My mother's eyes followed his finger and she held out her hand to Sonja, "Give it here." We watched as she gave our candy to the soldier, who took a piece for himself and passed the bag to his friends. They unwrapped the cellophane and laughed as they ate. They were young and tired and far from home. Those candies might have been the first purely sweet things they had eaten in months.

I began to cry. Sonja began to cry. When the men finally noticed, the original soldier returned to my mother's window and rattled the bag in Sonja's direction. There was something daring in his expression. Would we really take it back? My mother cradled her hands around his and gently pressed against them. "Keep it," she said. "It's just candy." In that moment, I hated her.

I looked at Sonja. Her face was blotchy, her eyes blazing. Words burned in our throats.

The soldier told my parents that we were free to go. My father restarted the car, and we drove away, just like that. For a long time, the only sound was our reproachful snuffles. "I'm sorry, girls," my mother said, finally. "I'm really sorry. Someday you'll understand."

Perhaps she felt sorry for the soldiers. They were somebody's children, conscripted into the military and sent to Uganda for who knows how long. Or perhaps she was afraid. The soldier had seemed annoyed at our tears. Or perhaps she was embarrassed at her daughters' privilege. Crying over candy, indeed! Or perhaps, as we thought at the time, she was worried the soldiers might yet confiscate the oil and flour at her feet. She had been relieved when their eyes landed on something so inconsequential. A bag of candy, praise the Lord.

Maybe it was everything.

We spent the night at the Adventist guesthouse in Kampala. My mother said that she for one didn't want to drive at night, and when my father told her that people might be expecting us in Bugema, she just patted her hair and said she didn't care. "Tomorrow's probably better anyway," he said.

Since the roadblock, I had worn my resentment, refusing to play car games or chatter to my parents about the lineation of the world. But in the morning, it was impossible to be sullen. Our car rushed up hills and bumped down them. We passed clumps of elephant grass, the blades swaying like dancers. From the window, they looked soft, almost velvety, a trick of the eye. I knew how fiercely the grass could resist small hands. From the window, everything was magical. The road was a red swath through the countryside. It was the road home.

"I remember that tree," I told Sonja.

"I remember that goat," she said.

"I remember that chicken," I said.

"No," she said. "You remember the chicken next to it." We began laughing. The joke was that we couldn't possibly remember. We had been gone, and Uganda had become a stranger. As we tried to reclaim our memories, we laughed. There was nothing more Ugandan than rueful laughter.

"I sure remember that pothole," my father said. My mother said nothing.

Our car turned into campus. Sonja and I bounced on the backseat like kernels of popcorn. There was the clinic. There was the mango tree. There was the Villagomez's house. There was the turnoff for the dairy. We sang, "We will soon be home, soon be home, soon be home."

The bright day dimmed as my father turned up the hill. It was like entering the mouth of a dragon—the branches a canopy above, the tall grass scraping the car below. My father drove slowly, trying to find a course up the washed-out road. Nobody spoke. Sonja and I craned our necks and watched for the water tank, the frangipangi tree, the red brick house.

We pulled into the clearing, the sky blue and cloudless. A monkey chattered peevishly near the garage, and the tree branches shuddered as it disappeared with its troop into the jungle. My father unlocked the verandah, and Sonja and I dashed into the house, leaving footprints upon the thick sheet of dust. We were home.

The school year had already begun, and my father threw himself into teaching. My mother cleaned and unpacked, and Sonja and I explored. One morning, our cat appeared at the backdoor, meowing. Another morning, an old python sunned itself beside the verandah like a log, like several logs. I had never seen such an immense snake. My father killed and skinned it, tossing its flesh far into the bushes. Years later, I would take the snakeskin to show-and-tell.

At night, my mother sat again at the dining room table. Moths fluttered above her, tapping against the bulb, and mosquitoes landed soft as kittens on her bare ankles. She lined up her two pens and wrote:

Dear Father,

It goes well with us. This morning, I opened the oven and with a thump, a small snake (about 80 cm) came out and fell to the floor next to my feet. It tried hard to get away, but Gary killed it. We can't be sure what it was as we haven't found it in our snake book!! It may be a baby mamba! Now before opening the oven, I always knock on the door and get ready to jump out of the way.

We retrieved your package last week from Kampala. It came quick and the coloring books were a great happiness for the girls. The mail has been arriving here more quickly. Sabene has begun to fly to Entebbe once a week and it helps. Here at school, it has been fortunately peaceful. I cannot say the same of Kampala. I don't believe the Tanzanian's presence has helped in the least. Rumor has it that the soldiers will stay.

Now it is soon time to put on nightclothes. Luckily the lights are on again and the water too. May Father in heaven keep you, we hope and hope.

CHAPTER 16

───── ❧ ─────

Waiting for Jesus to Come

IT WAS SABBATH afternoon, and I was waiting for Jesus to come. The day was bright and beautiful. "Glorious," my mother would have said, despite herself. The frangipangi tree was covered with creamy yellow flowers, and swallows were chattering under the eaves. Above the jungle, white clouds billowed. Maybe it would rain later today—we were all waiting for the dry season to break—or maybe Jesus would come. I searched the sky for the right cloud. The Second Coming would begin like this: a cloud that looked at first like a man's hand would draw nearer and nearer until, finally, we would see Jesus sitting on His throne, surrounded by angels.

I sat on the verandah steps and looked at the sky, my fingers peeling at the moss that grew in the crevices. The porch was in a pool of shade, and the cement felt cool, almost damp, through the cotton of my hand-me-down shorts. The branches that my mother had once paid Samson to cut down had mostly returned, and she knew better than to have them cut again. The shade was a "welcome commodity" (her words), and snakes would find their way into the house regardless. *Didn't she know?* Samson had tried to tell her, but she had believed in being proactive.

My mother now believed we were at the mercy of God, and God, she told us pointedly, expected people to use their common sense. It wasn't common sense to take children into danger. And yet, here we were, back in Uganda, living in the house on the hill.

"Trust the democratic process," my father said. "It takes time."

"The democratic process, my foot," my mother said.

My parents' disagreement became the backdrop of our ordinary life. My mother boiled water in the mornings and set it aside to cool. My father dashed about the house looking for his Bible, his Bible commentaries, his stack of student papers. My mother gathered up what he needed and handed it to him as he careened out the door, always late. "Watch for snakes," she called. With my father gone, our morning slowed. We ate breakfast and had worship on the verandah, and my mother read from Psalms, even the ones she might take issue with:

Make a joyful noise unto the Lord, all ye lands. Serve the Lord with gladness: Come before his presence with singing.

My mother didn't hide her feelings. We knew she worried about civil war on the horizon, about military checkpoints, about snakes and malaria and iron deficiency. We knew my father didn't like making mountains out of molehills, and that relative to human history, most anything we faced was a molehill. Their openness made their dispute boring news. Also boring: their love and commitment toward each other. I felt fully secure in the permanence of my family.

The only thing more dependable was God. We prayed before meals and after worships. Everyone we knew did the same, and because most of our children's books were religious, everyone we read about also prayed and worshiped a Christian God. I believed in God with the same certainty that I believed in the sky and in gravity and in music. Stories about doubt were confusing. Nothing was more certain than God.

Since Vacation Bible School, I had been particularly attentive to the Second Coming. My favorite hymn was "Lift up the Trumpet," and when I heard the opening chords, a martial bum-bum-ba-*bum*, I would stop squirming beside my mother and stand straighter, ready to belt out the lyrics: "Lift up the trumpet and loud let it ring: Jesus is coming again! Take heart, ye pilgrims, rejoice now and sing: Jesus is coming again!"

It was after we moved back into the house on the hill and I noticed how blue the sky was, how evocative the clouds, that I began watching for Jesus to return. I would sit for five minutes one day, ten another, and then I would go weeks without searching the sky.

During this time, my mother spoke often of heaven. While we had been living in Kenya, there had been a telegram, a hasty trip to Finland, and a winter funeral. After my grandmother's death, my mother found comfort in what she called "the beautiful resurrection morning." She would, in the hazy future, be reunited with her mother, and she spoke about that day with the same assurance that she spoke about our coming shipment of supplies.

She was not expecting heaven now, of course, and if she knew her daughter was watching for Jesus, she might have been concerned. We were a religious family; we weren't fundamentalists. The difference was in how literally you took the word "soon." On Sabbath, everyone said reflexively that Jesus was coming soon. Fundamentalists planned accordingly.

A troupe of monkeys chased each other on the edge of the jungle. When they leapt from a tree, the branches swung back and forth. It was the movement of leaves I saw more than actual monkeys, until they finally congregated on one of the branches and began to groom each other's fur. I looked at the sky. Clouds hovered over the horizon. I held my fist up to measure them. The clouds were much too small. I wondered if I should look instead for a chameleon in the jungle. We hadn't seen any since we had been back, and I was anxious to have one as a pet. If I got up, I wouldn't be able to keep an eye on the clouds. Chameleons were hard to find. Jesus's return felt as likely.

My father walked up the road just as I was about to give up on it all: in both Jesus and in chameleons. If my father was here, fun would follow. Maybe he would play a board game with us or read stories. We held hands as we walked into the house.

CHAPTER 17

———— ❧ ————

Bat Valley

NOW THAT THE Adventist faith was legal, church leaders viewed Uganda as fallow ground, waiting to be planted. Evangelists from California began a crusade in Bat Valley, the aptly named suburb of Kampala. The evangelistic team promised free Bibles for those with perfect attendance. You could trade a Bible for soap or rice, or you could read it and pray for a better hereafter.

My father didn't volunteer to lead out—a miracle that my mother observed with quiet surprise. He did offer to bring his students once a week to tally attendance, stack chairs, and learn the prosaic realities of a crusade. Even my mother agreed that this was a good learning opportunity for his students.

On the evenings he was gone, my mother fretted—worried at first that he would volunteer for a larger role, and then, as the night wore on, that he had been killed. Kampala was dangerous in itself, and the road between Kampala and Bugema was notorious for carjacking. Every few weeks, masked men stopped a vehicle and shot the occupants. The missionaries called that stretch of highway "the road to Jericho."

During the day, the violence felt far away. Students walked to class in crisp uniforms, carrying books under their arms and laughing with friends. Weaver birds sang in the pasture trees, and a few bony cows lay in the shade. On the dirt road beside the pasture, boys pushed bicycle wheels with sticks they had carefully selected. They would race each other, propelling their one wheel and urging it to go faster. The winner would throw his hands into the air and kick his legs high.

My mother turned her attention to our education. After morning worship, we would do an hour or two of school. She might place workbooks on the table and have us practice our numbers or letters, or she might read a chapter from *Little House on the Prairie* while we drew and colored a scene, or she might have us bake bread, the baking measurements our math for the day.

After school and lunch and a nap—the Fordham sisters did not neglect their naps—Sonja and I fetched milk. Sonja carried the pail, and I carried finger bananas, which I took to feed to the cows.

Collecting milk was our favorite part of the day. Our house was like a boat bobbing in a green sea. When we looked up, we could see the sky, the clouds blowing in and bringing rain, the stars following their faithful paths. We loved the house on the hill, and we loved escaping its solitude. We followed the same road that carried our father to work. It was a green tunnel, the trees rising on each side, the branches clasping each other from above. As we entered the road, we were plunged into shadow. Our mother took this road only a few times each week. She did most of her traveling through her words—*We are still here. We are still here.*

As we walked, Sonja and I spoke sometimes of mambas. Once Sonja drew them with her words, I imagined them everywhere. Our eyes swept the nearest branches and trunks. Before taking our stompy steps, we inspected the dark road where our feet were and where they would be next. Sometimes we sang, "He holds the whole world in His hands. He holds the whole world, in His hands. He holds the whole world, in His hands." The snakes would hear us a mile away.

More often, we didn't think of snakes at all. We told our own elaborate stories, spoke passionately about our pets, or narrated the plots to one of the two films we had watched in Florida. Adventists didn't go to movie theaters, and my mother usually turned off the television after *Sesame Street*, but we had attended a free showing of *One Hundred and One Dalmatians* at an Adventist Community Center and attended again when they showed *The Incredible Journey*, giving Sonja and me hours of adventure to relive.

At the bottom of the hill, the road spit us back into the sun. The jungle, which had seemed so vast from our verandah, ended here. The only monkey on campus was a pet, tied up in a missionary's yard. It would groom your hair when you held it, but when you tried to put it down, it bit you, hard. This unhappy monkey ensured we never wanted one for ourselves.

Our father continued straight here, toward campus, but we turned right, to where the road followed the pasture. Grass grew in the center, tickling our calves. I tugged at the longer strands and absently chewed their stems. The dairy was a small building: a roof, a frame, two stalls, a trough for food and water. The dairymen would sometimes already be here, sitting on a stool, milking a cow. Often, though, they were elsewhere. They came when they came. We set our pail in line with the other children's pails and ran to find Tigist.

Tigist, our best friend, was tall and slender. Technically, she was Sonja's best friend, but I inserted myself into their company, no matter how mystifying it could be. Sonja and Tigist would spend hours talking about Johnny— an older missionary boy I had known nearly my whole life. Sonja, who still had to be reminded to use her fork *for goodness sakes*, giggled and giggled and tossed her braids.

At other times, the three of us bragged about our countries, about their most important resource: food. Sonja and I claimed both Finland and the United States, giving us plenty of material. We described nectarines and pizza and chocolates that looked like tiny loaves of bread. Tigist rolled her eyes— that was nothing. No lousy candy compared to the bounties of Ethiopia. I remember being particularly impressed with the lemons. She told us they were larger than grapefruits, and she held out her hands to demonstrate their size. Oh, I was jealous about those lemons.

Years later, after we had moved to Texas, one of my classmates made a terrible joke about the famine in Ethiopia; the punch line involved hungry people swirling down a drain. It was, incredibly, the first I had heard of the war and the hunger that Tigist and her family had fled. I mumbled something and walked away, yanked back to the dairy, to the scent of manure and the chatter of weaver birds and to Tigist sitting across from me, drawing circles with her feet and describing lemons.

At supper, Sonja was full of stories about Tigist. I spoke mostly of cows. I had named one of the calves Honey, and the dairymen called her my cow and told me that when she was old enough to milk, they would set it aside for me. I came home each day bustling with self-importance and spoke so seriously and so obsessively that my father finally told me not to believe everything I was told, sometimes people were just being nice. "Gary," my mother said, but she didn't contradict him. They would laugh later, I suspected.

And yet, when my parents talked about food shortages, I couldn't stop my interjections: "Do you think we'll get extra milk when Honey is old enough?" or "Honey seems like she'll be a good milker. The dairymen say it's because of the bananas I bring her."

In the middle of the evangelistic crusade, the Californians told my father that their vacation was about over and they were returning to the States. They hoped he and his students could finish the meetings. My father stood before them, too shocked and responsible to object. He collected the remaining sermon scripts, the attendance logs, and the boxes of Bibles. He shook their hands and wondered what he would tell my mother.

"So they're leaving," she said. "What scared them off?"

"Nothing," he said. "You really won't believe this. Their vacation is over. That's it. At least they could have told someone their schedule ahead of time."

My father resented the Californians. They were as showy and impulsive as his mother. Except they were worse. They had known all along that they wouldn't finish their meetings. They needed a chump, and he had shown up. Now, he would have to drive the road to Jericho three times a week. *As soon as the thieves know one goes to Kampala every Wednesday, Saturday, Sunday, they will be waiting to hijack the car,* he complained in a letter.

My mother insisted that we travel with our father. Carjackers would be less inclined to kill a man in front of his children. When we complained, she told us it wasn't her idea of fun, either. Three days a week, we wore Sabbath dresses and pinchy shoes. Mosquitoes whined at our ankles as we colored in our books and worked on our letters. When I got malaria, my mother packed a metal bowl and a blanket.

The meetings were held under a tall grove of trees. I remember resting my head in my mother's lap and gazing at the bats above. They looked like dark, plump leaves hanging from the branches. While my body shivered and lurched, my eyes focused on the leathery creatures. I watched for movement—a bat shifting its shoulders, repositioning its feet—and I waited for that grand moment when all the bats would swoop off the trees and into the coming night. Such a wonderful racket of wings.

Once I became too sick to travel, my mother stayed home with Sonja and me, her fear swinging like a metronome between her husband and her daughter. *Sari had another long night,* my mother wrote. *She had a fever like a battery. She got aspirin and we rolled her up in dripping wet sheets. And she threw up. These are the tropical happinesses.*

It was a bad case of malaria. The nurse came up and gave me a shot of chloroquine, and accompanying him was my father, a kitten cupped in his hands. If my parents were giving me a kitten, then I knew they were worried. I wondered if I was dying. Late at night, as the flame tree scratched at the windowpane and I felt shaky and scared, I made a bargain with God: If He spared my life, I would become a doctor and open a clinic in the mission field. For years, I felt beholden to this promise, and when I changed majors in college—from biology to history—I felt as if I was having a theological crisis as much as a career one.

After I recovered, my mother did not resume taking us to the crusade. She sent us down to Tigist's house and traveled alone with my father. She continued to have faith in her charms.

On the crusade's final Sabbath, my parents were gone the entire day. We went to church with Tigist and spent the afternoon dashing around her yard, scattering their chickens. We played Bible hide-and-seek and the Bible board game that Sonja and I had gotten for our joint birthday celebration. We had memorized all the answers and had brought the game with us specifically because we wanted to impress Tigist's sisters. As Sonja and I moved our pieces around the board, her sisters laughed and laughed, knowing what was what. "You are so smart," they kept saying, and Tigist kept shouting, "Because they're cheating!"

As it got dark, Sonja began asking—What time is it? What time is it? Tigist's parents assured us our parents would come soon. Still, we waited. Tigist went to sleep. Her sisters went to sleep. We lay on the floor and wondered.

"They're never coming back," Sonja whispered. "Something's happened. I know it." Sonja and I faced each other, and whispered the word "orphans." Who would take us in? We hoped Tigist's parents would.

We were asleep when our parents arrived, their voices energy at the door. The adults were all whispering with exclamation points. I followed Sonja into the kitchen. She hung onto our mother's hand and swayed back and forth. "I thought you weren't coming back."

"We almost didn't," our father said.

"Never mind," our mother said, thanking Tigist's parents.

My father couldn't not mind. He was more rattled than he had ever been. The next morning, he sat down and typed my American grandmother a letter and didn't even share the aerogramme with my mother.

He was a man who believed in lining up his details before plunging into the plot. In his letter, he described the crusade, the vehicle they were in, the missionaries they were with, and how on the drive back to Bugema, they had pulled over to the side of the road. With the preliminaries out of the way, he began the story that still made him wince:

All of a sudden a pickup comes heading straight for us, coming from the other direction. I thought it was the end. It was sure to be a head on collision. (I was sitting in the front seat.) The other driver must have been drunk. He was coming about 50 or 60 miles an hour. Just before impact, I turned my head. Miraculously, he didn't hit us head on, but instead scraped down the entire left side of the car. He then turned sharply to get back on the pavement and turned over and slid half a block down the road. Everyone was telling us how lucky we were. The bystanders picked up his vehicle and he got in and drove off—without even apologizing for scrapping up V.'s car.

As these things often go, the night's troubles were just beginning. My father described how they got stuck in the mud, how a tractor pulled them out, how they accidentally paid the wrong man, how the actual tractor driver yelled at them, how they had no more money.

Buried within his narrative is a story I would have led with: *If that was not enough for one night, when we finally got about one mile from the school, some Bugema people came to warn us that there was a roadblock ahead with some masked gunmen.*

My father would later identify that night as one of the most harrowing of his life. He was sitting in the front passenger seat and saw death coming. My mother only said it was scary; her tone suggested that living in Uganda was itself harrowing, and that a car accident would be the least of it.

Both of them shrugged off the masked gunmen who were waiting for them. The point of the story was always the thwarted collision. They expected carjackings and troubles with soldiers; they weren't expecting something as mundane as a drunk driver.

CHAPTER 18

———— ❧ ————

Murphy's Law

WHEN THE POWER cut out, we didn't know whether it would come back in an hour or a day or a week or if, in fact, it would ever return—though so far, it had. "Murphy's law," one of my parents would say when the refrigerator stopped humming. The other would nod, expanding on why today was a particularly bad day to be without electricity. Maybe my father had just returned from Nairobi, and the precious cheese and butter would have to be tossed. Maybe my mother had used the last of the flour to make gluten. She didn't cry anymore. She just blamed Murphy and went on with her day.

My parents might not agree about Uganda, but about Murphy, they were of one accord. Murphy had impeccable timing.

In Kampala, a roll of toilet paper cost $5.00 (*wait for God to notice*, wrote my mother), and pineapples were cheaper in the United States than in Kampala. Sugar was intermittently available. Petrol was intermittently available. Soap could only be bought in Kenya. No wonder there was looting.

The rainy seasons came. The dry seasons came. We spent Christmases in Kenya, as well as the weeks before and after elections. In Nairobi, my parents bought oats, oil, sugar, and (of course) lots of soap. The 1970s turned into the 1980s. New decade, old story. The monkeys harvested our jackfruit. The monkeys harvested our peanuts. There was fighting in Kampala. Our mother, bored and anxious, volunteered to teach. Her news reporting class met around our dining room table. While Sonja and I climbed trees and scattered monkeys, she taught the inverted pyramid.

There were elections. There were coups. There were rebel attacks. Obote returned to Uganda. My mother wrote to her father, *Yesterday as we listened to the news from VOA [Voices of America] we heard that 2 Adventist American missionaries in Zimbabwe were brutally tortured to death. We didn't get the names clearly. It was a couple. One should be thankful that we are still breathing here. Also in the same broadcast it was told that Kampala is again without peace. The state began price control and the cost of food fell at the stores. We didn't hear if you can even find bananas at the market square.*

My mother began to plot our departure. She asked family members to write the church headquarters and express concern for our safety. She suggested that they quote from our letters—particularly my father's—and tell the church leaders that Uganda was too dangerous for a family with children.

She ate less for breakfast, until finally she ate nothing at all, waving her hands, "I'll just have lunch." She slept longer. In the mornings, she watched the light falling across her sheets. When we had first arrived in Uganda, she had learned to close the curtains carefully, overlapping the fabric; otherwise, children would be lined up outside, looking in. We were no longer so interesting.

My mother sat on the edge of the bed. Her cotton nightgown draped modestly over her knees. She used to be astonished that she was a missionary. The very word was exotic and pious. She believed in the church's goodness then, or at least she remembered believing in it. Now she felt cynical and old. She was forty. *The weather is usually so exhausting*, she wrote her father, *that you cannot get enough exercise. From our place to school it is over a km and Gary goes that way sometimes three times a day. I go three times a week.*

The little ones got sent to Uganda, she liked to say, and the big ones assured you the country was safe, even as they withdrew their speaking appointments. My father had laughed at that one. He wrote his mother, *It is rather funny that all the people scheduled for camp meeting in Uganda have seemingly canceled since the taking of the Sec. Tres's car. Forty cars a week are taken; how does it make a difference that it belonged to a missionary?*

She wanted to stay in bed. But she should bake some bread before the power went out, she should wash some clothes. She felt Ecclesiastical. Everything was meaningless. Two thieves had been captured a mile from campus and had been tied together and set on fire.

She dressed and walked out to check the tomatoes. She was wearing flip-flops, and her hair, she knew, was crushed on one side of her head. That was the problem with her perm. Otherwise, she appreciated its simplicity. She stood with her hands on her hips and faced the road. It was a beautiful morning. It was always beautiful here; even the rains, stern and lashing, were beautiful. Some leaves in the jungle jumped, and she watched the monkeys chase each other and disappear. She had never walked directly into the jungle. She took the path or the road, but mostly, these days, she stayed in the yard. She could spend a week at the house and never walk beyond the clothesline.

The mimosa tree was in bloom, and so was the frangipangi. Samson was right: Every tree had flowers. She had tried so hard to get the branches off the roof. Her efforts had resulted in the permanent destruction of some trees, but the branches of others had returned. You couldn't stop them. Samson could have told her that.

The tree nearest the house was a royal poinciana, though everyone called it a flame tree. When she was braiding Sonja's hair, she saw it. When she read from Psalms, she looked up and saw it. In her Bible, she'd underlined: "But I am like a green olive tree in the house of God: I trust in the mercy of God for ever and ever."

Trust was in short supply, hers particularly. But when she stood outside, she could feel her stomach unknot. The world was a mess, but God was here somewhere. No matter how bad the news on the radio, birds would sing brightly in the morning, and the sky would be blue. She could smell smoke—someone was making matoke—and she could feel, more than hear, her daughters moving through the house. They were little ladies now—well, not ladies, not with their manners, but they were growing into their own selves. She stood and watched the swallows, and for a moment, she didn't want to be anywhere else.

This was the exact feeling my father had on most days. The Bachelor of Theology program was now accredited by both the government of Uganda and the Adventist church. When students graduated, they would have options. They could work as pastors, or they could apply to graduate programs in the West. Already his students were talking about attending Andrews University. The ministerial program was young, though, and Uganda was teetering on the precipice of civil war. If my father left, who would replace him? My father was committed to Bugema's success. His teaching hours were long and satisfying. When he left class, he was invigorated from the discussions.

The Adventist church was undergoing a doctrinal crisis. Desmond Ford, an Australian theologian, was questioning the church's position over what had actually happened on October 22, 1844. He argued that the investigative judgment—the Adventist belief that on October 22, God moved from the Holy to the Most Holy Place to begin judging the world— was poor scholarship, which caused Adventists to worry, unnecessarily, that they weren't good enough to be saved. Church leaders believed Ford was questioning the very foundation of Adventism, and eventually, they fired him.

Though several months behind, my father followed the controversy as closely as he could. He adjusted the curriculum in his Old Testament class so that students could wrestle with the Book of Daniel. They got into the minutiae of the debate, examining key verses in Hebrew. "A good scholar knows his Hebrew," my father said. "You win arguments in Hebrew." Word reached Kenya that Gary Fordham was teaching heresy in his Old Testament class. A bigwig was sent—despite the theft of the Secretary Treasurer's car—to observe my father's class and return any wayward students to theological orthodoxy.

My father sat in the back of the room and listened as his students asked question after question. The church official, who had begun the session with jokes and reassurances, grew more and more aggravated. When the students brought up the Hebrew translation, he took no more questions and launched into a speech. My father came home gleeful.

The official returned to Kenya and recommended that Gary Fordham be immediately relieved of his duties. My father's friend, a well-known Adventist with a lot of pull, told the administrators that Gary might be a bit of a heretic, but he was the heretic you knew. A replacement might be even more liberal. Also, who else would stay in Uganda? "Oh, I saved your job," he told my parents. My mother could have kicked him.

My father, the goody two-shoes, was delighted that anyone would consider him subversive. He was relieved that we were staying. These were exciting theological times. Who wouldn't want to be teaching? Why would we leave Uganda intentionally? He was not one of those wazungu who panicked at the first sign of trouble. When others fled the country, my father felt a jolt of pride. The Fordhams knew how to stick around.

Yet there were times when my father was driving at night and a pair of headlights bumped ominously behind him. He turned down road after road, and still the lights followed, acceleration matching acceleration. Carjackers didn't always leave the driver alive. At these times, these driving times, he wished he had not been so stubborn. He thought of his wife, a widow (*who would tell her?*), his two daughters forgetting their father piece by piece, as they did each time they were in Finland. These nights when he returned home, he didn't say "Murphy's law." Rather, he told my mother how he almost got killed. "They stopped following me at the roadblock. Imagine a roadblock coming in useful."

She responded by letting out her breath and saying, "So, you'd rather get killed than leave, I see."

Then they would argue.

When the electricity cut off, there was first a groan from my father and then wild excitement. Sonja and I groped around the dining room, hands out.

We slammed into each other, collapsed onto the floor, laughing. My father turned on a flashlight and walked through the darkness, opening cupboards and drawers. Candles rolled next to papers and pencils and bits of unknown. It was always the matches that were impossible to find.

"Ah," my father said in disgust. "You can never find anything in this house." We heard him in the bedroom pulling open drawers, and we watched the bobbing flashlight return and travel into the kitchen.

"Well, where did you put them?" my mother asked. She stood and followed the light. From the tangle of searching, she emerged triumphant. "If it were a snake, it would have bitten you." It was her favorite saying. If we came whining into the kitchen, looking for a lost toy, she would dismiss us with a wave of her hand. *Don't be helpless.* But if we were searching for our church shoes or a schoolbook, she would sigh deeply, sweep a hand under the bed, and pull it out. *If it were a snake, it would have bitten you!* Her ability to know where everything was sent us to her.

My father lit the candles. "Just great," he said, picking up his pen and setting it down. "I have all these papers, and I can't see a thing." The flames leaped up and down to an inaudible beat. Beyond the candles, the darkness took on the quality of something solid. We were here together, a family in a boat.

Sonja and I spent these nights happily. We poured wax into our palms, molded it into the creases, peeled it back to reveal our fortunes. When we took turns trying to strike matches, our mother finally said, "Good grief, do you think matches grow on trees?" Our father snorted. She turned back to her letter. We ran our fingers through the flame. She looked up crossly. "Make up your mind. Leave your finger in or out."

"Leave it," Sonja said. "I dare you."

"I can," I said. I held my index finger just outside the ring of warmth. I counted in my head, and then I cut my finger swiftly through the flame.

"You didn't," Sonja said.

"So. You didn't either."

The power went out for many reasons. Sometimes the guerrillas blew up something, throwing us into darkness and reminding us of the civil war that had not yet been called a war. Sometimes a body would get stuck in the Owen Falls Dam. Sometimes a storm would blow a tree into the wire. Most often, the fuse blew. The whole area depended on one generator.

It would have been a simple matter for my father to hike to the generator and fix the problem. He had gotten adept at making things work. But my father, who took many risks, was not overly eager to take on this one. He wrote his mother: *The fuse blows every day and someone must drive 10 miles to Bombo to fetch the electric company man, drive him here, and then return him after he replaces the fuse. We could do it ourselves except the penalty is several weeks or months in prison. The last time, the electrician just took a wire from me and wrapped it around the old fuse and left. He said it takes an 80 amp fuse (we have 120 amps of fuse in our house alone). No wonder it blows all the time.*

We apparently had more to do with the outages than Murphy.

My parents went weeks without arguing. My mother held her tongue and boiled the water in the morning and boiled the water in the evening and pressed her lips together. Only rarely did she stew like this, but when she did, watch out. Open your eyes, Brother Fordham.

We avoided Kampala. The new President Obote was also former President Obote. Those who didn't like him in 1971 also didn't like him in 1981. He was now warier and more violent. The civil war that was not yet called a war had already begun.

"You should tell the church that it's getting too dangerous for us to stay," my mother said. "Remind them that you have two young daughters. Tell them that you've noticed that nobody from Nairobi is particularly keen on visiting Bugema these days."

"We'll see," my father said.

"I've seen plenty," my mother said.

CHAPTER 19

A Red Line

O N MARCH 5, 1981, my mother sat at the typewriter, her back straight against the wooden chair. A colleague was traveling to Kenya and had offered to mail a letter there. Usually, my mother wrote her letters by hand, lounging on the sofa. She had beautiful handwriting and disliked the cranky typewriter, with its ribbon of ink that so often snagged. She disliked also the formality of the table. She was typing because she had to share this aerogramme with my father and because she had so much to fit into her allotted space.

Dear Nana and Gordon:

I finally did it. And all by myself. I have asked the union to transfer us to Kenya by next September so the girls can both go to school. I told them that both our parents would like us to ask for a transfer out of this country. I also mentioned the hardships and the isolation in which we live. I don't know what they will do since the request comes from the wife and Gary didn't sign it. He says he would just as well stay here. I and the girls are very anxious to leave. If we don't get transferred, you might ask someone at church headquarters when they are transferring us. Just don't mention anything we wrote. There must be some items in the news about Uganda that would justify your concern.

She concluded the letter with breezy questions about my father's brother John, who rarely wrote, and about his wife and children: *How is Johnny? How is the house? Are there changes in furniture, etc.? What is Alisa studying in college? How does she like it? How is her social life? How are Jacky and Josh? How is Mamma Martins health? I would be very happy if you could answer these questions one by one and give us any other information you have. It's so frustrating to be stuck in the bush and not know anything about one's family and loved ones.*

After my mother's message, one of my parents—probably my father—drew a red line across the aerogramme. It was a precise boundary, as if a ruler had been laid across the sheet. Never before had they divided a letter with such sharpness.

Below the line, my father typed: *Now it's my turn. The last letter I wrote was mailed from Kampala so I don't know if you have received it yet. In it, I sent a picture of the water pump. I hope you have received it. I need a couple spares so that we have them in case the spare I bought goes kaput.*

The letter continued for half a page, but my father didn't mention my mother's request for a transfer or his refusal to sign it. He didn't argue that Uganda was a relatively safe country, that we could also die in Kenya or the United States, that there were no guarantees in life. Instead, he typed a complicated story about how our family and another was harassed and robbed by soldiers. The only indication that he even knew what my mother had written was the tone of his first sentence: Now it's my turn.

Two days later, my father wrote his mother again. This time, he didn't share the aerogramme. He repeated his argument over and over, as if he already knew that his mother was another audience to persuade: *Kaarina has written the Union requesting a transfer. I feel we should stay until after the next graduation which will be in December. Kaarina wants to move before September. I think we could last another four months and finish the task we came to do. By December we will have graduated nearly all of the students.*

When my grandmother read my father's letter, she must have wanted to wring his neck. She loved her son, but he was blind to reason. In every letter, he described some new and menacing danger, and then he complained that his wife had had enough. Well, Kaarina wasn't the only one with common sense. God helps those who help themselves. Wasn't that in the Bible?

At my mother's request, my father's relatives—including his mother—had been sending letters to the Adventist mission headquarters in Maryland. Their message: Move the Fordhams. Word eventually reached Nairobi, and my father was called in to answer for the trouble. For an uncomfortable hour, he sat in the office as his bosses told him about the calls they had received and read from some of the more outlandish letters.

My father had the gift of listening expansively, without interrupting or looking disturbed. He leaned forward and didn't speak until they were through berating him. "Are you unhappy in Uganda?" they finally asked.

My father began with the obvious—my mother was worried about our safety in Uganda. It was such old, old news that he considered it a prudent place to begin. But when he said it, the men pantomimed astonishment. *Why on earth hadn't she told them?* Out of politeness, my father ignored their questions and continued: He would like to fulfill the commitment he had made. He would like to stay at Bugema until the senior class graduated in December. He had been encouraging Kaarina to take the girls and wait for him in Finland. He would do so again.

These big men, whom my mother considered adversaries, were finally on her side. They arranged for my father to teach through the summer, completing his courses several months early.

It was a good agreement for our family, but as my father walked to the guesthouse, he felt as embarrassed as he ever had in his life. He sat down and wrote his mother a hotly worded letter. When she received it, she was so offended that she threw it in the trash and wrote a fuming reply. My father's eventual apology is all that remains from their exchange:

I'm sorry to have made you feel bad for having written to the Division. You did not say too much about what I wrote, only you left it wide open for the imagination to work overtime and they thought I must have written some really bad stuff. It's O.K. I suppose I have the right to write what I want to family. I think though that Uncle Merrill got a little melodramatic. I do not have a Mercedes here and we were not almost killed at a roadblock (though we could have been—recently two diplomats were shot for driving through a roadblock). Nor are we in danger 24 hours a day, nor is Uganda currently worse than the worst battlefield during the second world war. It's this kind of writing that makes us look bad.

The long rains were returning when my father came back from Nairobi. In the afternoons, we kept an eye on the clouds, and when they darkened, we hurried home. From the living room, we watched the rain cut through the jungle, we watched water pour off the roof. Each day, the tank held more rainwater. Each day, the grass in the pastures grew greener and more lush, and the cows produced more milk. Slugs crisscrossed the outside walls of the house, and our cats stayed indoors. Beside the verandah steps, my mother's tomato garden died.

The civil war between my parents was over. They had both won. My mother was getting what she wanted: We were leaving Uganda. My father was getting what he wanted: He was leaving on his terms. But there was no easy happiness. Not when things were so bad in Uganda.

My mother greeted my father with a hug and a sympathetic smile. "This has been a good home," she told him.

In later years, though, my mother would remember our departure as her triumph. "I was proactive," my mother said. "I wrote a letter of resignation all by myself."

CHAPTER 20

———— ❧ ————

Maybe This Is Reincarnation

O N THE DAY we left Uganda, I had malaria.
"What a time to get sick," my mother said, handing me a chloroquine tablet and a glass of water. "Don't throw up." Throwing up meant another pill, another glass of water. We didn't have time for this.

I swallowed the pill—gagging on its bitter taste—and then pressed my palm to my mouth. We both waited. "You're doing good," my mother said. She brought a metal bowl from the kitchen and set it behind me, just in case. I tried not to hear the clink on the floor. Its presence, I knew, would call the contents of my stomach.

My mother moved through the house singing not a hymn, but the opening song—"Oh, What a Beautiful Mornin'"—from the Broadway play *Oklahoma!* The next academic year, my father would teach theology at Kamagambo College in Kenya, my mother would teach English part-time, and my sister and I would begin a formal homeschool curriculum.

My father came into the house. "Are we ready or what?"

"We're ready," my mother said. "Everyone go to the bathroom first."

The car sunk low under the weight of our things. There was luggage at our feet and even a box on the seat between Sonja and me. My mother handed me a pillow and the bowl. "See if you can just sleep." Sonja looked glumly out the window. It would be a long drive, and she had to share the backseat with Pukey Sari.

"Let's have a word of prayer, shall we?" my father said. We all closed our eyes and folded our hands. My father asked God to protect us on the road, to be with the pets we were leaving behind, to watch over the families still living near Kampala. I opened my eyes and looked up at Sonja. Her hair was in two braids, and her bangs were blunt across her forehead.

She blinked at me: *Will this prayer ever end?*

I blinked back: *No! We will never leave.*

Our father prayed for each of his students by name, for the administrators, for the church in Uganda, for president Obote, who needed wisdom, for me and my possible malaria. Outside, the sky was blue. We were parked under the mimosa tree, and I could see the lacy leaves and the tufts of pink flowers. Every tree has flowers here. Our father prayed for our future, a vast and unknowable topic. His tone shifted into the sounds of a man winding down. I closed my eyes to join him at the end of his prayer. "Amen," he said, and my mother echoed him.

"Okay," our father said. "Let's go like a herd of turtles." He turned the key in the ignition, the engine caught, and our car bumped down the hill. I lay on the pillow, my eyes gazing up at the jungle's green roof.

Maybe this is reincarnation. For years, you're someone who is surrounded by jungle. You see monkeys every day and occasionally find a chameleon and carry it around like a pet. At night when the chickens squawk, your father puts on his boots to check on them. Sometimes, he will find driver ants streaming through the coop, and he will release the chickens into the night. Other times, he will find a genet cat or a mongoose.

At the breakfast table, he asks, "Guess who came last night?"

Once your father goes to work, you and Sonja will sit on the verandah while your mother reads to you from Psalms: *The Lord is my light and my salvation; whom shall I fear? The Lord is the strength of my life; of whom shall I be afraid?* Never again will you have morning worships so religiously. You will go to school, and you will learn how to hurry. Maybe this is reincarnation. You will grow up. You will become a different person, a person who does not live on the edge of a jungle. You will stop watching for a cloud the size of a man's hand.

Your former life, though, will always be there. Tug at any moment, and a thread will carry you back to Uganda. It will take you to a time when you lived in a house on a hill with your parents and sister. You will hear the sound of rain coming toward you and will remember how you used to run outside with your family to gather the clothes. Your mother would have arms full of laundry, and when the rains caught you all, she would laugh and shout, "Hurry, hurry," even as she slowed her steps and gazed at the sky.

PART III

Secrets

CHAPTER 21

———— ❧ ————

We Don't Belong Here

THERE IS AN omission in stories about missionaries. A secret. No one talks about what happens to the family when they return to their country of origin. Do they adapt and survive, or do they muddle along, ever nostalgic? What happens when they encounter their own small troubles? Will their faith survive? And what about their children? Will they ever find a way to belong?

Sonja was twelve when a dentist in Nairobi told our mother that he had done all he could for her teeth and that Sonja needed braces before it was too late.

Since leaving Bugema, we had lived pleasantly in Kenya. The country was politically stable, and if we drove into Nairobi, we could buy flour, sugar, and even, oh glory, butter. On vacations, we camped in game parks or lounged on the wide beaches of the Indian Ocean. Sonja grew tall and bossy. She babysat other missionaries' children and read romance novels, when she could find them. I remained small and needy, my mother's baby. I was passionate about drawing, tree climbing, and my pet guinea pig. We missed life on the hill—the birds jabbering in the jungle, the green shade of the verandah, and, most of all, our friends—but in Kenya, our happiness had fewer complications. Even our mother was content.

After discussing the dentist's upsetting news, my parents were in agreement: Something had to be done for Sonja's teeth. They began planning our return to the United States. My father would attend a Ph.D. program in Texas. My mother would get a teaching job and support our family economically. Sonja and I would attend a real school, and we would discover if our mother's philosophy—that as long as we were readers, we would do fine academically—was actually true. We sold our books and clothes, gave away our pets, and flew to the United States.

That is one story.

Here is another.

Sometime before we left Kenya, our family visited Baraton Junior College, an Adventist school in the Kenyan highlands. The altitude was too high for mosquitoes, and the cows grazed on plush, rolling hills. The missionaries lived in a small neighborhood with lawns and paved roads, and the children attended a school with a bell that brought everyone in from recess. We called Baraton "little America." It was the plummiest mission assignment in East Africa, and the missionaries there were glamorous and confident, several cuts above the rest of us.

During our visit, we took a Sabbath afternoon walk with a few missionary families. Sonja and I ran ahead with the children. We poked sticks into streams and picked flowers and bragged about our countries of origin. Though we Americans were in the majority, we couldn't match the passion or confidence of the Norwegian sisters. I kept trying to interject that in California, I had once seen a lollypop as big as a plate, but the Baraton children didn't care. They were now organizing a game of freeze tag. I was a fast runner, and ordinarily, I would have been thrilled at the opportunity to impress these cool Baraton kids. But Sabbath games were supposed to be at least arguably religious. With our usual crowd—the Cochran brothers—Sonja and I played a lot of Bible board games, Bible charades, and especially Bible tag. I was about to suggest we shout the name of an apostle as we unfroze someone, when Sonja shot me a look: *Don't. Just don't.*

While I was fretting about breaking the Sabbath, our mother fell into step with a trusted friend. The two women dropped behind the other adults and traded gossip. On our campus, a petty conflict between two missionaries had escalated until one missionary had dumped a bucket of cow dung on the other missionary's head. "Can you imagine?" my mother said happily.

The gossip at Baraton was even juicier: Two missionaries were having an affair. They weren't even being discreet. My mother tsk-tsked encouragingly. She could have spent the entire walk discussing the affair, but her friend steered the conversation to our family.

"So you're finally leaving," she said. "You know, your girls might have a hard go of it. Several of us were talking, and we're all concerned. Don't get me wrong, they're sweet girls. But you've always lived way out in the sticks, and your girls are quite shy. They don't know about fashion or hairstyles. If you move to the States, they're going to get crucified."

On the drive home, our mother told us what her friend had said. Maybe she was preparing us for the coming apocalypse. Maybe she was hoping we would tell her we were more sophisticated than the other missionaries suspected. More likely, though, she couldn't keep a secret. If she knew something, we knew it, too. Already our mother had told us about the affair—or rather, she had told our father, while Sonja and I sat in the backseat and gaped at each other. Now, as she recounted the missionary's warning, Sonja and I shifted uncomfortably. We didn't know the word "nerd" yet, but we felt it.

A few weeks later, our father told us he had gotten a letter from missionary friends who had moved to London. Lori, the youngest daughter, was Sonja's age. Our father held the letter out for us to see. "Lori's father writes that on the first day of school a boy teased Lori about being from Africa. Well, you know what she did? She hauled off and punched him right in the nose. Everyone's scared to tease her now."

It wasn't long ago that we had all been on safari together. Sonja and Lori had passed a romance novel back and forth, giggling over the kissing scenes. "You're too little," they had told me when I asked to read the passages in question. At our campsite, they had set aside their superiority, and we children had run barefoot together, exploring the scrubland beside the river bottom, pulling out thorns when we stepped on them. Missionary kids are generally scrappy, but Lori was fearless. Her golden hair floated behind her as she clamored over rocks and ran between acacia trees. I wasn't surprised that she punched that boy. Everyone knew you didn't mess with Lori.

Our father smiled at us. "Lori's father says she's really enjoying school now. She's made a lot of friends. Isn't that great?"

Sonja and I murmured something and wandered off. Of course, the story was exhilarating. Lori—*our* Lori—had punched a city boy. But our father had an agenda, and we could feel it. When we fought with each other, our parents forced us into false apologies ("I'm sorry I bit you" or "I'm sorry I scratched you") and lectured us on getting along. Now, our father was encouraging us to hit a future classmate. Beneath this extraordinary subtext was a darker message: If we didn't punch at least one classmate, we would be teased. Or worse.

Sonja and I were doomed.

When we left Kenya, we flew with our mother to Finland, taking advantage of our last church-funded airfare. Our father flew to Texas to begin the difficult task of moving a family from one continent to another. He wrote my mother letters about finding a house to rent and getting the electricity turned on, and she wrote him letters about going to sauna and picking blueberries. My mother sank into Finland. Daughter again. Sister again. Sonja and I ran to the woods and sea. We ate salted licorice and viili and piirakka, and all the other foods that identified us as Finns.

Finland was our mother's land. Motherland. Outside of Kenya and Uganda, it was the country we had spent the most time in. We had once stayed in Finland so long that our mother had enrolled Sonja and me in school. The local newspaper did a human-interest story about the arrangement. We had been newsworthy because we had just left Uganda, a country on the verge of civil war, and because our mother was Finnish and Sonja and I were not. We were exotic creatures: foreigners.

Sonja and I were comfortable with our identity as foreigners. We were conspicuous in all the obvious ways, but we were also disregarded. Kenyan mothers didn't shout at us the way they shouted at other people's children. Without a shared language or culture, there were fewer expectations. Our strangeness was an expected quality, and we were given the benefit of the doubt. *That's just how Americans are.* I might be a particularly awkward child or I might be a typical foreigner. Even I wasn't quite sure.

That's not to say I didn't yearn to belong, first to Uganda and then to Kenya. My parents bought Sonja a t-shirt that read, "I am not a tourist. I live in Kenya." When Sonja outgrew it, I wore it proudly. Only later did I consider how that t-shirt underscored our status as outsiders. If you needed the t-shirt, well, then. Sonja and I weren't Kenyans or Ugandans. We weren't Finns, either. We were called "the Americans" by everyone except real Americans. What we were was missionaries, and now, we weren't even that.

It was August when we flew into Texas. The sun was a white disk, and the asphalt radiated heat. We stepped out of the terminal, struggling under the weight of our luggage and still wearing the light jackets we had put on that morning. Without talking, we lurched away from the automatic doors and released our bags into a pile. We hurried out of our outerwear, wiping at our foreheads, feeling the sweat gathering under our arms and spreading across our shirts. We wrapped our jackets around our waists. We squinted. Texas felt like the end of the world: hot and loud and bright. And people said Africa was hot.

My father was full of news. He had enrolled Sonja and me in the local Adventist school and signed us up to ride the school bus. The academic year had already begun, but our teachers knew we were coming late and had promised to help us catch up. Sonja would be starting seventh grade, and I would be in fourth.

My father flagged a taxi. We were anxious to see the house my father had rented, anxious to unpack our bags and start the hard work of making this place, this blistering place, feel like a home. Of course, our desire meant that no taxi would stop for hours. That was Murphy's law, and Murphy, Sonja and I knew, liked to keep a close eye on our family. Yet as soon as my father held out his hand, a taxi stopped. Here it was: a positive omen. It meant that we were going to love America, and America would love us. Sonja and I were going to make friends at school. We would live in a real neighborhood and eat ice cream and go biking on summer nights. When our family had enough money, we would buy a poodle, and Sonja and I would send a letter to the Cochran brothers, who had been infuriatingly proud of the poodle their family had brought over from the States. See our poodle, we would write, and please notice how very, very American we are.

The driver and my father tried to fit our luggage into the trunk. We had six suitcases and three carry-ons. My mother watched, a hand up to shield her eyes. She shook her head. She had hardly spoken since we had left the airport. The driver conferred with my father and then shouted to my mother not to worry. He was from India. We all nodded as if this made any sense. We watched as he put as many suitcases as he could fit into the trunk and stacked the rest in the backseat. Sonja would sit in the middle, my mother by the window, and I would sit in her lap. "See?" the driver said and laughed. It was such an American notion that everyone had to have their own seat. Lucky we weren't *really* Americans.

As Sonja struggled to keep the suitcases from teetering, my parents and the driver chattered like old friends reunited. My mother asked after the driver's family and sorted out who lived in Dallas and who still lived in New Delhi. They talked about fitting into Texas. My mother was concerned.

It was hard to imagine a state less compatible with her disposition. While Texas women were opinionated, they wore the agreed upon uniform: heels, lipstick, hair. A well-coiffed woman could be brassy and bold, a real ball breaker. Of course, she also had to be charming. She blessed your heart and meant the opposite.

My mother was incapable of blessing anyone's heart. She considered forthrightness a virtue, and if someone didn't like it—well, that was their problem. She was too old to bother, she said, though I realized later that she cared more than she let on. She was forty-four. At some point, people had stopped telling her she looked so young, like a girl. Her accent no longer delighted Americans the way it had when she was in her twenties and thirties. She wore slacks, a t-shirt, and comfortable shoes. She didn't look like a glamorous European. She looked like a missionary, and she knew it.

In Finland, she had heeded her friend's warning and spent our entire clothing budget on school clothes for Sonja and me. She had an artist's eye and was drawn to off-kilter fashions. She selected A-line dresses and terrycloth jumpers and velour tracksuits and flouncy skirts. Maybe she had forgotten how orthodox children could be, how they punished differences. More likely, she had no idea how American children dressed and just bought what she would have liked to have worn as a child.

The taxi driver dropped us off in a rundown neighborhood. Our mother walked into the house and dropped the bags she was carrying onto the shag carpet. "Oh boy," she said. Sonja and I rushed past her, determined to compensate for her disapproval. *Look, the bathroom has crystal faucets. Look, the backyard has a chain-link fence. Look, the mirrors are actually closet doors.*

"Rent is cheap," my father said.

"Well, that's something," my mother said. "Here we are, huh?"

We arrived in Texas in 1984. Hair was big, and jeans were name brand. The radio played Madonna and Prince and Michael Jackson. The cool Adventist kids knew all the lyrics, and the rest pretended they did. On Saturday nights, after the sun went down, children played putt-putt or hung out at the mall.

When they invited friends over for slumber parties, their parents served Godfather's pizza with black olives and extra cheese. Kids perched around the living room, eating pizza and watching *Raiders of the Lost Ark*. Older siblings zoomed through the house, saying "hey" to the children and telling their parents they were going bowling, but instead piling into a friend's car to go cruising. On Sabbath, the whole family attended church. They dressed nicely and styled their hair. They were Texans. They were Adventists. It was impossible to know which identity was more important. In the fall, the Cowboys played heart-rousing football, and in the spring, bluebonnets and Indian paintbrushes bloomed across the plains. God loved Texas.

Monday morning, our mother wrestled Sonja's glossy hair into two French braids. She tied them off with ribbons. There was no time for morning worship, but while Sonja and I ate breakfast, our mother let us watch the end of *Wild, Wild World of Animals*. Besides the news, it was one of two television shows my parents approved of; the other was *The People's Court*. In a couple months, Sonja and I would discover *Little House on the Prairie*, *The Cosby Show* and reruns of *Bewitched*, but for now, we were pleased with any distraction. We ate Raisin Bran and watched giraffes glide across the Serengeti plains.

Our mother walked us to the bus stop. Sonja and I each carried a Care Bear lunchbox. We had met a non-Adventist girl in the park, and she had been so friendly and so effortlessly American, chattering to us in her Texas twang, that when we had spied her lunchbox in the store, we had both wanted one. Sonja hadn't even complained that I was copying her.

We waited for the bus under a majestic American tree, maybe a maple or an oak. It was the kind of tree that would turn colors in the fall and drop its leaves. My father had bought a rake to prepare for our first autumn, and I had doggedly found a few leaves in our backyard and dragged them into a pile. This was the sort of thing Americans did. Sonja took photographs as I held the rake at a jaunty angle.

My mother looked at her watch, looked at the road, looked at her watch. If we had already missed the bus, then what? She had her own job to get to. Well, she would figure something out. She wasn't helpless. What she *was* was tired. Perhaps Texas was a particularly hard place to fit into, or perhaps she had forgotten how unwelcoming America could be. Whenever she spoke, someone would ask dismissively, "Where are *you* from?" She felt embarrassed and lonely. The school bus turned the corner and drove toward us. "Oh, thank goodness," my mother said, and when she spoke, I couldn't hear her accent. She just sounded like my mother.

The bus slowed, and I could feel something shift. America had always seemed like Disneyland, a fun and artificial place. It was loud and bright and sweet, and I was always relieved to return to the authenticity of home. The school bus was yellow, just like in the movies, and like in the movies, children gazed out the windows. Soon, Sonja and I would join them. We would be inside, looking out. More than our passports, attending school would stamp us as citizens of this place. Whether I liked it or not, I was home. The bus squeaked to a stop. The doors opened, and I followed Sonja up the stairs.

"Sonja and Sari," our mother said. "Look at me." She rummaged around in her bag, emerging with a camera. "Smile."

Mortified, I stuck out my tongue.

The Adventist school offered kindergarten through twelfth grade. Students studied in one sprawling building. Outside was a playground, a baseball field, and a gymnasium. School buses lined up at the chain-link fence, and kids shouted greetings to each other. Though there were fewer than two hundred students in the school, it felt immense and official. School with a capital S.

The secretary walked me to my classroom. The hall smelled of floor wax. "The third and fourth grade classes are together right now," the secretary said, "but if we ever find another teacher, you'll have your own class. It will be smaller, and I think that will be even nicer." She pointed to an open door. "And here we are."

The room was large, with windows along the far wall. Students stood in groups talking; others rummaged in their backpacks. A girl with purple hairclips set her lunchbox in the back cubby, and for no observable reason, a boy ran loops around the rows of desks.

I wanted to turn around and walk away, but even if I could find my way back to our rental house, no one would be there. My father was in class, and my mother was at another school, working as a teacher's aide. She had applied to teach here, to be the fourth grade teacher, in fact, but the principal said her master's degree made her "overly qualified" for the position. At home, my mother sniffed. "Such malarkey. Americans think that if you have an accent, you must be stupid. Now I get to empty wastebaskets and pull gum off the rug. At least I'm not *overly qualified* for that."

"Okeydokey," my new teacher said. "Time to get started, class." He was an older man with a narrow face and heavy eyebrows. He wore a brown suit and sat on the edge of his desk. "Hey, everyone. We're beginning class. Y'all need to sit down now. Did you hear me, Todd?"

A pretty girl looked up and noticed me standing by the door. She gestured toward the desk beside hers. Could she actually mean me? Were we going to be friends? I walked over, hesitant. "Hey," she said, her smile wide. I sat in the desk beside her and slid my feet around. On the far side of the room, another girl waved.

"Looks like you're going to be fine," the secretary said and patted my back. "Good luck."

"Okay, gang," the teacher said. "We have a new student. Her name is 'Sorry,' and she just moved here from Africa. I'm sure she has exciting stories to tell about the mission field and how God has worked through the lives of her and her family. Let's all say welcome."

"Welcome," my classmates said, a chorus of reluctance. I stared at my hands. My nails were short and ragged, and the cuticle on my thumb was bleeding. I wrapped the bottom of my t-shirt around and around it.

During handwriting, the girl beside me whispered, "Hey, Sorry. Are you bored yet?"

"No," I whispered back. As soon as I spoke, I hated myself. The right answer was clearly yes. "My name's not really Sorry," I said. "It's Sari, rhymes with Mary." Before we had moved to the States, my mother had coached me on being proactive about the pronunciation of my name. The rhyme was the key. *I don't want people calling my child Sorry. We weren't sorry you were born.*

"Oh, that's cool. My name's Priscilla, doesn't rhyme with anything," the girl said.

I smiled, hoping we would be best friends, hoping it would be this easy.

Throughout the morning, Priscilla helped me find the books I needed for each class period. The work wasn't difficult. The work was beside the point. I had a friend, and I hadn't even punched anyone. At recess, Priscilla and her friends Becca and Jennifer told me about the boys and warned me about specific ones who might look cute, but were actually horrid. As we sat on the monkey bars, the boys ran past in a laughing, shouting, hitting herd, and I was grateful to be a girl.

We fourth graders were the oldest kids on the playground, and when my new friends walked over to the swings, they told the first graders to "get lost." I had never been on this side of the age divide, and it felt wonderful. I sat on one of the relinquished swings, the chains warm in my hands. I pumped my legs back and forth, back and forth, tipped my chin upward. The sky was bright. Texas was beautiful. I flew so high that the chains jerked. I allowed the swing to slow and when the arc was right, I leaped off. Becca jumped after me. "I think Jeremy's really cute," she whispered in my ear. "Don't tell Priscilla."

During the last recess of the day, Priscilla said she had something important to show me. She called for Jennifer and Becca, and they obediently followed. The girls led me into the school and down the hall. They stopped outside a bathroom. "I dare you to go in, lock the door, and say 'Bloody Mary' three times," Priscilla said. The way she asked and the way the other girls kept glancing at each other, I knew they expected me to refuse. But why? It was so easy.

When we visited Nairobi, older missionary children had sometimes paid me to kiss one of the large slugs that emerged after a storm. I would give the slug a peck and the kids would scream and then turn over their shillings. I knew they were laughing at me, but I didn't care. I could do something that they couldn't, and that was a type of power.

"I can do that," I told Priscilla, feeling a familiar surge of capability. "That's *easy.*"

"You have to turn out the lights," Jennifer said after I had stepped into the bathroom. "And you have to turn around while you're saying it."

"Okay," I said. I locked the door and switched off the light. As I turned, my sneakers squeaked on the cement floor. "Bloody Mary, Bloody Mary, Bloody Mary."

When I opened the door, the girls were alert and fidgety.

"Did you see the ghost?" Priscilla asked.

"Huh?" I said. We were all Adventists, and Adventists didn't believe in ghosts. *The living know that they will die, but the dead know not anything.* That's in Ecclesiastes. But even I knew you couldn't go around quoting Ecclesiastes to your fourth grade classmates. Adventist school or no Adventist school. "I didn't see anything," I said.

"There must have been a ghost," Jennifer said. "Maybe it was behind you and you just didn't see it. Maybe you didn't see it 'cause the lights were out."

The girls nodded.

"Last year, the teacher's wife committed suicide in that bathroom stall," Priscilla said. "She cut her wrists and bled everywhere. There was blood *everywhere.* She was there for hours before they found her dead." Priscilla's voice hit the word 'dead' hard, and I felt it almost as a slap. "My sister says that if you lock yourself in here and say 'Bloody Mary,' her ghost will show up."

The girls nodded.

My hands and face felt clammy. I leaned against the hallway wall and hoped I wouldn't throw up. In Uganda, the whole country was haunted with the disappeared. Anytime our parents were late, Sonja would just know that they had died. But how could I say this? I didn't even think it. I was struck instead by the new and dreadful knowledge that someone could willingly do violence to themselves. I had never before heard of suicide. I looked at the girls, who were giggling, and though I didn't believe the bit about ghosts, I was certain the story about our teacher's wife was true. My mother would later confirm it. "It didn't happen at your school," she said. "It happened at church. But it doesn't matter. Just be extra nice to your teacher, okay?"

"I didn't see anything," I said. The girls laughed and ran back to the classroom, and I knew somehow that I wasn't invited.

On the bus ride home, Sonja and I sat apart. I looked out the window. Texas was ugly, ugly, ugly. I squinted my eyes and replaced the billboards and strip malls with a big, open sky. I extended the straggly grass all the way to the horizon. Telephone poles and cars became termite mounds and acacia trees. Maybe a secretary bird was stepping through the brush. I imagined we were riding again in our old Ford station wagon, and my father had just told Sonja and me to stop singing about cars bursting into flames. It was a familiar joke, both the request and the song. We were easy in each other's company. My mother sat in the front seat, handing back dried bananas. She analyzed some campus gossip while Sonja and I searched the horizon for vultures, a sign that somewhere ahead there were lions.

"Hey, monkey," a boy said, leaning over the back of my seat. "Did you live in a tree? I heard you did. I heard you lived in a *jungle* tree."

Our parents weren't home when we got off the bus. Sonja had a key, and she unlocked the door. We watched Judge Wapner dispense justice and shared a box of grape and strawberry Nerds, the irony completely lost on us. Once *The People's Court* was over, we turned off the television, as our parents had instructed. Only later would Sonja discover that obedience was optional, and what our parents didn't know wouldn't hurt them. It was still too hot to go outside, and the backyard was mostly dirt. We bumped around the house, restless and bored.

When our mother later asked how our days had gone, I chattered about Priscilla and Jennifer and the playground and what subjects I liked (reading and social studies) and which ones I didn't (handwriting and spelling). I asked my mother about the suicide but said nothing about how my classmates' interest in me had soured. When I finished talking, Sonja said her day was fine and her classes were easy. "It's just fine, Mom," she said, when our mother pressed for more details.

For now, we were each holding our secrets.

It would be years before Sonja would talk about her first day.

While I had followed the secretary to my class, Sonja had stood in the school office alone. She watched students walk or dash past and felt exhilarated. Sure, she was nervous about the day before her, but she was also optimistic. She had a particular habit of liking wherever she currently lived. Why yearn for the past? The past was the past, and change might be a good thing. It might be a wonderful thing. School might be great. She might finally delve into the complexities of math, a subject she particularly enjoyed, and she might get a boyfriend. She wouldn't just be reading romances; she would be living them.

"Your sister's going to be fine," the secretary said when she returned. "She's already making little friends."

"That's good," Sonja said, one adult to another. She declined the secretary's offer to walk her to her classroom. After getting directions, she picked up her lunch pail and set off down the hall, her flats clack-clack-clacking on the floor. She used her free hand to retuck her blouse and then to straighten the suspenders on her flouncy skirt. She was wearing an outfit our mother had bought in Finland, an outfit too sweet to wear without irony. Sonja looked as if she had stepped off a Swiss Miss box.

Class had already started when Sonja opened the door, and the teacher was taking attendance. He fell silent when he saw her and everyone turned and stared. She stood in the doorframe for just a moment, but it was enough time for her to have an epiphany: Everything about her and her Care Bear lunch pail was terribly, terribly wrong.

Sonja's seventh grade classmates looked at least twenty-five. The girls had woken early to tease and spray their hair. They had lined their eyes with blue or green pencils, curled and painted their lashes, applied foundation and blush, and at some point before class, they had taken compacts out of their purses and dabbed at their noses. This was the first year most of their parents had allowed them to wear makeup, and the girls were certain that more was more. The boys ranged in height, though Sonja would remember them all as tall. One boy had the beginnings of a mustache. Another boy's hair curled into a mullet. Boys fidgeted in their jean jackets, their legs draped across the aisle. *We are Texas men,* their posture said. *Who are you? And what do you want?*

Sonja ducked toward the closest empty desk. She murmured answers to the teacher's questions and said nothing further. She was so silent that as the day progressed, her classmates began to believe she was mute. They would ask her questions (*Can you talk? Do you understand English? Are you retarded? Do you think Steve is cute?*) and she would look away. During Texas history, her teacher forced her to read aloud from the textbook, and when she rhymed *Waco* with *taco,* she could hear the whispers: "What did she say? What did she say? Maybe she *is* retarded." She ate lunch in a bathroom stall.

That night, Sonja begged God to send her just one friend.

We were like a family of polar bears plodding across the savannah. We didn't belong. We didn't belong in Texas.

But if there was one thing my parents knew how to do, it was to persevere. We would not be one of those missionary families who hustled back to the mission field, unable to hack it in the States. We could hack it just fine, thank you. Besides, Sonja had braces now, and it looked as if I would need them, too.

My father attended classes, wrote papers, and drove us to our appointments. My mother applied for U.S. citizenship, worked as a teacher's aide, and clipped coupons. We lived together, but carried our problems separately. Our parents worried about money, while Sonja and I worried about making friends. We believed that if we just wore the right brands—Guess jeans, Keds sneakers, Swatch watches—we might fit in. But how could we tell our parents? They dragged us to Kroger's on double coupon days, and we spent what felt like hours on the world's most boring scavenger hunts. We couldn't add to their difficulties, and so we hid our own. Sonja and I became secretive about school, even with each other.

Each time I started to fit in, things somehow went sideways. For show-and-tell, I took Maasai gourds and a python skin. My father had said the boys would be impressed, and they were. At lunch, they sat at my table smelling the gourds and gagging dramatically, and then smelling them again. My stories about mambas and cobras were met with genuine fascination. Priscilla watched from her table, and I—devoid of pride—smiled back, *Let's be friends!* But even this wasn't my error. While regaling the boys with stories, I decided to detour into the culinary world of Finland, describing my enthusiasm for lingonberries. "Dingleberries," shrieked the boys. "Dingleberry Sari." I began to live in the pages of books.

For Sonja, it was even worse. That first year, she spun herself into a cocoon. She grew quieter and quieter. At church, she looked so thoughtful and serious that parents of young children plopped their restless toddlers into her arms. Without even trying, she lined up babysitting jobs. She spent her money on candy, which she shared with me, and, more covertly, on the accouterments of girlhood.

When eighth grade arrived, Sonja emerged as an American teenager. Our mother had permed her hair, and she had told our parents that she was too old for the Care Bear lunch pail. For once, our parents didn't say, *"If all the kids jumped off a cliff, would you?"*

On the first day of school, Sonja locked herself into the bathroom and painted her eyelids blue and teased her hair. Our parents had left before we woke up; my father had to drive my mother to her job and then get to his own morning classes. "Mom's not going to like it," I said.

"I don't care," Sonja told me, "and you'd better not be a tattletale."

Sonja carried a purse to school. She said "cool" and "chill out." She made friends and spent hours talking on the phone, the long cord disappearing under her bedroom door. On Saturday nights, she went cruising, telling our parents she was going bowling or helping a friend write a paper. While no one in her class would forget that she had once pronounced *Waco* like *taco*, she could laugh and laugh. She could pretend it didn't matter.

CHAPTER 22

———— ❧ ————

She Couldn't Keep a Secret

WHEN I WAS fifteen, I flew with my mother to Finland. The Fordham family was settled. Americans. American*ish*. We were living in Atlanta, my mother's final home. To pay the bills, my father had left his Ph.D. program, the first time he had quit anything, and was now the pastor of two small churches. My mother had a real teaching job. She had gotten her U.S. citizenship and, more astonishingly, her driver's license. She drove to school on the winding roads of Georgia, and if she wanted buttermilk or peaches, she just took herself to Safeway.

We had two poodles, an abundance I couldn't have imagined as a child. Of course, as a teen, I found them, like everything else, deeply embarrassing. What must my classmates think? I attended a small Adventist high school, where I sang in the choir, worked on the yearbook, and played varsity basketball. Despite my involvement, I still didn't fit in. And so I carried novels in my backpack, which I read during class or when friends didn't save a seat for me in the cafeteria. I was too embarrassed to ask why or what I had done. I just turned on my heels and took my book to the abandoned playground equipment.

I read at home, too. I read so much that my mother would toss up her hands when she saw me. I was the kind of teen who wrote letters to all her grandparents, who walked the dogs with her mother, who tamed the backyard squirrels, who watched figure skating on TV, who cross-stitched gifts for relatives, and who still thought it was her parents who were embarrassing. My father shouted "jambo" when he picked me up at school, and when friends visited, my mother fed them weird Finnish foods and asked what their mothers cooked. "Oh, your mother doesn't bake much?" she would say, visibly pleased. "Let me get you some more piirakka." I would kick her under the table. "Why are you kicking me?" she would say. "Oh, am I embarrassing you?"

Sonja was the kind of teen who was never embarrassed by our parents. When she had friends over, she asked our mother to cook weird Finnish food. She laughed when our mother interrogated her friends about their dietary habits. Laughter was her secret. She laughed so much that she was known at school as an airhead, a title she cultivated. Sonja excelled academically, effortlessly getting the As I studied so hard for. She attended church functions cheerfully—well, cheerfully enough—and she washed dishes without being asked. She was the kind of teen every parent wishes for.

But in our family, Sonja was the kind of teen who got sent to boarding school. Our mother thought Sonja wore too much makeup, wasted too many hours fixing her hair, and was probably up to no good. Why else did she shut the door every time she talked on the phone? Why did she get so angry when our mother investigated? Sonja was trying to hide something, that's what. Sonja was entirely too anxious to fit in with these fast American girls.

When our mother read her diary, Sonja didn't laugh. She shouted and cried and slammed her bedroom door. None of her friends had to deal with this baloney, so why did she? Why did our mother ask so many personal questions? Why didn't she trust her? Why couldn't anyone in this family respect her privacy? The two argued more and more. Finally, Sonja asked to attend a nearby Adventist boarding academy, and our mother didn't say no. Their relationship improved immediately.

When Sonja came home on weekends, the whole family brightened. My mother baked cinnamon rolls, and my father made what he called his "world famous" enchiladas. On Sabbath afternoons, we hiked in the Georgia woods. Conversations would, inevitably, turn to Uganda or Kenya. *Remember this. Remember that.* Sonja and I would listen. It had only been a handful of years since we had left East Africa, but it felt so long ago. Who were we then? Who were we now?

The summer Sonja turned seventeen, our mother took her to Finland. It was the first time any of us had been there since we had moved to the States. Finland was as familiar as a fairytale, and felt as unlikely. When my mother and sister returned, I pored over their photos. To see them swimming in the Baltic or rowing on a lake was a promise that those experiences still existed. But the pictures I kept returning to were less about Finland and more about them. They were dressed breezily and standing on a mossy rock. In the first picture, they were side by side—smiling, relaxed, happy. In the next, my mother, with exaggerated effort, was holding a piece of driftwood high above her head, while Sonja crouched beneath, both her hands raised and an expression of mock alarm on her face. My cool sister and my square mother were fully committed to being silly. They were, I realized, approaching something like friendship.

"She's just so companionable," my mother said when they returned. "It's sure nice to have such smart and interesting daughters."

Now it was my turn to visit Finland.

My mother and I filled our suitcases with gifts—hypercolored t-shirts, Levi jeans, and Take 6 cassettes. Everything had been on sale. Fifty percent off fifty percent. Our tickets had also been purchased at a discount. The Fordham family prided themselves on thrift.

At the boarding gate, my mother and I sat in comfortable silence, alert to the drama of the airport. The flight from Cairo was about to board, and the flight from Panama City had been delayed. An urgent voice rattled off a family of names, requesting that the passengers please report to a distant gate. Wheels rolled on the terminal floor. Grandmothers hugged grandchildren and cried. Flight attendants walked past in crisp groups. It felt as if the radio was playing a song I hadn't heard in years, but whose words I had always known.

And then the tune changed to electric guitar and percussion. There, beside the airline counter, was another teen. An extraordinary teen. His mouth was humorous, his eyes blue. He was, perhaps, the most attractive boy I had ever seen. He looked toward me, and I looked away.

I had just finished my sophomore year of high school and had never gone on a date. I nurtured crushes on the good boys, the ones who competed with me for grades and who didn't drink or smoke or cause problems for the teachers. They, in turn, had crushes on the girls who got suspended for impertinence. One of these girls was my neighbor, and outside of school, we were friends, and she would speak to me for hours about her love life, never imagining that I, too, might harbor romantic aspirations. Only my mother seemed to know. One Sabbath afternoon, she joined Sonja and me in the living room and told us that if we ever got pregnant, we could come to her for support. She spoke with such earnestness that Sonja and I looked at each other and began to laugh. We laughed until we were weeping. "You're such smart alecks," she said and walked out.

The boy at our terminal appeared to be traveling alone. His backpack rested at his feet, and he leaned his shoulder against the large glass window. Occasionally, he checked his watch, but mostly he looked out toward the runway, flicking his hand through the blond hair falling into his face. He appeared intelligent. And funny. Maybe he played basketball. I imagined meeting him and discovering that we both liked Boyz II Men, geology, and building puzzles.

Our plane boarded, and my mother and I found our seats. The one beside me was empty, and my hazy daydream began to sharpen. The teen would sit here, and somewhere over the Atlantic, as we flew below the stars, he would discover that I was quirky and smart. Perhaps he would even think I was beautiful. Of course, such a thing would never occur in the history of the world, but wouldn't it be something? My mother flipped through the inflight magazine, and I watched for the teen, and still I was astonished when I saw him slouching down the aisle, his sunglasses holding back his hair.

He stopped at our row (could it be?), looked down at me, and said in accented English, "I think this is me."

He was a Swedish exchange student and was even more striking up close. He looked as if he should star in one of those teen movies where the exchange student falls in love with the nerdy American. If only my mother wasn't sitting beside us. She leaned over and introduced herself, and he shook her hand and said his name was Erik or Lucus. I was too dazzled to hear. I just knew it was something cool and effortless and Swedish. She said, "Nice to meet you," and then she settled herself into her seat and closed her eyes. We began to talk. He was a year ahead of me in school and had been staying with his host family in the suburb of Fayetteville. He thought Atlanta was kickass.

"Yeah, Atlanta's pretty cool," I said.

He was bummed about returning to Sweden but was taking it philosophically. I asked about school, and he said English was his favorite subject. "Do you like to read?" he said. I felt as if I had slipped into an alternate universe where everything I wanted was possible. I showed him the novels I had brought with me. "Oh, you're one of those smart girls, huh? That's rad. I like smart girls."

Is this flirting? I wondered.

When the flight attendant took our drink orders, the exchange student asked for a beer. I waited for the attendant to ask for his ID, but she just handed him the can and a cup. He smiled and when he did, his eyes crinkled at the corners. I decided that I could overlook his drinking problem.

I imagined my mother would ruin everything, though. She would tell him he was too young to drink alcohol—she would call it "alcohol," too—and then she would ask whether his parents knew he drank. But my mother either didn't hear or didn't care. She ordered an orange juice and flipped through the inflight magazine and sipped it. When the lights were dimmed for a movie, she closed her eyes.

The exchange student and I unfolded our thin airplane blankets and tucked them around our bodies. We talked about how cold planes were, and we smiled at each other. Now would be the perfect moment for him to reach over and take my hand. Nothing in our conversation had suggested this could happen, but nothing had suggested it couldn't. I was flying to Finland, and anything was possible.

"Let's hope this doesn't totally suck," he said.

"Totally," I said.

During the movie, he looked over during funny parts and we shared a smile. My face flushed as his knee bumped mine. "Sorry," he said, and it didn't happen again. When the movie finished, he yawned. He said he hated sleeping on planes. He adjusted the pillow behind his neck and tilted his head toward the aisle, away from me. I shut my eyes and the word *idiot* scrolled across my brain. Romance was never going to happen. I was too skinny, too awkward, too shy, too weird. What was wrong with me?

When I woke, my mouth was sour. My head was angled toward my mother's shoulder. Both she and the boy were asleep. I wrestled my backpack out from under the seat and climbed over my mother's lap. In the tiny bathroom, I changed into a favorite shirt and tussled my hair. I was experimenting with a wavy bob. I brushed my teeth, washed my face, and applied brown lipstick. I looked as presentable as the circumstances allowed.

My mother's face brightened when she saw me. Carl or Otto (what was his name?) still hadn't woken. "Oh, good. You're here," she said. She rummaged in her bag, emerging with a fake pearl necklace and matching clip on earrings. The pieces were large and tacky. An Adventist joke. She put them on and then peered into my compact, tilting her head this way and that. She asked to borrow my lipstick and applied a thick coat.

"What do you think?" she asked. She took off her glasses.

"Maybe blot your lips a bit," I said.

"The lips are exactly the point," she said.

By the time the Swedish exchange student had woken up, I had already decided that the electrical possibility between us had existed only in my mind. *I don't care,* I thought. *He had a drinking problem, anyway.* I set my lips and refused to indulge my disappointment. Sometime before exiting the plane, though, his eyes met mine. They were studying me the way Gilbert studied

Anne at the end of the movie version of *Anne of Green Gables*. We owned the miniseries, and on Saturday nights, I watched as the Nova Scotia winds blew Anne's hair, and I watched Gilbert reach out and touch her check. Here was my moment. We could, at least, exchange addresses. He looked so serious and swoony and available. But what exactly was I supposed to say?

I panicked. I lunged for the bag under the seat in front of me, nearly knocking my head against the tray table—*idiot, idiot, idiot*—and took out my novels and then returned them and then turned to my mother to ask a question. When I finally glanced back at him, he was wearing headphones.

As my mother and I exited the plane, I tried not to hate myself. He lived in Sweden. What did I think was going to happen? My mother bounced beside me. She had a child's capacity for sheer joy, unfiltered by irony or self-protection. It had been three years since she had last been in Finland. She was the point. This was our trip. I reached for her heavy carry-on and told her that her earrings looked outrageous.

At baggage claim, my mother and aunt clutched each other and laughed. They laughed so long and so hard that they ran out of air, their hands pinching into their sides. "Oh boy, oh boy, oh boy," my mother said. "Don't I look fancy?" Then she launched into a torrent of Finnish, words held captive in her mouth.

They say Finland has two seasons: winter and August. We came in June. The sky was grey and spitting rain. I read books, ate halvah and Finnish chocolate, and traded good-natured insults with my cousins.

We spent a week at my aunt and uncle's summer cottage. Each day, my uncle heated the sauna. It took hours to get hot enough. All afternoon, we could step out into the wet grass and walk under the wet birch and smell wood burning, a dry scent amidst all that water. The sauna was small, and we used it in turns, first men and then women, and though we were separated by gender, my cousin Riikka and I had no intention of going nude, and we protested when our mothers suggested it, and when they shrugged and entered the sauna in only their skin, we looked away, embarrassed.

The four of us—two prudish teens, two naked mothers—sat on the highest bench. We leaned against the wall and talked. Mostly our mothers talked, speaking in English out of courtesy to me. They traded affectionate complaints about family members who weren't there and gossiped about people I didn't know.

Have you heard that So-and-So is doing such and such?

What? No! I can't believe it!

My mother and aunt liked the sauna mild, and as they talked, they allowed the logs to burn low in the stove. When it was time to go swimming, Riikka began throwing water on the rocks, trying to create enough heat to chase us to the lake. My mother was first out the door. I followed. She walked cautiously down the wooden walkway, and when I ran past her, she called out "careful, careful." Her voice—"Don't slip and hit your head"—followed me across the dock as I sprinted toward the water and dived into the lake.

When I surfaced, she was easing down the stone steps. She walked until the water reached her hips. She didn't have far to walk. And there she stood, palms against a tabletop of water. She stood, bending and straightening her knees. It looked as if the lake was yanking her nude body down and then pushing it back up. She was still acclimatizing like this when my aunt arrived and marched robustly down the steps. As she swam past my mother, she said something in Finnish, and they both laughed. The sky was finally darkening. We weren't far enough north to see the midnight sun, but the days stretched on and on, and the summer nights whisked past like an express train.

My mother had been a child here. Not generally here, but specifically *here*, at this lake. The cottage sat beside the Adventist Youth Camp. She had walked past these birch trees or ones like them, and she had sat with her friend on the large rock beside the lake. They had chattered about boys or books or faith, or something else altogether, and then they had posed for a photograph that I now have tucked into my drawer. It is black and white, and my mother is smiling at the camera. Forever here.

My adult mother, usually awash in sentimentality, didn't seem particularly nostalgic about being back beside the Adventist Youth Camp. In Finland, it was normal to return to the lakes of your girlhood, for your many selves to walk past the same trees, to swim in the same water, to sit in the same saunas. Returning wasn't extraordinary. It was leaving that had marked her.

Accustomed to the water's temperature, my mother finally pushed away from the floor of the lake and began to swim. She swam breaststroke, her head and shoulders high above the water. She circled the dock twice, returned to the steps, and rose out of the lake like a cat.

On our last full day in Finland, the skies cleared and the sun shone. We were back in Turku, and my mother and I were alone in the house, everyone else at work or school. I sprawled across my aunt's couch with a book and a generous slice of halvah. I had fallen deeply into a novel and was reading to find out whether the protagonist would emerge intact.

My mother walked in, carrying her shoes and smiling in such a kind and hopeful way that I knew my afternoon was ruined. She was going to invite me for a walk, and because I also knew I would eventually say yes, I felt particularly irritated. *Fine. Fine. I would walk fast.* But it was worse than I expected. She wanted us to take the bus into town.

"I'm just feeling lazy today," I said. "Go on without me."

"You'll feel different once we're there." She smiled that sympathetic smile again. "Come on. We'll have fun."

"I just really want to finish this book."

She stopped smiling. "You've been reading this whole trip. You can read anywhere. You won't be in Finland again *for years*."

"I know that."

"Of course you do. You know everything. I always forget how very much you know."

"Fine." I set down my book. "Are you happy?"

"Yes," she said.

I found my shoes and purse, complaining as I moved through the house. We walked to the bus stop. My mother led the way, humming, as I dragged far enough behind that she would know I was annoyed, but not so far that she would stop tolerating me.

She could veer abruptly from peeved to ferocious, and when she was angry, it was as if she was angry at the world. And maybe she was. She had once been her mother's cherished child, the smarty-pants daughter who spoke five languages and showed so much academic promise that she had been allowed to hide away and read when she should have been helping with the chores. After she got married, she had learned how to put meals on the table, and when she had children, she had learned how to put herself third and then fourth, and in the process, she had become someone who was rarely taken seriously. She was an English teacher with an accent. For years, she had lost teaching jobs to less qualified candidates. She finally had her driver's license, but she hated driving and stayed on the routes she knew. She joked that if she ever left my father, she would only get as far away as her school or the grocery store. Worst of all, she had the temerity to get older (she was fifty) and *look* older. She wore glasses and comfortable shoes. She dyed her hair, her one concession to vanity. Occasionally, strangers would ask if she was my grandmother. Oh, how she laughed then, her unhappy laugh.

When she was especially furious, she would tell me, "You're just like me." It was the coup de grâce. I was quiet at school, but we both knew that I had a high regard for my own intelligence. She wanted me to know that I shouldn't sit on my high horse and look down at her. Maybe she was also warning me.

At the center of town, we got off the bus. It was a glorious day. It seemed as if everyone in Turku was out. In the park, families lounged beside the river. Parents ate ice cream, children ran shrieking across the grass, and a woman biked down the sidewalk, her hair blazing behind her. So much joy. Even my teenaged peevishness couldn't withstand such an assault of happiness, and though I wouldn't have admitted it, I was glad to be here and not back at the house, cooped up—as my mother liked to say—and reading.

We entered one shop after another. My mother plunged into racks of clothing in the back, while I circled the stores, admiring the blouses and dresses. "Let's get you something dressy," my mother said. I stopped and looked at her. Clothes in Finland were expensive, and our plane tickets were already more than we could afford.

My mother smiled at me, a conspirator, and I smiled back.

I carried a rayon blouse to the changing room. It had structured shoulders and a Peter Pan collar, and it looked as if it belonged to a *woman*. My mother knocked on the door and asked me to turn for her. "Straighten your shoulders," she said. It was no use. I was a ruler, sharp and flat.

We moved on, from piece to piece, from shop to shop. My thoughts returned to the book I had been reading and to the half-eaten block of halvah that I had returned to the fridge. It felt churlish to suggest we go. My mother was trying so hard. She held up a greenish-brown jacket, with a boxy cut and copper buttons. It looked like a military jacket, like something from the Soviet Union. "Ha ha," I said, continuing to shift through a rack of pretty dresses.

"No. I think this is a very special jacket. Not everyone can wear it, but I think you can pull it off." She held it out to me. "It suits your coloring."

To humor her, I slipped on the jacket. I buttoned the front. I looked in the store mirror. My bobbed hair was tucked behind my ears, and my jeans were worn at the knees. With this green-brown jacket, though, I looked like someone else. I came closer and smiled at my reflection. This was how I decided things: How did I look while smiling? My braces flashed, but I didn't notice them. I was too taken with the jacket, too taken with myself. I looked sophisticated and—was it possible?—a little edgy. Maybe even dangerous. A girl in this jacket could do anything. She could ask an exchange student for his address, and he would want to give it to her. I imagined wearing the jacket to school. I imagined the compliments and my breezy response: "Oh, this? I got it in Finland."

My mother came up behind me, adjusting the shoulders. "Wow. You look like a model," she said. "I think we should get it. What do you think?"

I turned the tag over in my hand. The jacket was more expensive than anything I owned.

"Well," my mother said when she saw the price and that it wasn't on sale. I could tell that she was calculating the cost in dollars, dividing the price tag by four. I knew then that she wanted it as much as I did. "You're not in Finland every day. If you really like it, we get it."

I turned around slowly. "It's so expensive," I said. "Too expensive."

"Nonsense," my mother said.

I walked with my mother through an outdoor market. The women wore colorful handkerchiefs that held back their hair. They sold raspberries, strawberries, bilberries, and black currants. They sold chanterelle mushrooms and potatoes dug up that day from the ground. My aunt's pantry was full, and so we walked, enjoying the sun on our faces and the spectacle of so many berries. In my hand, I carried a paper bag, and in the bag, the jacket crinkled. My mother stopped at the last booth and bought a packet of peas, which we ate as we strolled to the bus stop, two ladies of leisure.

On the bus, my mother began to riffle through her purse. She smoothed the bills she found and placed them in her wallet, and still she searched. She opened her purse wider and ran her hand across the bottom, scooping up coins. "I had five hundred markka," she told me. "I broke my thousand in the shop, and I know they gave me back a five hundred markka bill. I just stuffed it all in my purse. Did you see anything fall?" I shook my head. She kept searching, now dumping out the contents of her purse and returning the items one by one. "I'm so asinine." She sorted through everything again. The jacket was already too expensive, and now this.

As a child, I viewed prayer as a panacea for my troubles. God was like a kindly uncle, more tangible than most of my relatives. When our life worked out, as it generally did, it wasn't just luck; it was divine providence. And when things didn't work out, it was also an answer. Maybe God was saying no, or maybe we didn't have enough faith. As a child, I had secretly prayed that Jesus would sew up a rip in my beloved teddy bear. My Finnish grandmother had given it to me before she died. I worked hard at my faith so that God could do his work, never considering how my grandmother once prayed for her own more substantial miracle.

As a teen, my beliefs about prayer shifted. I had come to believe that prayer changed me, not the world around me. At night, I piously asked God to improve my character, to make me kinder and more helpful. But in moments of panic, my theology dropped away, and I treated God like the invisible uncle he had always been, waiting, specifically, at my elbow. "Please, dear Jesus, help me find my keys," I prayed as I looked under papers and between couch cushions. "Please. Just this once."

The lost money was more serious than misplaced keys, but I didn't consider prayer as a solution. My lost keys were always going to be found; it was a question of time. Unless we planned to retrace our steps, the money was certainly gone.

"I must have dropped it in the market," my mother said. "I could just kick myself for being so careless. Listen, don't tell your father. Okay?"

"Of course," I said.

When we arrived at my aunt's house, I retrieved my book, while my mother hurried into the room where we were sleeping. I could hear her shifting through her things and probably mine. I knew that she was hoping that she had misremembered the encounter at the store and had left the one thousand markka bill here. She came out of the room, disgusted.

"Did you find it?" I said, setting my book on the arm of the couch.

"Never mind, never mind," she said. "It's only money. Maybe whoever found it really needed it."

I nodded and returned to my book.

That night, my father called. I talked with him first, telling him about our trip to town and the jacket my mother had bought me, omitting any mention of money. I handed the phone to my mother, and she took the receiver hungrily. "Oh, Gary," she said. "You'll never guess what I did today. I lost five hundred markka."

My mother couldn't keep a secret. It was the most reliable part of her temperament. She liked to go to bed early and sleep in late. She placed tremendous importance on food, and when I returned from a friend's house, she would quiz me with exasperating thoroughness about what I had eaten for each meal. She was fascinated by weather. If the forecast was on TV, everyone would be wise to shut up. She was a woman comfortable with the words *shut up*; she was comfortable, in general, with directness.

She told stories to everyone, and they told stories to her. We were amazed at what strangers would tell her. When her daughters didn't reciprocate the way others did, she had no qualms about snooping. Why should we have secrets? Why should she?

We teased her sometimes about her inability to keep news to herself, and at other times, we complained bitterly. "You can't keep *anything* a secret," we told her again and again. Yet that last year, she showed a strange skill at hiding her growing fear, her certain panic.

CHAPTER 23

—◦◦◦—

You Better Come Home

SONJA AND I were in our twenties when our mother felt a lump in her breast and started monitoring it. She continued her days as before—teaching Latin at an area high school, fixing dinner, reading the paper, watching the weather forecast, attending church, writing her daughters—but in sudden moments, she must have felt the pull of panic and turned over her options: Go to a real doctor, find a homeopathic practitioner, check herself into a Lifestyle Center. *And then? And then?* She couldn't imagine doing any of these things and not being found out. Late in her life, she had discovered secrecy.

One afternoon, my mother sat down to write her sister. Her small desk, which had once been my small desk, overlooked our backyard woods. She had wanted this house because the thicket of Georgia pines reminded her of the jungle in Uganda. How was that for irony? Except, of course, it wasn't ironic at all. Even on the hardest, most isolated days, my mother had loved the house on the hill. It was on that verandah—such a verandah—that she had cultivated her habit of correspondence. In the years since, her wry observations and humor had only sharpened. And so, she wrote.

My aunt already knew the basics of Fordham family life—my mother was teaching, my father was pastoring, Sonja taught in South Korea, and I had begun graduate school in Iowa. My mother filled in the particulars: Sonja had taken up hiking and was the first up every mountain, I had just been to the Iowa State Fair and had written about butter cows, and in Georgia, a church member had stopped taking his bipolar medication and was once again causing havoc. Periodically, my mother paused to watch squirrels eat from the bird feeder. Near the end of her letter, she wrote that she had felt a lump in her breast and wasn't sure what to do.

My aunt was traveling when the letter arrived in Finland. It sat on her table with the accumulating mail until she finally came home and fished it out of the stack. She read through the customary Fordham news—*Joo, joo, joo. Everyone was busy with something.* At the end of the letter, she stopped short. She checked the date. My mother had mailed the letter weeks earlier. My aunt calculated the time difference, and once she was certain my mother was awake, she telephoned. After brief chitchat, she told my mother to see a doctor immediately.

"False alarm," my mother said and wouldn't speak of it further.

My aunt imagined my parents learning the mass was benign. Maybe to celebrate, they stopped for Thai food. My aunt knew she ought to be relieved, but she couldn't shake her unease. My mother turned everything into a story. It was strange that she had nothing more to say about this, the embodiment of all her fears, and that she was so dismissive of my aunt's questions. My aunt considered asking my father for more details, but she pushed away her concerns.

"You don't get something small when you already have something big," my mother told me at Christmas. I was home for vacation, and everyone had the flu except her. She made us soup and rotated the electric heating pad from person to person.

I looked up at my mother and knew what she meant by "something big." For as long as I could remember, she had had a premonition that, like my grandmother, she would get cancer and die relatively young. It was a topic I had no interest in. It wasn't so much her fears about cancer that annoyed me; it was her obsessive distrust of oncology. My grandmother had received radiation, and though I knew it had been horrific, I believed that cancer treatments had since improved. My mother did not. "The cure is worse than the disease," she said. "The Hippocratic oath says, 'First, do no harm.'"

My mother's determination, which had once fueled our departure from Uganda, was now at least partially directed toward cancer. She would do what she could to avoid it, and when she got it, she would beat it naturally. She walked briskly each day, stirred BarleyGreen into her orange juice, and referenced the Lorraine Day video *Cancer Doesn't Scare Me Anymore!* without embarrassment. At dinner, she might tell us about someone in Pennsylvania who had been given weeks to live but was now in remission thanks to this herb or that supplement. We changed the subject or tuned her out.

Her enthusiasm for kooky cancer treatments contradicted everything else we knew about her. When church members were skeptical about conventional medicine, my mother was aghast. Diet and prayer for mental illness? Someone better do something. She took it upon herself to be that someone. "Are you still taking your meds?" she would ask between Sabbath School and church. "Good, good. And have you seen your doctor recently? Good." At home, she reported her conversations. As she talked, she stirred BarleyGreen into her orange juice. When we teased her, she shrugged. "Your body, your choice. My body, my choice."

For all my mother's talk about cancer, she had never, until now, suggested that she actually had it. "You don't get something small when you already have something big." Of course, I knew what she meant. But I didn't ask if she actually thought she had cancer now, and if she did, why. I packed her sentence away and didn't think about it again for months. I didn't even say anything to Sonja, who was visiting from South Korea.

Later, I imagined an alternate spool of our lives. One in which I heard my mother's statement for what it was and did something. Maybe I asked her why she thought she had cancer. Or maybe I said something to Sonja. I didn't know it then, but for months Sonja had been having dreams about our mother's death. She would have been alert to the warning and asked our mother what was going on. And then what? I don't know.

Later, I wondered why my mother told me. Was it because she thought I was the family member most likely to respond or because she knew I was the least likely?

"You have to stop this," Sonja tells me now.

In the actual version of our life, those of us with "something small" recovered, and we had a bright Christmas, the kind one sees in sentimental movies.

Sonja had brought her boyfriend, Jong-hak, home to meet her family. He asked us to call him "Kramer," the English nickname he had acquired while studying in the States and watching lots of *Seinfeld*. Kramer had an infectious laugh, and he used it often, making us feel like the smartest and funniest family in Atlanta. After meeting him, our mother pulled Sonja into the kitchen and told her, "Your Kramer's a teddy bear. I like him!" We all suspected Sonja would marry this man.

Home again, Sonja and I fell into the role of daughters, and Kramer became the third Fordham child. The three of us set the table for meals and then cleared it afterwards. We took the poodles for walks with our mother and bought a Christmas tree with our father. In the evenings, we ate cookies and watched old Christmas movies or sat around playing board games. Sonja had bought five or six to take back to South Korea for game days with her students. We were thrilled when she opened them immediately. "I have to learn the rules," she said.

Our father committed to the board games the way he committed to life, without any sense of urgency. When it was his turn, he would stare at the board for long minutes, thinking aloud: *If I move here, this could happen. If I move there, this could happen.* We Fordham women would implore him to just move already. "Hold on, hold on," he would say. "You're making me lose my train of thought."

Sonja and I had inherited our mother's impatience and our father's competitiveness. Kramer, we soon learned, also played to win. No matter how silly the game, the four of us tilted forward, calculating our various paths to victory, while my mother got snacks from the kitchen, lifted one of our poodles into her lap, shared a story she had heard at church. She often took an early lead, but as the game dragged on, she would make whatever move amused her most. If we were playing in pairs, her gaming partner might protest: "But that doesn't even make any sense." Oh, how she laughed then. She would rock back and forth, taking off her glasses and wiping her eyes. Whoever teamed up with her was doomed.

During that Christmas break, which in my memory stretches on and on, we drove north to show Kramer the Appalachian Mountains. We hiked the Bear Creek Trail to see the Gennett Poplar, which our guidebook described as the largest poplar in Georgia. My father took a picture as we circled the base of the tree like a string of paper dolls. We held hands and faced outward, our backs against the bark. My mother stood between her daughters. In Uganda, she had marched, adept and certain, pulling us along. She had been the comet, and we her tail. Now, we were both taller than her, and she was more likely to receive letters about our adventures, particularly Sonja's, than to travel with us. Though so much had changed, we still relied on her for guidance and support. She was our mother, and nobody was as invested in our happiness.

Absent my aunt, my mother was surrounded by those she loved the most. Her husband was behind the lens. "Girls, marry a man like your father," she always told us. On each side of her was a daughter. She had read to us during long afternoons of rain, and when we were sick, she had nursed us back to health. She had seen us through our teen years, and now we were finally adults, people she enjoyed spending time with. We were the ones who knew her best of all.

My father counted to three. My mother grinned, as if to say: *Isn't it great?*

At some point, my mother purchased two homeopathic books about cancer: *Beating the Odds* by Albert Marchetti and *Herbs Against Cancer* by Ralph Moss. When she wasn't reading them, she left them on her desk. If we noticed them at all, we thought it was just Mom being Mom. Kaarina being Kaarina. After she died, the books were a rebuke. Even as we gave away more and more of her things, my father continued to store these books. None of us could open them.

Finally, I asked for them. I wanted to understand my mother better, and what she had been thinking. I put the books at the bottom of my bookshelf. I would read them later. Each day, it seemed, my eyes got caught on their titles, on my mother's fears. *Okay*, I thought. *Enough.* I took the books to a coffee shop, and out of habit, I set my things on a table and went to order. At the counter, I saw the two books and their titles exposed. What must everyone think? After all these years, my mother could still embarrass me. I don't have cancer, I wanted to say. And I certainly don't believe in kooky medicine. I'm not my mother.

"You're just like me," my mother said, her voice sharp. I was a teen and we were arguing again. That was her closing argument.

"I'm nothing like you."

I carried my latte back to the table, picked up the first book, and opened it.

My mother had read these books with a highlighter, and now I followed behind, reading only the sections she had marked. I expected the books to be an autopsy of her fears, but they were as much about her hopes, the optimism she was trying to conjure up. She had noted all the foods she should be eating (papaya, asparagus, garlic, beans) and those she shouldn't (red meat, milk, butter, eggs). She highlighted the name of a legitimate cancer center in Massachusetts, and I wondered how close she came to calling it. She marked sentences about the power of positive thinking ("My faith was as important as the diet itself") and sentences that validated her decision to use food in place of medical treatment ("Macrobiotic experts . . . firmly believe that a change of diet will reverse the cancerous process and actually eliminate the disease, even when standard therapy is abandoned.")

And then she highlighted this sentence: "She viewed her cancer as a personal challenge and endeavored to cure it on her own."

I closed the book.

In April, my mother had phoned. "I have some bad news, I'm afraid."

It was spring in Iowa. The ground was turning green, and on campus, students gathered on the great lawn before the clock tower. They threw frisbees or studied on picnic blankets. A man known as "the preacher" appeared beside them, drawn by the sun and the sinners. "Don't be an Eve," he said as I declined a pamphlet. He walked beside me, "Jezebel, Jezebel." I quickened my stride, my mouth a scowl, but inside, I felt pleased. He hadn't seen the earnestness that Adventism and my missionary childhood had drawn onto my features. I, Sari Fordham, was fitting into a public university. "You're traveling to hell, missy," the preacher shouted at my back.

My mother called on Friday night. I had done a little Sabbath cleaning and was now flung across my bed, reading a novel and listening to hymns on my wonky CD player. There were parties on fraternity row, just as the preacher imagined, and somewhere, students were laughing and flirting. Even the bookish English types were out at a bar tonight, though my classmates would be the first to agree that staying home and reading was a solid alternative. Life was good. In one year, I would finish my degree. The world lay before me with compelling possibilities. I might become an English teacher or a writer or, my secret hope, I might go overseas (maybe to Uganda) and work for a nonprofit organization. I felt buoyant and optimistic.

"What's going on?" I asked my mother. When she didn't answer, I turned the volume down on my music. "Is everything okay?"

"I went to see the doctor," she said. She had been feeling increasingly fatigued and nauseated, and had finally made an appointment. Her doctor referred her to a specialist, who ordered a series of tests. At the end of it all, she had sat with my father in a bland office, and a young someone had fidgeted and cleared his throat and told her that she had metastatic liver cancer. In an email to friends, she called the news "a two-by-four to the head." The doctors didn't yet know where the cancer had started, but they knew it was terminal. "It probably started in my colon," my mother told everyone with a chart. She told them that her mother had died of colon cancer. About the lump in her breast, my mother said nothing. Not to her family. Not to the doctors. When a mammogram eventually revealed she had breast cancer, she seemed surprised.

The cancer was stage four, she told me. She was going to treat it with diet, exercise, and homeopathic herbs. She had read some really promising things about Essiac Tea. She sounded almost cheerful.

"What does Dad say?"

"He's hanging in there."

I didn't know what to say. My mother filled the silence by talking about prayer warriors and the healing power of sunlight.

Prayer and sunshine? My mother was dying. There was absolutely no hope to hold onto.

I had been home a few weeks earlier for spring break. I had spent my vacation working on a linguistics paper. During my writing breaks, I hung out with my parents, but mostly with my mother. We watched the news together. An Adventist youth pastor had disappeared at a nearby lake, and his students had put up missing person fliers while divers searched for his body. My mother and I had followed the story obsessively. As we walked the poodles in the afternoon, we speculated about what had happened. We both thought that he had staged his disappearance. Something just seemed fishy. "Probably an affair," my mother said.

When the pastor was found, alive, many states away, I felt sorry for his wife and children, but mostly I was pleased with our intuition. You couldn't pull one over on us.

I couldn't say the word *terminal* to my mother. It sat between us. I couldn't tell her that I loved her, either. We weren't that type of family. Even my mother, who was always hugging me, rarely told me in person that she loved me. Instead, she closed her letters and emails with the phrase "love and prayers." If I now told my mother that I loved her, it would be the same thing as telling her that she was dying.

Of course, she knew she was dying. What she wanted to know was whether I was as devastated as she was. Would I remember her the way she remembered her own mother? Years from now, would I cry about her death at the dining room table, while my husband and child—whom she would never meet—shifted uncomfortably?

My mother was teaching two Latin classes at a public high school. She planned to finish the school year, then see how she was feeling. She didn't tell her students she had cancer. During class, she sat more, assigned more in-class readings. When she got too tired to drive, my father took her to work, carried in her school bag, and then went back to the car to wait. At some point, my mother called in sick. A substitute teacher showed up, and her classes became study halls. The students were told that my mother was ill, but they weren't too concerned. They thought she was ancient, which my mother found hilarious and probably encouraged more than she should have. Old people got arthritis and stuff. When my mother died during her students' last week of classes, the school had to bring in grief counselors. "Why didn't she tell us?" the students asked. "We didn't even get to say goodbye."

We learned all this from our mother's colleagues. After the memorial service, they brought us a roasted chicken and a condolence card signed by her students. It was a comfort to hear that my mother's students needed grief counselors. I wanted the world to be ruined.

When our mother told us she had cancer, Sonja and I didn't come home. Our academic years were almost over, and we would finish our responsibilities first. We were Fordhams, after all. I went to class, wrote papers, taught my students, graded speeches, emailed my family, called home. I didn't tell anyone in Iowa that my mother was sick. Instead, I accepted a date from a classmate who had spent the last few months telling everyone he liked me. The more I had heard about his crush, the more I had avoided him. He was too young, too needy, and I just wasn't interested. But when he stopped me after class and asked me for a date, I surprised myself by saying yes. On Saturday night, I sat on his couch and watched *Rushmore* with him and wondered, *What am I doing here?*
Here, so unkindly. Here, nearly motherless. Here, so far from home.

Sonja and I talked to our mother often, and for a while, she sent us email updates.

April 12
Thanks so much for your concern and advice. I'm a proactive person as you may know and am carefully researching my options. After all, the Hippocratic oath said above all do no harm. I'm exercising. Walked 5 miles today with dad. Am trying to get sun and drink like a winebibber. We got the specialty teas mamma even used to drink and do carrot juice. I eat as much as I can get down. Nausea seems to be a small problem. One has to eat liver friendly stuff these days.
Wow. What a life change. I am doing ok so far and poor dad is even starting to eat and sleep. God is so good and healing comes from Him alone. So many people are praying and that is encouraging. Jokes are slow in coming though.

April 19

Went to school today. Dad drove and carried my heavy bags. It went quite okay. It's hard to keep much down these days. The juices are so acidic that I get this acid reflux and have to fight nausea all the time. Tonight is THE night for Essiac! It is not the most pleasant looking concoction, but you're allowed to add a little honey. Tomorrow, I could be jumping over mountains.

April 20

Essiac was fine last night and again this morning. We even walked 1.5 miles. And will try another small walk later. God is so good and He has healing under his wings!

At night, I knelt on the wooden floor and prayed, "Dear Jesus, please heal her. Please. Please. Please. Help the cancer to go into remission. Make it all be a terrible mistake. Please, let her live. Or at least, let her live longer."

The prayer was a loop with variations. What was there to say? As I prayed, I critiqued my hypocrisy. I no longer believed God reached down to Earth and rearranged things to my advantage. To believe in an interventionist God in the face of war and poverty was to believe in a God who valued some lives more than others. My mother was dying. She had refused chemotherapy, and no one was talking about surgery. What good was prayer? What good was God?

In a letter to her father, my mother had once written "wait for God to notice." It was 1979, and Ugandan women couldn't afford beans or nubs of soap or toilet paper. Children died of malaria. Husbands and brothers disappeared. In our cupboards, we always had food, though it never seemed like enough. When we got sick, we went to the clinic or the hospital, and when things got too dangerous, we left. There were two realities: ours and theirs. The year my mother was diagnosed with cancer, the life expectancy in Uganda was forty-seven years. My mother was fifty-nine.

Heaven was the equalizer.

"We have this hope," Adventists sang in church, "that burns within our hearts. Hope in the coming of the Lord." Life on Earth might be unfair, but God was coming soon. In heaven, there would be no malaria, no war, no hunger, no cancer, no death. Heaven was the destination that we were all traveling toward.

During Sabbath School, it wasn't unusual for church members to describe the mansions they wanted in heaven or the exotic animals they would keep as pets. At the Adventist college I attended as an undergraduate, a professor made a heavenly appointment with us on the last day of class. She would meet us, along with all her other former students, three trees down from the Tree of Life. How my father had laughed when I told him. "People are kidding themselves if they expect heaven to be anything like Earth," he said. I respected my father's more intellectual views, but they didn't sound nearly as fun.

When my mother talked about heaven, she talked about her mother. Heaven was the place where they would be reunited. Of course my mother paid lip service to seeing Jesus, but we knew who she particularly wanted to meet. At the dinner table, she would meander into a story about her mother, and soon, she would be removing her glasses and wiping her eyes. We, her daughters, were so accustomed to her mealtime tears that we would continue eating our potatoes. Finally, our mother would return her glasses to her face, pick up her fork. What to say? Maybe someone would tell an unrelated story. Maybe my mother would speak about heaven, about a time when we would finally all be together.

Before her death, my grandmother had joked that she should sleep in a box on the balcony. It would be good practice, she said. It was bitter humor. Like all Adventists, my grandmother believed that at the second coming, Jesus would wake the dead. Until then, the spirits of those who had died would rest in the ground. *The living know that they will die, but the dead know not anything.* As pleasant as a long nap sounded, no Adventist really wanted to die. And so my grandmother did what she could to prolong her life. She didn't drink or smoke. She tried to eat healthy. She prayed for God to watch over and protect her. How many times had my parents written letters from Uganda, asking relatives to keep us in their prayers? We were all barnacles clinging to this beautiful old Earth.

Before my Finnish grandmother died, we rushed to Finland. Afterward, my mother wrote a letter to my American grandmother: *Just a note from us to tell you we're O.K. The girls and I arrived here in Finland. Just in time for me to see my mother before she died. We came here at 5 p.m. and by next morning, she was no more. But it was good she was laid to rest. She was nothing but skin and bones. Now she is safe until that beautiful resurrection morning. But she left behind an empty space and unutterable longing and sorrow.*

My mother had brought beautiful big walking dolls for Sonja and Sari. It was real hard for me to contain myself as I was watching them enjoy those dollies. Sonja said: "I have to give Mamma a kiss for the doll in heaven. I hope I'll not forget for heaven is such a long time away."

The day before my mother died, I picked up my uncles at the airport. As I drove, I talked about my mother and how she was doing. "She's still waiting for a miracle, so don't mention death to her. Just talk about your childhood and Finland. Talk to her in Finnish."

"What is all the fuss about?" one of my uncles said. "Everyone is so hysterical. We're all going to die. Kaarina will just go to sleep sooner, and the next thing she'll know is heaven. There's no need for such hysterics. It's just death."

My hands tightened on the steering wheel, and I found myself speaking, my mother all over again. "You wouldn't say that if one of your children was dying or if you were dying. You treasure your own precious life. You're wearing a seat belt, aren't you?" I cried as I spoke. "So you know, it's a big deal to me, okay? It's a big deal to my mother."

For a long time, we were quiet.

At my mother's memorial service, the afterlife again became a point of contention.

A non-Adventist neighbor attended. She had recently moved to Atlanta, and although my mother had just been diagnosed, she had taken the new neighbor a loaf of homemade bread and a Tupperware of soup. Soon, the two women were trading coupons and telling each other their life stories, though my mother neglected to mention cancer. When my mother grew sicker and stopped visiting, her new friend chased down my father as he was walking the poodles and asked, "Where is Kaarina?"

Where indeed?

After my mother died, we believed she was waiting for the second coming. We held a memorial service in Atlanta, and as our neighbor listened to the sermon, she must have felt increasingly puzzled. The minister was neglecting the most obvious and comforting detail: that Kaarina was now in heaven. *Did he think she was in hell?* When the minister asked the congregation to share their memories, our neighbor leapt up and preached my mother directly into heaven.

Oh, how I wished my mother could have witnessed all those Adventists shifting in their seats and looking about. She would have laughed over it for weeks.

A month before my mother died, I was still at Iowa State University, still fulfilling my responsibilities. My mother answered the phone less and less often, and her emails stopped altogether. When I did talk with her, she asked about my students.

I told her about my class of troublemakers. They turned their work in late. Their grandmothers were all dying on the days of their scheduled speeches. They made inappropriate jokes. They saw me for who I was: a graduate student with no pedagogical background in communication. They didn't respect me. My mother—my strict mother—advocated for them all.

"Oh, they sound cute. Let them turn in their papers late. Let them make up their missed speeches."

And so I did.

"I'm not trying to scare you, but it sounds very bad," our aunt emailed Sonja and me. She was flying to Atlanta, and she thought that we had better do the same. Sonja found a substitute teacher and booked a plane ticket. It was my last day of class when I got the email, and I had already purchased my bus ticket. My college friends offered to fly me home instead, but I told them no. That old Fordham instinct. I packed most of my things and stored them in the garage of an Adventist church member.

At the Greyhound station in Chicago, I transferred buses late at night. The terminal was bright, and passengers were moving across platforms, lugging bags and babies. Drivers were buying coffee. As I hauled my own bag, I saw a payphone and decided to call home, never mind that it was late, never mind that payphones were for emergencies, never mind that Fordhams weren't sentimental. After a couple rings, my mother answered and said "hello" in her old voice. I remember being surprised. She hadn't answered the phone in quite some time. We talked about small things, mostly my trip home. She wanted to know if I had a pillow, snacks, a book on tape. She asked if I had sat next to anyone interesting. I remember how attentive she was to my well-being.

Even as I remember it, I know our conversation couldn't have happened. While I was transferring buses, my mother was in the hospital where she had been admitted hours earlier for an electrolyte imbalance. If I had called home, I would have only heard the phone ring and my father's voice on the message machine: "This is the Fordhams. We're not here right now, but if you just leave a message, we'll call you right back. God bless."

I know I didn't speak to her, yet I still remember the clangs and hollers of the terminal and the enormous relief I felt when I heard her voice.

A church member met me at the Greyhound station in Atlanta. She told me that my father and aunt were bringing my mother home from the hospital. "Oh," I said. "Oh, I see." I hadn't known until then that she had been admitted. I followed this nice church lady to her pickup truck. When she offered to help me carry my enormous bag, I waved her off. "I got it." Somewhere inside the bag, a black silk skirt was getting rumpled. It was an elegant affair—too fancy, too fussy, too dry-clean-only—and I rarely wore it. But in Iowa, I had packed it, trying not to think about why I needed something black and dressy. I heaved my bag into the bed of the pickup truck and climbed into the passenger's seat. I watched this nice church lady, who I had never known well and hadn't seen in years, work the truck's stick shift. She talked about her grandson and her garden, and I was grateful that she didn't ask any questions or expect anything of me at all.

My father's car was in the driveway when we pulled up, and I could see him and my aunt still sitting in the front seats. They must have arrived moments before us. My aunt leapt out of the vehicle when she saw us. She was like one possessed, taking my bag out of the back and setting it on the driveway, greeting me, thanking the church lady, thanking the church lady again. I sensed that the church lady was hoping to see my mother. She kept looking at the closed door of our relic of a car, not unkindly, and when she finally realized my mother wasn't coming out, she wished me luck and got back into her truck.

It was only then that my father opened the back door and my mother's legs dropped out. She was wearing a long, vibrant dress. All that was visible was the fabric from her dress and her small feet. She was wearing leather sandals. I couldn't move. My father and aunt reached into the car and helped my mother sit. She then stood with their help, and I saw her.

Seven weeks ago, I hadn't noticed that my mother was sick. Now it was as if she had fast-forwarded through her life, arriving on the far side of ninety. She didn't just look older; it was as if she had already died. Her face was a skull. Her starving body had absorbed all the softness. Her eyes were yellow and sunken in their sockets, her cheeks were hollowed out, her skin was a tent over her bones.

My mother looked at me standing in the driveway, holding my enormous bag, and said nothing. She turned to the house. Walking on tiptoes, she leaned heavily on my father's and aunt's upheld hands. They were so tender, so cautious; it was as if they were moving a glass bookcase between them.

I waited until she was in the house, then I carried my bag inside. My father and aunt had helped my mother to the couch, and she was sitting with her feet on the coffee table when I walked into the living room. I sat beside her. "Hi, Mom," I said.

She reached out her arms and held onto me with surprising ferociousness. "I'm so glad you're home."

CHAPTER 24

The House on the Hill

SABBATH MORNING, AND Kampala was bustling. I peered over the balcony of the Aponye Hotel and down into the alley. A cluster of men and women bent over fires, boiling water to sell. Laundry day. A line of customers scooched forward, and a woman left with a pail, her arm pulled down with the weight of water. The sidewalk was wet from all the sloshing. A man, dressed for the office or maybe church (there were a lot of Adventists in Uganda), edged around the proceeding. Over the din of conversations, I could hear the ting-ting-ting of metal hitting metal. A construction crew was building another high-rise on William Street.

I was in Uganda. I was really here. I wanted to pinch myself. I wanted to pinch someone else. Instead, I took a photo of the alley. Since arriving on Thursday, I had been taking pictures of the city: roads, fruit stands, construction crews, billboards, banana trees, marabou storks, the mosquito net over my bed. I would share them with my father and Sonja, of course, but I had another audience primarily in mind. In a few months, I would be marrying Bryan, a non-Adventist man from Arkansas. His mother and grandparents still lived on their family farm, and he understood how place could shape a person's identity. I had seen his land. He should see mine.

Two women walked briskly beneath the balcony, their voices animated. I turned off my camera. If I didn't start moving, I would be late for church. The original Fordham sin.

I hustled into the hotel room, counted enough money for a trip to Bugema, and then stopped at the mirror. Goodness, my hair was wild. Crazy-lady wild. The humidity had caused it to shoot upward and outward, and I hadn't packed any hairbands or clips. *Why? Why? Why?* I pulled a brush through the fuzz. In the grand tapestry of life, my hairstyle (or nonstyle) was too small a thing to matter, but there it was: I cared. Who goes to church like this? Who returns to their past looking like a banshee?

When I had left for college, I had thought it was clever to leave a single dress at home, something to wear to church when I visited. "Always the same dress," my mother said. "And such a raggedy one. The church members sure know how you feel about them."

I smoothed my hair as much as I could and then tamped it down with a scarf. Okay. Okay.

I had placed all manner of hopes upon this day, and also none. Almost despite myself, I was drawn toward the house on the hill. I wanted to ramble over the land I had once known so well. I wanted to be transported back to the past. Only that. And then, I also wasn't sure what I was doing here. Alone, again.

I had already been to Bugema once as an adult. After my mother died, I had finished graduate school and landed an internship at ADRA Uganda, an Adventist NGO. For several months, I had lived in the suburbs of Kampala, walking to work on a road strewn with jacaranda petals. The neighbor's goat stood on a mount beside the road and bleated as I passed.

Once, I had come upon a line of driver ants, and I squatted down to watch them cross the road. They were a river of ants, flowing, flowing, always flowing someplace else. The soldiers formed a sturdy bank, and when my shadow had fallen across them, they waved their pincers as if to say, *You! Again!* I stayed and watched so long I missed the morning worship that began our workdays at ADRA. It was just as well. When we sang hymns, my eyes filled with tears. I would drop my head, my hair a screen, and tell myself to get it together, and I would hope that nobody had noticed. Long ago, I had stopped being a crier, but in Uganda, I found myself always on the verge of weeping. As I watched the driver ants, I felt something different, a sturdier emotion. I felt curiosity and joy. For the first time since I had arrived, I felt familiar to myself.

That day, I rushed into the ADRA office and apologized for being late. "There were driver ants," I said, breathless from my sprint.

"In your room?" my colleagues said. "Pole sana."

"No, crossing the road." They looked at me. "The ants were really interesting," I said.

My colleagues broke into laughter. They passed the story around the office. "Come on, Sari. Are you a mzungu?" They were still teasing me at lunch. Never mind. The ants *were* interesting. My office mate Esther and I splurged on a bottle each of Bitter Lemon. We sat under the mango tree and drank our sodas and talked. After work, Esther went home, and I stayed to play badminton with a coworker whom I had known slightly during my childhood. His father had made trades with my mother. Passion fruit for soap and rice and oil. I remembered him as being too old and cool to play with Sonja and me. He remembered me as speaking Swahili.

"I wish," I said as I retrieved the shuttlecock.

"You did. You did," he insisted. "You can learn again."

As I swung my racket, I practiced new words.

I should have been happy in Uganda. Ever since we had moved to Texas, I had been navigating my life so that I could one day return. Uganda was the land of my heart. But moving back so soon after my mother's death had undone me. Adventists like to say it's a "small Adventist world." Everywhere I went, I met someone who had known my parents and wanted to know how they were doing. I recounted my mother's death over and over, my narrative growing shorter and shorter. "She got cancer and died last year. Yeah, it was sad, but we're doing okay." In the evenings, I sat on my bed and played solitaire. I played for hours. "Do you have malaria?" Esther asked, noting how much weight I had lost. I shook my head, tearing the chapati in my hand, unable to eat. Once, I attended vespers with a youth group and had to leave because I couldn't stop crying. It was embarrassing. I was embarrassing.

When Sonja set a wedding date, I saw an opportunity. I would attend her wedding in South Korea and start a new life there. Before I left Uganda,

I visited Bugema University. My father's former student was the president of the school and lived with his family in the house on the hill. They were away the day I visited, but they had invited me to look around. The road, the jungle, the house were nearly the same as from my childhood. What I remember most, though, was how alone I had felt. One Fordham, back again.

I stayed connected to ADRA Uganda, and for several years we collaborated on a project for displaced Batwa, which had resulted, finally, in the purchase of several tracts of land. It was both an insufficient solution and something tangible—a place for families to build homes and plant food.

I was in Uganda now to visit that land. On Sunday, I would meet my former colleagues and we would drive to Kisoro, a town on the border of Rwanda and the Congo, and we would hike far up into the hills. We would interview community leaders and talk about ongoing needs. I would fall back into NGO parlance, and through an interpreter, I would give small, ridiculous speeches.

But today, *today* I was the daughter of Gary and Kaarina Fordham.

As I walked through the lobby of the Aponye Hotel, one hand self-consciously smoothing my hair, the receptionist called out to me. She was a good deal younger than I was, but since I was the only mzungu staying here, and the only woman that I could tell who was traveling alone, she had taken a maternal interest in me.

"Where are you going?" she said, and in her voice, I could hear my mother sitting on the living room couch and asking my teenage self: *Hey, where are you going? Who are you going with? What time will you be back?*

"The New Taxi Park," I said.

"And how are you getting there, my dear?" she said. Her nails were painted red, and she looked at them frequently. I instinctively curled my hands to hide their chewed ends.

"Boda boda," I said, referring to the motorbike taxis ubiquitous in modern Uganda.

"But no," she said. "You must not take a boda boda. They have many accidents."

"And how did you get here this morning?" I said, knowing I had her there.

"But you're a visitor," she said. "You have to be more careful. If you are in an accident, your family will be calling me and asking, 'Where is our daughter? Why didn't you take care of her?'"

"Okay," I said. "I promise I'll be careful."

"No boda bodas," she called after me.

At the front of the hotel, a line of men straddled motorbikes and chatted. When they saw me, they called out, "Mzungu, mzungu, where are you going? Where are you going?" One of the drivers, the youngest in the group, walked beside me, gesturing toward his bike. He was barely a teenager. "Come with me, mzungu," he said. "I will take you."

"How much to the New Taxi Park?" I asked, disliking this game of bartering, which I knew was no game for the drivers who barely made a living wage. Why should I be stingy? But the child offered a price so high I nearly laughed. Did I look that much like a tourist? Of course I did. I was wearing a prAna travel dress and a pair of old Chaco sandals. With the scarf in my hair and a vinyl backpack slung over my shoulders, I was a mzungu cliché. I offered the driver a lower number, and he agreed, smiling over at his friends. Sucker.

There was a hierarchy to the road—first buses and trucks, then matatus, then cars, then motorbikes, and finally pedestrians. An older man pushing a cart full of pineapples was nearly hit as he crossed the intersection. He didn't change his pace or seem to flinch, but I yelped for him and then for myself as my knee skimmed against a car. When we lurched in front of a van and it really did seem as if the receptionist was a prophet, I leaned forward and shouted that I wasn't in a hurry. The child ignored me. The sooner he dropped me off, the sooner he could pick up his next customer.

My father would have recognized the roads and the roundabouts. Some potholes were so large I wouldn't be surprised if they had begun when we lived in Uganda—a pock then, a crater now. Many of the buildings were also the same. The bank. The Speke Hotel. But the general scene before me was one my parents couldn't have imagined. When we left Uganda, there were few cars, and the stores, of course, sold nothing. This city reminded me of Bangkok. The tiny shops opened to the street and had shelves jammed with things. You could buy watches, cell phones, radios, pens, calculators, wallets, and nail polish. In front of the stores, women from the countryside spread newspapers down on the sidewalk and stacked their produce: dodo, green oranges, bananas, pineapples, and passion fruit. Other women sold tabloids or used textbooks. Above us, billboards advertised cooking oil and diapers. There was so much to buy.

At the New Taxi Park, I paid the teen more than I had promised. Further proof, I knew, that I was a mzungu and didn't belong. Never mind. I was here now, wasn't I? The air smelled of rain, and high in a tree, a marabou stork gazed down at the street.

The matatus were white vans parked in a field. There were no signs. Everyone just knew where to go. "Gaza Road matatu?" I asked again and again, and each time, I was pointed farther down, until a man gestured toward his own van and cheerfully said, "Get in." I scrambled inside. There was still a window seat available, and I was amazed at my luck. Ever since I had purchased a ticket to Uganda, I had been thinking about this window and about the road that would carry me home. I was pulled to the house on the hill like one of those termites who came out after a good rain and pinged against our windowpanes.

In the United States, I sat at my computer each evening, tap, tap, tapping against time.

The Gaza Road had been paved, a recent development. No more whipping up red dust. As our matatu rattled by, children glanced up and then resumed whatever they were doing. A vehicle was no longer a spectacle, and teens were as likely to be carrying cell phones as they were to be following their parents' cows. Enough homes were painted a particular shade of pink or orange that I came to recognize the rival mobile companies: Zain and Orange. I asked the passenger beside me what homeowners got out of the deal. "Free paint," he said, looking at me in such a way that I understood how stupid my question was.

On the stoop of a Zain pink house, I saw two small girls, maybe sisters, sitting close together. They still carried the chubby cheeks of babyhood, but they were swinging their legs and laughing at some joke passing between them. I craned my head and watched for as long as I could. *I remember those girls*, I thought.

At Bugema, I got out of the matatu and watched the van drive away. I was here. My feet were again planted on the red roads of my childhood. There was the clinic in need of painting, maybe a nice Zain pink or Orange orange, I thought. There was the mango tree still in front of it. Even from the road, I could hear singing. I was late for church.

I slid into the last pew just as the guest pastor was being introduced. He was around my father's age, and when he saw me in the back—the one mzungu—he asked me to stand and introduce myself. I was surprised. Wazungu were old news in Uganda, boring news, often bad news. Your skin color no longer made you a special guest. But how the sins of colonialism still lingered. If the students near me wanted to roll their eyes, they resisted. It was Sabbath. They shook my hand and said, "You're welcome."

The sermon was about either Elijah or Elisha—I always got them mixed up. I looked around. I had come all this way and I couldn't pay attention. I thought about my parents, who were my age when they came to Uganda.

My parents liked to joke, "No problems, only solutions." It was the mantra of a distant relative that they had co-opted with ironic glee. As a child, I thought they used the phrase sincerely and found it comforting. While Sonja grew more anxious about our parents' safety, dreaming increasingly terrible dreams, I remained nestled in the belief that our parents, particularly our mother, would get us out of any predicament. And then we moved to the United States, and I grew up. My parents were stripped of their infallibility. I saw my mother for who she was, or so I thought. Even after she died, I didn't romanticize her memory.

In Finland, after I found my mother's old letters, my aunt drove Sonja and me downtown. Sonja wanted to buy presents for her Korean in-laws, and I wanted to purchase a pair of knee socks that I had had my eye on. It was raining, and as our aunt drove, she kept wiping at the condensation forming on the windshield. She shifted gears on the old, cranky van, and when she wanted to change lanes, she simply did so. This was not how our mother had driven. Our mother had avoided driving when it rained or when it was dark or when the route required getting on the freeway. When she did drive, she leaned forward, demanded silence. My aunt stopped at a light just outside Turku, and we watched pedestrians cross.

"Your mother was always scared," my aunt said. "I remember once we were at an intersection, and she looked and looked before stepping out onto the street. And then she had a vice grip on each of your hands. It was like she expected a car to come out of nowhere and—*zoom*—run you all over."

The description rang true. My mother had often seen dangers where none existed. Several years after we had settled in the States, we were traveling to visit relatives. My father was driving, of course, and my mother had the map on her lap. It was late, and we were tired. When we saw a sign for Motel 6, my father exited. We stopped at a light, and our poodles began yapping at men standing by the intersection. Their backs were to us, and if they were annoyed, we couldn't see it. "Shut those dogs up before someone shoots us," our mother had said. Sonja and I, who had been squabbling much of the day, locked eyes in mutual judgment—*Is she serious?* Her voice had enough fear in it that we each grabbed a dog without comment. We wrapped our fingers around their muzzles and whispered, "Hush."

"Do you know why your mother was always frightened?" my aunt asked.

"No," Sonja and I said. "Why?"

"Maybe frightened is the wrong word," my aunt said. "Maybe overly cautious is better. Do you know why your mother was so overly cautious?"

"No, why?" We believed the question was rhetorical, and the answer rested somewhere in their postwar childhood. We waited for our aunt to reveal our mother's secret self.

"I don't know," our aunt said. "I never thought to ask her. I thought you might know."

The light changed to green, and as she shifted into drive, the conversation moved to other things. As my aunt talked, her hands flew off the wheel, and when she looked into the rearview mirror, it was to observe Sonja's son, Aidan. "Do you think he needs a snack?" she asked.

It had stopped raining, and most pedestrians were closing their umbrellas. Water rolled down the window. I remember watching the drops and wondering if I would grow into my mother. It was an old fear. "You're just like me," my mother would say. Would I become too scared to drive? Would I chew my pills? Would I see a couple of men and assume that because they were out late at night they might try to murder me?

Now, sitting in a pew in Bugema, I wanted to laugh. My mother, my poor mother. We see and don't see our parents in equal parts. Thirty years ago, she had sat in this church with two wiggly daughters. Her husband, standing at the pulpit, was dreaming up new ways to court danger. At game parks, he leapt out of the car to get better pictures. How close could one get to a crocodile before it was too close? Well, he was experimenting.

She was the counterweight to our father. If he was too adventurous, then she was too vigilant. When she saw men standing in the street, she feared they would shoot us. "Oh, Mom," Sonja and I would say. Each time someone told me I was just like my mother, my chest constricted. I didn't want to be a scaredy-cat.

I hadn't seen that all along, the inheritance she had passed on to her daughters had been one of courage. She never sat around and wrung her hands. When she saw a snake in the laundry basket, she used the handle of our hoe to remove most of the clothes, and then she turned the hoe around and killed the snake. To prevent anemia, she put a nail in the beans as they boiled. To get us through roadblocks, she chatted up soldiers with a friendliness that bordered on flirtation. She confronted whatever problem was before her with resourcefulness and tenacity. She was always capable, even after we moved to the United States. When she was deemed "over qualified" for teaching jobs, she became a poorly paid teacher's aide. Never mind. We needed the money. At night, she clipped coupons and dreamed up ways to skimp. Being capable wasn't glamorous, but it was the sort of bravery that mattered.

She insisted that her daughters also become capable. To my childish problems (*Where are the crayons? How do you spell hippo? Sonja is so mean.*) she would rattle off solutions (*Look in your room. Use a dictionary. Leave your sister alone*). If I continued to whine, she might stand up and come to my aid, or more often, she would tell me, "Don't be helpless." It was a refrain. It was a lesson her daughters absorbed, even as we were determined not to become her. Like our mother, we both traveled widely, took jobs because we needed the money, scrubbed our homes on Friday nights, spoke our minds at church and in our workplaces, laughed at ourselves and each other, and we both wrote home with the regularity of an alarm clock. We were our mother's daughters.

The closing hymn was "Shall We Gather at the River." How many times had my parents sung this song in this church? I shared the hymnal with the young woman beside me, but I didn't need to look at the words. I knew them through all the stanzas. "Shall we gather at the river, the beautiful, the beautiful river. Gather with the saints at the river that runs by the throne of God." Oh, how I had hated this song as a child. It was sung during baptisms, those long, excruciating affairs. Somewhere along the way, the hymn had grown on me. *Shall we gather at the river.* It was the hymn's sincerity I liked, the old-fashioned earnestness and hope.

After my grandmother died, my mother's faith in the resurrection deepened. She found comfort in heaven, in the certainty that she would one day be reunited with her mother. But when my mother died, I felt scrambled. For the first time, I considered, *really* considered, the logistics of the resurrection. I just couldn't imagine a cloud of angels floating through the atmosphere and arriving on Earth. I couldn't imagine the ground breaking open and bodies emerging from their graves. I didn't know what I believed anymore. I was an Adventist who read the Bible and prayed, whose faith was her most important identity. Yet I also lived with doubt.

"Do you still believe in heaven?" I asked Sonja.

"Of course," she said. "Don't you?"

"I don't know." I couldn't say more.

I held my end of the hymnal, and my voice united with those around me, "Soon we'll reach the shining river, Soon our pilgrimage will cease; Soon our happy hearts will quiver with the melody of peace." Our words were a river. The music was a river. As I sang, I didn't feel sad. I felt held by my childhood faith, and even though I still doubted, I knew I belonged to this church—to this specific building, certainly—but also to my particular religious upbringing.

I ate lunch with Mary, a woman I had met only once during my ADRA days, but who now took me into her home as if I were a family member. She served dodo and tropical pumpkin, and I almost laughed to see the latter. My mother had taken to serving it with a glare, daring Sonja and me to complain. She ate it herself without comment. In a letter, she wrote: *The only vegetable we've had for weeks is pumpkin and the girls can't stand it, and to be honest, I'm getting tired of it, too.*

Mary told me that the house on the hill was now the overflow dorm for boys. They were so far from campus that they might not be expecting company. Her tone suggested that they might be half naked. I promised to call out hodi before I reached the top of the hill. I couldn't come all this way and not see the old house. I had to see it for myself and for my father and Sonja. Before I left for Uganda, my father called me nearly every day. He wanted to make sure I had gotten an antimalarial prescription, that I had enough money for the trip, that I had a place to stay in Uganda, that I would be careful. I laughed then, and he caught the joke and laughed, too, before telling me, "Well, you should be careful. And you should make sure you see Uganda. Do more than just your research."

I walked, clutching my camera. The road was red, and it carried me forward. I knew this place. I remembered how the land once felt under my feet and how it smelled. The cassia tree was yellow with flowers, and the pods had fallen on the ground and been crushed. They smelled like *here* and *home*. I passed one of the old missionary homes, still painted white, the yard still wide and manicured. The missionary family who lived there used to have a miserable pet monkey. There was the tree where it was unhappily tied. I took pictures. There was the road to the dairy, and there was the road up the hill.

But the hill was no longer recognizable. If I had not visited earlier, I would have turned around here. There was no mouth through the jungle. There was no jungle. Branches lay in the long grass, and new lampposts lined the road.

This was progress, I supposed. I thought of my father rattling down the hill on his bike. When he came upon a mamba, he would raise his legs and hope. The last time I had walked this road, I had regretted wearing sandals. I had hummed, stomped my feet, watched the edges of the road, and eyed the branches above. Now, the road was benign. I could see the practicality in this, and yet, like Sylvia, the Finnish woman who had lived in the house before us and planted trees, I was aggrieved. She had always gotten a bad rap in our family stories because of her angry letter to my mother. Such audacity; we lived there, not her. Now, I sympathized.

I walked up the hill briskly, hungry to see the house. What else had changed? Was the water tank still there? Had the frangipani and the bougainvillea and the flame tree been cut down too? The last time I had visited, the jackfruit, star fruit, and the avocado trees were all gone.

Four teenage girls scrambled up through the grass. "Who are you? What are you doing? Where are you going?" they asked. I found I couldn't tell them without my eyes filling with tears, but they were so effervescent that they didn't notice. They weren't Bugema students, they told me. They lived down in the valley, and when they saw me walking up this road, they were curious. I had thought I wanted to climb alone, but I was relieved at their chirpy companionship. They made me feel less like an intruder.

As we rounded the final turn, we saw two teenage boys walk through the yard, towels looped around their waists. When they saw us, they darted inside. Today was laundry day—Sabbath or no Sabbath—and with the old clothesline gone, they had stretched their trousers and shirts over the bushes. I did not belong here. I would take a few pictures from where I was standing and leave.

"Hodi," my companions called out to the boys. "Hodi."

The teens returned with their clothes on and greeted the girls warmly and nodded at me. *What are you doing here?* They didn't ask, but I felt obligated to explain. They listened to me indifferently, clearly more interested in my companions. The past was fully the past, and the future for these students was surely bright.

I asked if I could walk around, and the boys nodded.

Here, my mother had hung clothes on the line. Here, she had greeted the soldier at the door. Here, my father had pulled open the garage door and dislodged that snake. Here, he had posed for a photo, the bush viper dangling from his outstretched hand. Here, Sonja and I had pushed our matchbox cars, creating towns out of dirt, and here, we had left our toys as we scrambled into the jungle. Through that window, my mother had sat on the school's red couch and written letters and then gazed at the road, wondering what to write next, wondering how to explain this life.

In the evenings, she would heat milk on the stove, divide it into two mugs, and tap a tablespoon of Milo into each one. Sonja and I sat at the dining room table, still damp from our baths. Often, we listened to music: "Only a Boy Named David" or "Heaven Is for Kids." Occasionally, my mother would select a Finnish record. We knew the songs only as themselves. She would hum along, sometimes singing the chorus. She had a clear soprano and was the only member of our family who could hold a tune. The melody sounded like weeping set to music. Only later did I think about how isolated my mother must have felt, how lonely.

The geckos would wait near the light, and the cat would weave between the table legs and our swinging ankles, liking us better as our bedtime approached. If the power went out, my mother lit candles. She moved between the kitchen and the dining room, doing mother things, and we felt safe and cherished and home.

I returned to the verandah. The teens were sitting together, laughing. I thanked the boys and told the girls I was leaving now. We waved merrily at each other, and then I turned to walk down the road I had walked so many times before. This would surely be my last time here.

And so, like Lot's wife, I stopped and looked back. For the sin of nostalgia, she was turned into a pillar of salt. Maybe I had been, as well. Ever since my mother's death, I had been looking backward, trying to find my way home. The kids were out of view, and I could stand and look at this house for as long as I needed. It was only a house. My mother was not here. *The living know that they will die, but the dead know not anything.*

Still, I took out my camera and placed myself in the frame. I wanted some tangible record that my adult self and this house had existed in the same moment. I took the photograph in "grainy black and white"—an actual setting on my digital camera—and then I turned my camera over to look at the image. It was as if time had fallen away. The remaining trees were framed in such a way that the house could once again have been in the jungle, and my smile was such that I could have been my mother, standing before the verandah.

"You're just like me," my mother would say. It was never a compliment. *Oh, mom*, I thought. *I see you now.*

EPILOGUE

———— ❧ ————

Shaking Hands with Idi Amin

IN JANUARY 1978, my mother stands in the Entebbe airport, a daughter on each side. Idi Amin has been up to his usual brutality. He has murdered four college professors, scores of Christians in the southeast, and fifteen men whom he personally called subversive. And these are just the killings reported in the *New York Times*.

My mother gently squeezes our hands and tells Sonja and me to "stop staring, for goodness sakes," and then she whispers, "You've seen people before, haven't you?" There are more soldiers in the airport than civilians, and in truth, she has never seen anything like this. What are the chances that he is here, too?

We are in this airport because my Finnish grandmother is dying. My mother received the telegram in Kenya after we had escaped by train: *Come immediately.* She and my father sat across from each other and considered their options. In Kenya, we didn't have enough money for one plane ticket, let alone three. Somehow, the plan developed: Our family would return to Uganda to sell enough of our belongings to buy tickets to Finland, and the three of us would fly out, and my father would take the bus back to Nairobi.

When the church administrators forbade my father from entering Uganda, my mother laughed. "So now it's too dangerous." She laughed and laughed, and then she wept. "Never mind," she said. "I'll go alone." She meant that we would go without our father. Of course she would take us. We were her limbs. Our father, ever pragmatic, nodded.

My mother sold her wedding gifts on the black market in Kampala. "Never mind," she said, knowing that she would never again see these plates and these bowls. Never mind. It was the phrase she used most frequently. She was brisk and certain, as if she had sold goods illegally her entire life, as if she wasn't little Oili, scared of her own shadow. She moved like a fury and didn't allow herself to cry for her mother. *Äiti-äiti-äiti*, she thought. *Mamma-mamma-mamma*. She took the shillings, good only in Uganda, to the Sabena Airline office and booked the earliest flight out.

At the Entebbe airport, we wait by the gate. My mother opens her purse for us, and Sonja and I pin brooches to our t-shirts and smear her strawberry chapstick across our lips.

A soldier approaches. "Excuse me, madam. How are you, madam?"

My mother jolts upward. She holds out her Finnish passport. Her eyes are wild. She assumes that Americans are in trouble again, and her daughters will be detained. Maybe her citizenship can protect us.

The soldier looks pained, embarrassed. He tells her to put her passport away. "Idi Amin would like to welcome you to Uganda," he says. Never mind that we are in the departure lounge. "Would you like to meet him?"

My mother thinks about my father, how willingly he steps toward danger. He is not here. "We would be honored," she says. There is no other possible answer. She takes a fast brush to our hair and holds out her hands. As we walk through the airport, people turn away, actively minding their own affairs.

Idi Amin is a large man dressed in khaki and exuding so much charm that he seems to fill the VIP lounge. A few other wazungu are already here, all of them women and children. A bodyguard gestures for us to stand in a row, and Amin stops chatting and walks down the line. A man takes photographs. We are political theater. The pictures will show that Uganda is safe. *Look at these foreign women bringing their babies here. See how happy they are to meet the president.*

When Idi Amin reaches us, he shakes my mother's hand and says, "You are welcome." It's the most Ugandan of greetings. My mother smiles and says thank you.

When Idi Amin reaches for Sonja's hand, she holds out her left arm. My mother has heard a story—maybe real, maybe apocryphal—about a cameraman killed over a left-handed shake. She hisses, "Your other hand." Sonja drops her arm and snorts back tears.

Idi Amin laughs. He's like a jolly uncle. He bends at the waist and takes Sonja's left hand in his. "Look at this one," he says. "You are welcome, little sister."

When we meet Idi Amin, he is kind and our mother is mean. This is one story.

Here's another: After we shake hands with Idi Amin, we board a plane to Finland and our mother says goodbye to her mother. At the graveside, she stands between us, holding our hands. The sky is grey with unfallen snow. We have not yet become acclimatized to winter or to our mother's sorrow. She smiles down at us. "Move your fingers if they're cold."

Years later, our mother will reside solely in the land of our memories. Some days, unexpected days, I will wake to the image of her sweeping through the Entebbe airport, holding our hands. Across the span of time, she will call to her daughters, and she will tell us that we must always do what we have to do. Never mind the rest.

SELECTED BIBLIOGRAPHY

Chapter 2: Soon and Very Soon

Knight, George R. *Millennial Fever and the End of the World: A Study of Millerite Adventism.* Idaho: Pacific Press Publishing Association, 1994.

Chapter 3: Jambo

Micalizio, Caryl-Sue. "Aug 7, 1972 CE: Asians Expelled from Uganda." *National Geographic,* July 7, 2014. https://www.nationalgeographic. org/thisday/aug7/asians-expelled-uganda/.

"Catholic Prelate Is Accused by Amin." *The New York Times,* December 4, 1972. https://www.nytimes.com/1972/12/04/archives/catholic-prelate-is-accused-by-amin.html.

Federal Research Division, Library of Congress. *Uganda: A Country Study.* Edited by Rita M. Byrnes. Washington, D.C.: U.S. Government Printing Office, 1992. http://cdn.loc.gov/master/frd/frdcstdy/ug/ugandacountrystu00byrn_0/ugandacountrystu00byrn_0.pdf.

Howgego, Raymond John. "John Hanning Speke – English Soldier and Explorer (1827–1864)." International League of Antiquarian Booksellers, April 18, 2011. https://ilab.org/articles/john-hanning-speke-english-soldier-and-explorer-1827-1864.

Mohr, Charles. "Discovery of Car Adds to Fear in Uganda That 2 Americans Have Been Killed." *The New York Times,* April 14, 1972. https://www.nytimes.com/1972/04/14/archives/discovery-of-car-adds-to-fear-in-uganda-that-2-americans-have-been.html.

Mohr, Charles. "112 in Peace Corps Seized by Uganda at Amin's Order." *The New York Times,* July 9, 1973. https://www.nytimes.com/1973/07/09/archives/112-in-peace-corps-seized-by-uganda-at-amins-order-african-leader.html.

Munnion, Christopher. "The African Who Kicked Out the Asians, Who Said Hitler Was Right, Who Has Made His Country a State Sinister." *The New York Times,* November 12, 1972. https://www.nytimes.com/1972/11/12/archives/if-idi-amin-of-uganda-is-a-madman-hes-a-ruthless-and-cunning-one.html.

Mutibwa, Phares. *Uganda Since Independence: A Story of Unfulfilled Hopes.* Trenton: Africa World Press, Inc., 1992.

Chapter 5: Fever

UNICEF USA. "Despite Progress, 1,500 African Children Die Daily from Malaria." April 25, 2013. https://www.unicefusa.org/press/releases/despite-progress-1500-african-children-die-daily-malaria/8240.

Chapter 6: Dividing Up the World Between Us

Briggs, Philip. *Uganda: The Bradt Travel Guide.* 4th ed. England: Bradt Travel Guides, Ltd., 2003.

Maberly, C. T. Astley. *Animals of East Africa.* Kenya: Hodder & Stoughton, [1960] 1976.

Poole, Oliver. "Idi Amin Encouraged the Slaughter, Now Uganda Is Saving Elephants." *Evening Standard*, August 5, 2015. https://www.standard. co.uk/news/world/idi-amin-encouraged-the-slaughter-now-uganda-is-saving-elephants-10439516.html.

Chapter 7: A Trip to Town

"A Clown Drenched in Brutality." *Sunday Times*, July 27, 2003.

Chapter 9: Archbishop's Murder

"Amin: The Wild Man of Africa." *Time* 109, no. 10 (March 7, 1977): 19-29, http://content.time.com/time/magazine/article/0,9171,918762,00. html.

Carter, Jimmy. "Remarks of the President During a Press Conference." Jimmy Carter Library and Museum, Atlanta, GA, February 23, 1977. Audiotape.

Kaufman, Michael T. "Amin Prohibits Exit By 200 Americans; Bids Them Meet Him." *The New York Times,* February 26, 1977. https://www. nytimes.com/1977/02/26/archives/amin-prohibits-exit-by-200-amer-icans-bids-them-meet-him.html.

Kiefer, James E. "Janani Luwum, Archbishop of Uganda, Martyr." Biographical Sketches of Memorable Christians of the Past, February 16, 1977, Society of Archbishop Justus, January 18, 1998. http://justus. anglican.org/resources/bio/101.html.

Kiefer, James. "Janani Luwum, Archbishop of Uganda, Martyr (16 Feb 1977)." The Lectionary, December 22, 2018. http://www.satucket.com/lectionary/janani_luwum.htm.

Kyemba, Henry. *A State of Blood: The Inside Story of Idi Amin*. New York: Ace Books, 1977.

Piwang, Georg. "Archbishop Janani Luwum." Archbishop Janani Luwum Trust UK, 2005. http://www.jananiluwumtrust.com/luwum.html.

Chapter 10: House Arrest

"Amin: The Wild Man of Africa." *Time* 109, no. 10 (March 7, 1977): 19-29, http://content.time.com/time/magazine/article/0,9171,918762,00.html.

Marder, Murrey. "Uganda Bars Exit of Any Americans." *The Washington Post*, February 26, 1977. https://www.washingtonpost.com/archive/politics/1977/02/26/uganda-bars-exit-of-any-americans/9d670846-dd0c-4a37-9f91-160b18d719d8/.

Chapter 12: Adventist Church Banned

"Amin Bans All but Three Christian Churches as Risks." *The New York Times*, September 21, 1977. https://www.nytimes.com/1977/09/21/archives/amin-bans-all-but-three-christian-churches-as-risks.html.

Chapter 14: Civil War

"Rejoicing and Revenge in Kampala: The Invaders Seize the Capital, as Amin Disappears." *Time* 113, no. 17 (April 23, 1979): 36, http://content.time.com/time/magazine/article/0,9171,920251,00.html.

"Saving Some Bullets for the End: As the New Regime Mops Up, Big Daddy Seeks Arms in Libya." *Time* 113, no. 19 (May 7, 1979): 32, http://content.time.com/time/magazine/article/0,9171,920309,00.html.

Schroeder, Barbet, dir. *General Idi Amin Dada: A Self Portrait.* 1974; The Criterion Collection, 2002. DVD.

Chapter 18: Murphy's Law

Kellner, Mark A. "Desmond Ford, 90, Adventist Theologian Defrocked for Controversial Beliefs, Dies." *Religion News Service,* March 12, 2019. https://religionnews.com/2019/03/12/desmond-ford-90-adventist-theologian-defrocked-for-controversial-beliefs-dies/.

Chapter 23: You Better Come Home

Marchetti, Albert. *Beating the Odds: Alternative Treatments That Have Worked Miracles Against Cancer.* Chicago: Contemporary Books, Inc., 1988.

Moss, Ralph W. *Herbs Against Cancer: History and Controversy.* Brooklyn: Equinox Press, 1998.

World Bank Group. "Life Expectancy at Birth, Total (Years)." Uganda, World Bank Data, 2019. https://data.worldbank.org/indicator/SP.DYN.LE00.IN?locations=UG.

Epilogue: Shaking Hands With Idi Amin

"15 Killed by a Uganda Firing Squad." *The New York Times*, September 10, 1977. https://www.nytimes.com/1977/09/10/archives/15-killed-by-a-uganda-firing-squad.html.

"Amin Said to Execute 4 Professors Who Fought Naming School for Him." *The New York Times*, August 7, 1977. https://www.nytimes.com/1977/08/07/archives/amin-said-to-execute-4-professors-who-fought-naming-school-for-him.html.

"Uganda Said to Kill Up to 20 Persons in Religious Purge." *The New York Times*, November 13, 1977. https://www.nytimes.com/1977/11/13/archives/uganda-said-to-kill-up-to-20-persons-in-religious-purge.html.

PUBLISHER ACKNOWLEDGMENTS

This World Is Not My Home (I'm Just Passing Thru), Albert E. Brumley
(c) Arr. Copyright 1936. Renewed 1964 by Albert E. Brumley &
Sons/SESAC (admin. By ClearBox Rights). All rights reserved. Used
by permission.

My Tribute (To God Be The Glory) - (CMG Song #393), Andrae' Crouch
Copyright (c) 1971 Bud John Songs (ASCAP) (adm. at CapitolCMG
Publishing.com) All rights reserved. Used by permission.

We Have This Hope Words and Music: Wayne Hooper
(c) 1962, 1995 Wayne Hooper (Admin. La Sierra University,
Riverside CA 92515). All rights reserved. Used by permission. Under
license #1023.

ABOUT THE AUTHOR

Sari Fordham has lived in Uganda, Kenya, Thailand, South Korea, and Austria. She received an M.F.A. from the University of Minnesota and now teaches at La Sierra University. She lives in California with her husband and daughter.

BOOKS FROM ETRUSCAN PRESS

Zarathustra Must Die | Dorian Alexander
The Disappearance of Seth | Kazim Ali
The Last Orgasm | Nin Andrews
Drift Ice | Jennifer Atkinson
Crow Man | Tom Bailey
Coronology | Claire Bateman
Topographies | Stephen Benz
What We Ask of Flesh | Remica L. Bingham
The Greatest Jewish-American Lover in Hungarian History | Michael Blumenthal
No Hurry | Michael Blumenthal
Choir of the Wells | Bruce Bond
Cinder | Bruce Bond
The Other Sky | Bruce Bond and Aron Wiesenfeld
Peal | Bruce Bond
Scar | Bruce Bond
Poems and Their Making: A Conversation | Moderated by Philip Brady
Crave: Sojourn of a Hungry Soul | Laurie Jean Cannady
Toucans in the Arctic | Scott Coffel
Sixteen | Auguste Corteau
Wattle & daub | Brian Coughlan
Body of a Dancer | Renée E. D'Aoust
Ill Angels | Dante Di Stefano
Aard-vark to Axolotl: Pictures From my Grandfather's Dictionary | Karen Donovan
Scything Grace | Sean Thomas Dougherty
Areas of Fog | Will Dowd
Romer | Robert Eastwood
Surrendering Oz | Bonnie Friedman
Nahoonkara | Peter Grandbois
Triptych: The Three-Legged World, In Time, and Orpheus & Echo | Peter Grandbois, James McCorkle, and Robert Miltner
The Candle: Poems of Our 20th Century Holocausts | William Heyen

ETRUSCAN PRESS IS PROUD OF SUPPORT RECEIVED FROM

Wilkes University    Wilkes
                                                 University

Youngstown State University    Youngstown
                                                 STATE UNIVERSITY

The Ohio Arts Council    Ohio Arts
                                                 COUNCIL

Community of Literary Magazines and Presses   [c|mp]

The Stephen & Jeryl Oristaglio Foundation

The Nathalie & James Andrews Foundation

The National Endowment for the Arts
                                                 NATIONAL
                                                 ENDOWMENT
                                                 FOR THE ARTS

The New Mexico Community Foundation

Founded in 2001 with a generous grant from the Oristaglio Foundation, Etruscan Press is a nonprofit cooperative of poets and writers working to produce and promote books that nurture the dialogue among genres, achieve a distinctive voice, and reshape the literary and cultural histories of which we are a part.

etruscan press

www.etruscanpress.org

Etruscan Press books may be ordered from

Consortium Book Sales and Distribution

800.283.3572

www.cbsd.com

Etruscan Press is a 501(c)(3) nonprofit organization.
Contributions to Etruscan Press are tax deductible
as allowed under applicable law.
For more information, a prospectus,
or to order one of our titles,
contact us at books@etruscanpress.org.